MENDING THE CRACKS
in the
IVORY TOWER

MENDING THE CRACKS
in the
IVORY TOWER

*Strategies for Conflict Management
in Higher Education*

Susan A Holton

Editor

Bridgewater State College

ANKER PUBLISHING COMPANY, INC.
Bolton, MA

Mending the Cracks in the Ivory Tower
Strategies for Conflict Management in Higher Education

ISBN 1-882982-21-5

Composition by Lyn Rodger, Deerfoot Studios
Cover design by Lyn Rodger, Deerfoot Studios

Anker Publishing Company, Inc.
176 Ballville Road
P.O. Box 249
Bolton, MA 01740-0249

ABOUT THE EDITOR

Susan A Holton is professor of communication studies at Bridgewater State College in Bridgewater, Massachusetts, where she also served as assistant to the president and chair of the department of speech communication, theater arts, and communication disorders.

Intensely involved in issues of teaching and learning, Dr. Holton is on the steering committee of the Center for the Advancement of Teaching and Research at Bridgewater State College and was the founding director of the Massachusetts Faculty Development Consortium. She was also a founding member of the Massachusetts Council on International Education and served on the culminating study group for the Study of the Undergraduate Experience for the Board of Regents of Higher Education in Massachusetts.

As a conflict management specialist, Dr. Holton works with educational, religious, nonprofit, and for-profit institutions. A certified mediator, she is involved with the National Association for Mediation in Education, the Society for Professionals in Dispute Resolution, The National Institute for Dispute Resolution, and Massachusetts Mediation Programs and Practitioners. She is the editor of *Conflict Management in Higher Education* (1995) and was featured on the PBS teleconference, "Coping with Changing Campus Culture."

Holton received her B.A. in speech and drama, English, and education from Miami University, and her M.A. and Ph.D. in communication from Case Western Reserve University.

ABOUT THE CONTRIBUTORS

Cynthia Berryman-Fink is professor in the department of communication at the University of Cincinnati where she also has served as acting vice provost for academic affairs, head of the department of communication, and partner in Enhancement Training, a human resources consulting firm. She has provided consulting/training for numerous Fortune 500, governmental, civic, and educational institutions in the greater Cincinnati area. Dr. Berryman-Fink has published several books, including *The Manager's Desk Reference, Communication and Sex Role Socialization, Research in Speech Communication,* and *Communication, Language and Sex,* and more than 30 articles and chapters in communication, psychology, personnel, women's studies, and education publications.

Joel M. Douglas is professor of labor relations at the School of Public Affairs at Baruch College of the City University of New York. His fields of concentration and research include public sector collective bargaining and human resource management. He is widely published and has written primarily on public sector labor relations, the labor injunction, the emerging labor law of public sector labor relations, and collective bargaining in higher education. An active mediator, fact-finder, and arbitrator, Dr. Douglas served as the director of the Baruch College National Center for the Study of Collective Bargaining in Higher Education and the Professions.

Walter H. Gmelch is professor, interim dean, and former chair of the educational leadership and counseling psychology department at Washington State University where he also serves as director of the National Center for Academic Leadership. An educator, management consultant, university administrator, and former business executive, Dr. Gmelch has conducted research and written extensively on the topics of leadership, team development, conflict, stress, and time management, and has published articles and books on management, including *Leadership Skills for Department Chairs, Chairing an Academic Department,* and *Coping with Faculty Stress.* He is one of the leading researchers in the study of department chairs in higher education.

Gerald Graff is George M. Pullman Distinguished Service Professor of English and Education at the University of Chicago. He is the director and principal designer of the interdisciplinary master of arts program in the humanities at the University of Chicago. He is the author of the award-winning *Beyond the Culture Wars: How Teaching the Conflicts Can Revitalize American Education* and *Teaching the Conflicts: Gerald Graff, Curricular Reform, and the Culture Wars.* He is a member of the executive council of the Modern Language Association and helped found Teachers for a Democratic Culture, an organization aimed at combating conservative misrepresentations of recent changes in curriculum and culture. Dr. Graff has lectured and served as curriculum consultant at approximately 200 colleges and universities.

Mary Lou Higgerson is professor in the department of speech communication at Southern Illinois University, where she was also department chair, associate dean, and associate vice president for academic affairs. Higgerson's focus in her writing, consulting, and training activities is on the application of communication and management theory using video vignettes and case studies. Since 1990 she has taught on a variety of topics for the American Council on Education in both the fellows program and national seminars offered through the Center for Leadership Development. Higgerson has authored *Communication Skills for Department Chairs* and coauthored *Complexities of Higher Education Administration: Case Studies and Issues.*

John W. "Sam" Keltner is the principal of Consulting Associates, a member of the board of directors of two mediation projects, and an emeritus professor at Oregon State University. He is commissioner and training officer of the Federal Mediation and Conciliation Service. He is the author of *Mediation: Toward a Civilized System of Dispute Resolution* and *The Management of Struggle: Elements of Dispute Resolution Through Negotiation, Mediation and Arbitration,* as well as other books and numerous articles dealing with mediation, conflict, interpersonal communication, and human relations. Dr. Keltner is the author and host of two videotape series on mediation, depicting the nature of and role of mediation in struggles between people and organizations.

Gillian Krajewski is assistant director of the graduate programs in dispute resolution at the University of Massachusetts in Boston. She played a key role in establishing an interuniversity network of graduate dispute resolution programs in the United States. Recent activities in this connection include organizing the nation's first conference for graduate students studying conflict in a variety of disciplines and conducting research into the career paths of graduates of dispute resolution programs. Ms. Krajewski was the cofounder of Canada's first campus-community mediation program and has worked with several institutions of higher education to establish campus dispute resolution systems.

Clara M. Lovett is president of Northern Arizona University. She has been a professor of history at Baruch College and the Graduate School (CUNY), where she was also an assistant provost. She was chief of the European Division of the Library of Congress, dean of the College of Arts and Sciences at George Washington University, provost and vice president for academic affairs at George Mason University, and director of the American Association for Higher Education's Forum on Faculty Roles and Rewards. In addition to her faculty and administrative roles, Dr. Lovett is widely published, and has held research fellowships and grants from the Guggenheim Foundation, the Woodrow Wilson International Center for Scholars, the American Council of Learned Societies, the National Endowment for the Humanities, and others.

Ann F. Lucas is professor of organization development, former professor of clinical psychology, and former chair of two departments at Fairleigh Dickinson University, where she is also founder and former director of the Office of Professional and Organizational Development. A consultant in leadership in higher education on the international level as well as in the United States, she has published books, including her latest, *Strengthening Departmental Leadership: A Team-Building Guide for Chairs in Colleges and Universities.* She also has chapters in books, and journal articles in the area of leadership in the academic department, the chair's role in enhancing teaching effectiveness, increasing writing productivity, student motivation, performance evaluation, team building, conflict resolution, outplacement in a university setting, and faculty development.

Janet Rifkin is professor in the legal studies department and associate dean of the College of Social and Behavioral Sciences at the University of Massachusetts in Amherst where she served as the university ombudsperson from 1991–1995 and was the founder and director of the University Mediation

Project. She has written extensively about the theory and practice of mediation in the United States. Her work has focused on issues related to gender and cultural differences, and on the concept of neutrality in mediation practices. Dr. Rifkin is the cofounder of NAME, the National Association of Mediation in Education, and is on the board of directors of NIDR, the National Institute of Dispute Resolution.

Nancy L. Sorenson is dean of the School of Education at the College of Charleston. She is a former dean or associate dean at three other institutions. She is currently director of the management seminar for assistant and associate deans for the National Association of Academic Affairs Administrators (ACAFAD). Dr. Sorenson speaks and writes about the impact of change processes on various aspects of professional and public education.

Judith A. Sturnick is president of The Sturnick Group for Executive Coaching and Consulting to corporations, higher education, and health care, and is also a senior associate with The Education Consulting Institute in Washington, DC. She served as a campus president for 11 years. Author of numerous articles, chapters in books, and two books of her own, Dr. Sturnick is recognized nationally and internationally as an expert in leadership, managing the dynamics of organizational and personal change, communication, stress management, and board development. She has given hundreds of keynote addresses, workshops, and retreats for leadership teams and boards. Since 1993, she has also served as an executive coach for leaders and managers in higher education, health care, and the corporate sector.

Lynn Willett is vice president of student affairs at Bridgewater State College and chair of the Vice Presidents' Think Tank at the New England Center for Research in Higher Education. She is president of the American College Personnel Association (ACAP), a prominent national organization for student affairs personnel. She has worked in the public secondary schools as a speech and English teacher and on six college campuses in student affairs work. Additionally, she has served as presenter, consultant, and author on many higher education topics. In 1992, she received the Hopwood/Stewart Award from her alma mater, The Ohio State University, for her professional accomplishments.

TABLE OF CONTENTS

PREFACE

Conflict? In higher education? Certainly not!

For years, we in higher education were able to hide—or at least vociferously deny—the existence of conflict. When it emerged, we were able to divide a department in two, so that people who didn't get along didn't have to work together. We transferred the administrator to another division, and eliminated the conflict, at least for a while. It is not a generalization to say that much conflict in higher education was managed by avoidance.

But that doesn't work anymore. There is little money to throw at problems; we can't divide departments but are now combining them. It is harder to transfer the administrator.

It is time to face conflict rather than flee from it. It is time to learn how to manage conflict in higher education. But how? How do you handle the conflicts that occur within your realm of academia? Who can help when you feel "up to your doorway in alligators, with no way to drain the swamp?" This book emerged as an answer to that "how."

For years, I had two lives. During the day, I worked as a faculty member, department chair, and administrator in academia. At night and on weekends, I worked as a consultant to religious, nonprofit, and industrial institutions that were enmeshed in organizational change and conflict. The work that I did in these institutions had a significant impact on the life of the institution and in the effectiveness of the people involved.

It became apparent to me that the same work was required in academia. I began to do consulting and workshops on the theme of "Cracks in the Ivory Tower," dealing with organizational change and conflict management in higher education. *Mending the Cracks in the Ivory Tower* emerged as the next step in the understanding of conflict management in higher education.

It is important to explain my use of the term "conflict management" as opposed to "conflict resolution." I invite you to think of a conflict that occurred early in your academic life. Who did it involve? What happened? Did it take you long to think of a conflict? I imagine that it did not. Was that conflict completely dispelled? Or were there residual effects? Perhaps, in your life as a graduate student, you had a conflict with your thesis advisor. You worked through the conflict, but it was a painful experience. You used the experience and learning of this first conflict when you approached him with the next issue. So your conflict was "resolved." You came to some sort of agreement, and it was no longer in the forefront of your interaction. But it certainly was not dispelled; it did not vaporize. And it affected your future interaction.

That is why I use the term "management," because I believe it is a more accurate reflection of what actually happens. We manage the conflict, and we go on to other issues. But the impact of that conflict remains with us.

When you were involved in another issue with that person in your original conflict, did you approach your work together in a guarded manner? Did you worry about another confrontation? Did you wonder whether the person would bring up the issues from the first conflict? Most conflict is managed, not completely resolved.

This book enlists the aid of people who have been involved in academia and conflict management for years. Their expertise will help you to analyze the conflict and learn to "mend the cracks" in your own towers. It offers practical wisdom that will provide you with options for managing your own conflict.

No book can be completed in isolation. Special thanks must be given to the two people who make my life—and managing our conflicts—exciting and engaging. Thanks to my son, Christopher Holton-Jablonski, and my husband, Joe Snyders. And thank you to Adrian Tinsley, president of Bridgewater State College, inspirational mentor and friend.

Susan A Holton
Bridgewater State College
Bridgewater, MA

INTRODUCTION

Mending the Cracks in the Ivory Tower is intended to be a "mentor on a shelf" for those in higher education who are faced with managing conflict, particularly for department chairpersons and deans, who interact with all constituents. The book provides you with models of conflict management in the academy and is a book of practical wisdom that will provide ways to deal with conflict.

Each chapter provides insight into handling conflict in a different area of academia. Each contributor presents a map, a model, a step-by-step process—a guide to dealing with a particular type of conflict.

In Chapter One, What's It All About? Conflict in Academia, I discuss conflict in general; its manifestations on campuses; its sources, types, and precursors; and then give an overview of the process of conflict and conflict management.

In Chapter Two, Administration in an Age of Conflict, Gerald Graff provides a history of conflict in academia. He notes that the evolution of academic administration emerged with a presumption of circumventing or neutralizing conflict. Academia, he contends, has assumed that conflict is inherently destructive, and therefore administrators have long sought to ignore it. He answers his challenge to develop a new conception of administrative conflict management, one that seeks to make productive use of academic conflicts instead of trying to shut them down.

In Chapter Three, The Janus Syndrome: Managing Conflict from the Middle, Walter H. Gmelch examines the tightrope walked by department chairs and deans. He contends that department chairs try to look in two directions and often don't know which way to turn. They are expected to mediate the concerns of administration to faculty and, at the same time, to champion the values of their faculty. He helps chairs to find the balance between the two potentially different value systems and to find ways to resolve the conflicts inherent in their position.

In Chapter Four, Chairs as Department Managers: Working with Support Staff, Mary Lou Higgerson explores a conflict area which can make or break the chair or dean. Good support staff can enhance the administrator's job; ineffective staff can jeopardize the operation of the department. Conflict with the support staff can easily spill over to conflict with faculty members, students, and administrators farther up the hierarchy, as tasks do not get completed. Higgerson provides answers to the question of how to minimize destructive conflict that jeopardizes the welfare of the department.

In Chapter Five, Spanning the Abyss: Managing Conflict Between Deans and Chairs, Ann F. Lucas addresses the cultural climate of the institution and the differences in perceptions of chairs and deans because of their positions in the organization. She suggests that managing conflict and preventing dysfunctional conflict in higher education is particularly difficult, perhaps because being a team player in academia has been neither required nor rewarded, and because roles and responsibilities are not clearly defined. Lucas notes that differences in leadership styles contribute to conflict between deans and chairs, and she suggests ways for both to effectively handle conflict.

In Chapter Six, The Cutting Edge: The Dean and Conflict, Nancy L. Sorenson notes that the role of dean is largely defined by the need to mediate and manage the various manifestations of conflict that they encounter. Explaining that the lack of effectiveness in dealing with interpersonal issues is a problem for deans, she gives guidelines that can help prepare the dean for conflict. She gives premises about the dean and conflict, principles for dealing with conflict, and strategies and tactics for handling conflict.

Judith A. Sturnick looks at the great divide between faculty and administrators in Chapter Seven, And Never the Twain Shall Meet: Administrator-Faculty Conflict. She presents 15 principles that faculty and administrators can use to understand and manage the conflict which they encounter. She encourages faculty and administrators to deal with conflict as soon as possible, noting that many institutions are contaminated by old conflicts.

In Chapter Eight, Managing Conflict on the Front Lines: Lessons from the Journals of a Former Dean and Provost, Clara M. Lovett notes that like the proverbial physician who is unwilling to heal himself, the academy in the past 30 or 40 years has built a culture that is unwilling to internalize and apply to itself the advice it dispenses with authority to other sectors of society. Because of it, she contends, we do not manage conflict effectively. She discusses academic exceptionalism and how it impacts the way we deal with conflict.

If we approach the institution as a system, then all parts of the institution must learn to work effectively together. Lynn Willett gives a model for such collaboration in Chapter Nine, Student Affairs and Academic Affairs: Partners in Conflict Resolution. Using Mr. Chips, she explains the evolution of the responsibilities of student affairs and academic affairs. In celebrating the yin and yang of the two, she explains how to work together to benefit our students.

In many institutions, faculty-faculty conflict is taking increasing amounts of time for chairs and deans. It is also one of the most unpleasant aspects of the administrator's job. In Chapter Ten, Can We Agree to Disagree? Faculty-Faculty Conflict, Cynthia Berryman-Fink examines academic culture and the changes in higher education which fuel faculty-faculty conflict. She explores the nature of interpersonal conflict and presents strategies for managing faculty conflict.

The 1996 shooting of three graduate committee members reminded all in academia of the extremes of faculty-student conflict. In Chapter Eleven, Views from Different Sides of the Desk: Conflict Between Faculty and Students, Sam Keltner examines the many conflicts that are possible between faculty and students. Using a struggle spectrum, he provides a vehicle for analysis of conflict and guidelines for management of the conflict.

Janet Rifkin calls upon deans and chairs to be problem solvers, challenging the managerial paradigm in Chapter Twelve, Student-Student Conflict: Whose Problem Is It Anyway? She notes that the power relationships between various constituencies require management. The dean and chair, she contends, need to define their work and themselves as multidimensional, as agents of the students, the faculty, and the administration. Using that model, she provides a variety of conflict management strategies for dealing with student-student conflict.

Conflict management within a unionized setting of higher education, primarily with faculty associations, is the focus of Chapter Thirteen, Conflict Resolution in the Academy: A Modest Proposal, by Joel M. Douglas. He notes that the romanticized vision of the academy as a bucolic workplace is today replaced by a traditional industrial prototype of labor relations. Significant problems have resulted. This chapter explains those changes and provides an organizational framework to assess conflict in higher education employment relations.

The perspective of each chapter in this book is that conflict can be managed successfully. Effective conflict management can be a tool to help the institution and the people in it move from stagnation to a new level of effectiveness. The final chapter, Academic Mortar to Mend the Cracks: The Holton Model for Conflict Management, provides a model which can be used to manage any conflict. The process is explained in theory and then applied to a specific conflict.

Is there training for administrators who want to be more effective conflict managers? In the Appendix: Conflict Management Programs for Administrators, Gillian Krajewski provides a list of training programs which are affiliated with academic institutions.

You are not alone as you face the crumbling of your own "ivory tower." I join with all of the contributors to this book in our hope that we have given you mortar—concrete ideas—for mending the cracks.

1 Susan A Holton

What's It All About?
Conflict in Academia

Conflict is not new to the academy. Our earliest roots are contentious ones. The educational establishment of the early Greeks, including Pythagoras, Isocrates, and Aristotle, was destroyed by conflict. Instances of conflict, both internal and external, led to destruction of educational institutions in Greece, Rome, and the Byzantine Empire. But conflict does not have to end in destruction. In the more than two thousand years since the downfall of Isocrates' institution, I certainly hope that we have learned something about the management of conflict.

Conflict can be positive. It does not have to lead to the destruction of the academy, the relationship, the division, or the department. It can lead to increased understanding, development of synergy, and positive engagement. Having successfully worked through a conflict, colleagues will be more willing and able to confront issues as they occur, rather than waiting until a crisis erupts.

But in order for that to happen, we need to understand the complexities of conflict. What is conflict all about anyway? Donohue and Kolt (1992) identify the parameters of conflict. First, conflict must be an "expressed struggle." It may be expressed either verbally or nonverbally. We can all tell that something is wrong when a staff member slams the door on the way out of the room! While no words are expressed, the presence of conflict is clear.

1

It is often the nonverbal communication that gives us the impression that something is wrong. At one institution with which I worked, I walked into a meeting and found half of the people on one side of the room, and half on the other. It was clear that a division existed, and it was clear where the sides were. You can think of other nonverbal signals that have forewarned conflict. If you hold a department chairs' meeting and everyone is late, there is a message of potential (or actual) conflict. However, relying solely on nonverbally expressed conflict presents great difficulties as some people have difficulty encoding, and others decoding nonverbal messages.

With conflict that is expressed verbally there is less room for misinterpretation. When you tell me that you are frustrated because you are teaching an overload every semester, I can immediately register the message. I don't have to guess that your crossed arms and glare mean something significant, and then guess what that significance might be. Clear, effective verbal communication of conflict takes much of the guesswork out of the problem definition.

SOURCES OF CONFLICT

For conflict to occur, there must be interdependence. Too often in academia, divisions, departments, and individuals act as if they are dependent upon no one. They work as if their part of the institution is the only one—or at least the only one that matters. In fact, each of us within an academic community is dependent upon other divisions, departments, and individuals. This interdependence may not be noticed, however, until conflict arises. I don't realize that the facilities office has anything to do with my classes—until it decides to renovate a floor of a building, and I must move. Or student affairs and academic affairs seem to be quite disparate—until the softball team wins its division, and the players need to go to the national tournament during finals week. This interdependence requires a systems approach to conflict, acknowledging that all of us are a part of the larger system of the college or university. What happens in every division, department, and office influences what happens in every other. Are you still unsure? Think about the repercussions when someone in your institution was profiled unfavorably in the local (or national) newspaper.

Incompatible Goals

Does everyone in your department or division have the same goals? Have you ever checked? Too often, we don't know the goals of others, but we perceive that the goals are incompatible. How could offices so diverse as student affairs and administration and finance possibly have the same goals? How could the physics department and the leisure studies department have the same purpose? We may perceive incompatible goals even where there are none. One institution had a large, complex faculty that included faculty specifically hired as researchers and some specifically hired as teachers. Assumptions about the goals of the two groups were made. What I discovered after some interviews, however, was that their assumptions were wrong. The goals of the entire faculty were essentially the same.

As you well know, perception is not necessarily reality. You are probably familiar with the perception exercise which features a picture that, depending upon the way you view it, shows either an old woman or a young woman. Your perception determines whether you see something as a problem or opportunity, whether you can visualize conflict as a positive, energizing force or only as a frightening prospect. And so we in academia must have conversations with others—others in our departments, our schools, our divisions, our institutions—to understand the goals of the others and to determine the overarching goals of the institution. If your institution has a clear mission statement at every level, and one that has been developed via an inclusive process, then this problem of disparate goals may not exist. If it does, it would be helpful to take the time to undertake a complete mission statement process.

Scarce Resources

One of the most significant changes in higher education during the past decade is the reduction of resources. The perception of scarce resources is usually present in conflict. A brief conversation with most departments and divisions in academia will reveal that many believe that others have different (more, better) resources than they. There is also the perception that there used to be money and resources available that no longer exist. In fact, this lack of resources is a significant factor in the increase of conflict in academia.

But too often, there is an assumption of scarce resources that is not necessarily true. In academia, as in other institutions in our country, there is often a scarcity mentality which says that there is only a small amount of anything (money, power, authority, students). If you get more power, the theory goes, then it takes away from me. If your department gets more equipment, mine cannot.

This conflict can be managed in a number of ways. First, everyone needs clear information about reality. What is everyone else's budget? Is there truly more money per person for academic units than for administrative units?

It is also a time when everyone must be more creative. One challenge and joy in working with institutions is to try to get them to identify alternatives. Yes, we want a forensics program that will send students to events throughout the country. And yes, the budget for that has been severely cut. So in what other ways might I find the resources to send the students? How else might I find funding for the program? This is a time for creativity in academia so that resources can be found to do what we want to accomplish. Until this happens, the conflict over resources will be one of the most significant in higher education.

Interference from Others

Sometimes we feel that all of our problems would be solved if only (fill in the name of your least favorite gatekeeper) would not get in our way.

Who is standing between you and your goals? Is there truly anyone else, or is it yourself or your issues standing in the way? The perceived interference in goals often occurs because we negate an idea before we fully form it. "The department will never go for it" stops many chairs from coming forward with a new idea. We assume interference before it is given. Instead, we should prepare the best case possible to support our interests and ideas and take it to the appropriate people for them to affirm it. When we develop a clear plan of action, then we think through those possible obstacles and determine ways to counter the possible interference. Many ideas go down the drain because we say no for others before they even have a chance to say yes.

When something truly interferes with the attainment of your goals, conflict management allows the opportunity to sit down and find out what the true issues are (not the positions, but the issues—what people really want). When you discover these issues, you may discover that the goals are not different, but that you were defining the problem differently, or that you perceived different methodologies for managing it.

Conflict, then, is defined as "an expressed struggle between at least two interdependent parties who perceive incompatible goals, scarce resources, and interference from others in achieving their goal" (Donohue & Kolt, 1992).

WHAT IS THE PROBLEM?

In higher education, as in other parts of our world, there are two different types of conflict: content and relationship. Many conflicts contain elements of both, and both must be acknowledged in order for conflict to be managed.

Content Conflict

Content conflict centers on objects, events, or persons that are external to the parties involved. When the students ask what questions are important to study for the test, that is a content conflict. Some other examples of content conflict include: Who is going to move into the new building? Should the academic advising center be located in student affairs or academic affairs?

Each one of those conflicts can be defined as clearly objective conflicts. However, for the people in the middle of the conflict, they are usually more complex.

Relationship Conflict

Relationship conflict centers on interpersonal relationships between the parties involved in the conflict and others in the institution (who may or may not be directly involved in the conflict). Relationship conflict centers on such issues as: Who is in charge here? How important am I? What power do I have?

As with each of the conflicts mentioned above, the relationship element can also be identified: Who is going to move into the new building? On the content level, that is a clear question external to the parties. Given the space of the new building, and the space requirements of the divisions, departments, and schools, what will be the best fit? What departments or divisions are most appropriate to be housed in that campus location? People external to the conflict can look at it and logically, rationally analyze the problem to come up with solutions. However, there is also a relationship element implied. What is the relationship of the building and its location and the departments or divisions? Is the building central to the administration, and therefore perceived to be closer to the seat of power? What are the perks for being in that location? Is there a perception that the department is being punished by being moved to the new location, or is it being rewarded with new space?

Should the advising center be under the auspices of student affairs or academic affairs? Again, on the surface, this is a clear content question. We could define the purposes of the center, analyze that based on the mission statement of the divisions, and determine which would be most appropriate. But is that how it is perceived? Is the center seen as a reward? Does it give more power to one area or the other?

Every conflict has both content and relationship components. Both must be identified and analyzed, or the conflict will occur again, perhaps in another guise.

PRECURSORS OF CONFLICT

What leads to conflict? Usually all conflict can be distilled to four substantive differences: facts, methods, goals, and values.

Facts

First, we may differ on the facts of the conflict. You and I may have different information. We may be working on the schedule for the next academic year, and I want to try an interesting new class time configuration. You have heard that there will be no manipulations of the regular schedule allowed. We have a conflict of facts. Or perhaps we differ on the definition of the problem. You see the issue as a question of room use, and I see it as a question of offering the students the most possible options. And finally, with conflict of fact, two people (or more) may have differing impressions of their own power or authority. You believe that as department chair you have the power to schedule classes at any time you wish. In reality, only the dean can make those decisions. And so your perception of your authority is inaccurate.

Conflict of fact is often easy to manage by getting the truth. Of course, if people have differing impressions of the truth, there is a problem. But for many conflicts of this nature, it is easy to make a phone call to check the facts. I can call to see if in fact I can schedule a class at this special time. Or we can identify our differing perceptions of the course offerings and discover that we are not really that far apart in our perceptions.

I frequently encounter conflicts of fact with institutions where the role and responsibility of individuals (usually department chairs or deans) is not clear. The facts can be identified and conflict averted if everyone's roles and responsibilities are clearly articulated.

Methods

Secondly, conflict may result from different methods. While we may agree on the facts, our method for handling the conflict or the situation may be quite different. We may have different procedures, strategies, or tactics that we think ought to be used to manage conflict. If you are a department chair who believes in making the ultimate decisions in an executive-consultative mode, and your department believes that all decisions should be made collaboratively, you have a conflict of methodology.

Goals

The conflict of goals has already been discussed. We often disagree over what should be accomplished. I want my department chairs to go on a retreat to learn to work together more effectively, and you want the chairs to go on a retreat to work out a mission statement for the school. While these may seem to be mutually exclusive, good conflict management can lead to an understanding that they are not. You can have a retreat in which the chairs learn to work effectively together while working out the mission statement. In this instance, and many other goal conflicts, both the process and the content goals can be accomplished at the same time.

Values

Finally, perhaps the most difficult type of conflict with which to work is the conflict of values. People may disagree about what is fair, about the way to exercise power, and about the moral considerations, about what is right. As a dean, you are often confronted with value conflict when two people, each with a unique story, come to you to ask for some sort of pardon—whether it be to get back into school after a disastrous semester, or to be allowed to take a semester off to pursue research interests. Your conflict often comes when one person says, "But you let him do it!"

Conflicts of values often surface when a department or division creates a mission statement. What is important? What are we truly trying to do here? What is our ultimate raison d'etre?

When working with conflicts of values, you must be very clear about the criteria you use to manage the conflicts. If someone asks you the basis of your decisions, you can lay out these criteria. You must be clear about the values that are central to your conflict management style.

THE PROCESS OF CONFLICT

Think about the latest conflict in your department or division. Did you see it coming? What happened? What was the precipitating moment? What was the process of the conflict?

Conflict doesn't just spring up overnight. As you think of some of the conflicts with which you have been involved, you can probably think of the often slow development of the process.

Allan Filley (1975) developed a six-element model of conflict that is an accurate reflection of the conflict process. His model includes 1) antecedent conditions, 2) perceived conflict, 3) felt conflict, 4) manifest behavior, 5) conflict resolution or suppression, and 6) resolution aftermath.

Antecedent Conditions

What leads to conflict? Why is it that you can be talking about an issue for a few weeks and no one raises a voice, but yesterday someone began screaming?

Antecedent conditions are the characteristics of the situation which generally lead to conflict, although they may be present in the absence of conflict as well. The saying "the straw that broke the camel's back" may sometimes be an accurate description of why the conflict erupted. Sometimes conflict lies fallow for months, or even years, and nothing happens. At other times, the very mention of a building, a person, or a situation triggers conflict. Levinger and Rubin (1994) noted three types of antecedent conditions: 1) physical context, 2) social context, and 3) issue context.

Physical context. Do you always have conflict when you meet in a particular room? Is there conflict when you have only a brief time to come up with a solution to a problem? Physical limitations often lead to conflict. People need to meet in a neutral space. If our departments are in conflict over the use of a television studio, we should not meet there. The very presence of that room may escalate the conflict. Of course, if you begin to realize that every time you meet in a particular room, your conflict escalates, you can try to understand what it is about that room that leads to conflict. One institution with which I worked had a particular issue with allocation of faculty offices. The group often met in the most palatial office on campus—one which many faculty coveted. Then they went back to their own woefully inadequate offices. And so the location of the meeting changed, and people were able to talk more civilly. The issue of inequality of faculty offices was also brought out on the table, and could be discussed.

Another physical antecedent can be time pressures. A group may work well together when they have adequate time to consider some divisional issues. But when there is a quick deadline—when something must be done within a few weeks—conflict may occur. The time regulation pushed the latent conflict into existence.

Social context. The social context is another antecedent condition. A group may be more willing and able to engage in conflict if there are no observers, if their discussions are not open to audiences or third parties. Sometimes the relationship between parties changes, thus changing the conflict dynamics. Two people used to be colleagues—but one has now been chosen to be the dean. And the previously concealed conflict may rear its head. The social context change is probably apparent as you work with a new group of directors or department chairs every year. Groups that worked well together in the past with one particular style may experience conflict when new players with different styles join the group.

Issue context. The third context of antecedent conditions is the issue context. A group may have been working well but become overwhelmed by the number of issues on their plate. The curriculum committee may become testy with each other when faced with the onslaught of requests at the end of the year. And the conflict that has been below the surface can no longer be ignored. Or sometimes the sequencing of issues can lead to conflict. That is easily managed by looking at all of the issues and determining the appropriate sequence for their consideration and management.

Perceived Conflict

The second step of Filley's process distinguishes between logical and emotional or personal conflict. Perceived conflict is a logically and impersonally recognized set of conditions which causes conflict between the parties. In perceived conflict, one can logically and rationally define what is wrong. Sometimes that accurate definition is enough to identify how to manage the conflict. Sometimes it is not.

Felt Conflict

Felt conflict is personalized, expressed in feelings of threat, hostility, fear, or mistrust. In felt conflict, people feel that the issue is not impersonal, but rather that it is contained in the relationship and within the individuals there. Mistrust is one of the most important aspects of felt conflict, because when mistrust occurs, there can be no effective conflict management.

An institution may be able to define the conflict as a disagreement between two student organizations about the use of Student Government Organization monies for a trip. The Archeology Club believes that a trip to the Painted Desert to participate in a dig is an appropriate use of funds; the SGO says that such a trip is not within the definition of use of funds. But the felt conflict acknowledges other issues. The members of the Archeology Club don't trust the officers of the Student Government Organization. The club believes that funds have been used for similar club trips in the past—of course for a club with which the SGO officers were involved. Or the SGO may feel that its autonomy is being threatened by a group that says it will go to the college's board to get the money.

Manifest Behavior

As a result of the perceived and/or felt conflict, manifest behavior occurs. This is the way in which the individuals handle the conflict. Do they flee the conflict, or pretend that it is not real? Do they decide to bargain? Do they work together toward consensus? Do they become competitive and compel the others, through authority or power or some reward structure, to "do it their way"?

Conflict Resolution

Finally, those involved in conflict bring it to conclusion through conflict resolution or suppression. How they do that varies greatly depending on the parties, the conflict, and the context. Effective conflict management techniques are found throughout this volume, and specifically in the last chapter.

Resolution Aftermath

What happened as a result of the agreements you and your colleagues made after the last budget cut? Do you still remember? It is this phase, the resolution aftermath, that reinforces the reality that conflict is not completely resolved, but rather is managed. There is always an aftermath of the resolution of conflict. It may be positive, as members of a department or division learn to work effectively together and draw on that goodwill for the next conflict. Or it may be negative as the "losers" in the conflict vow never to cooperate with the "winners."

Conflict patterns perpetuate themselves and conflicts often become a cause for disputants. The conflict often becomes cyclical. Conflict often reflects patterned behavior and is predictable. Especially in groups, such as departments or divisions, where the same people interact over many years, repeated conflict patterns are likely to occur. And so, using Filley's model, the resolution aftermath leads back to the antecedent conditions. The aftermath of today's conflict helps to determine how well we will interact when the next conflict surfaces.

How Do We Mend the Cracks?

Conflict in higher education is a complex phenomenon. For years, the cracks which appeared in our infrastructures in higher education were ignored or patched up. But quick fixes won't work anymore.

This book is devoted to analyzing those conflicts in higher education, to understanding the cracks and complexities of those conflicts, and to determining ways in which we might mend the cracks that are threatening the ivory towers of academia.

REFERENCES

Donohue, W. A., & Kolt, R. (1992). *Managing interpersonal conflict.* Newbury Park, CA: Sage.

Filley, A. C. (1975). *Interpersonal conflict resolution.* Glenview, IL: Scott, Foresman.

Levinger, G., & Rubin, J. Z. (1994). Bridges and barriers to a more general theory of conflict. *Negotiation Journal,* 10, 201-215.

2

Gerald Graff

ADMINISTRATION IN AN AGE OF CONFLICT

Let us begin with a proposition that I can't prove but that I think would be hard to refute. Since the dawn of educational institutions, a pervasive assumption has been that successful education and fundamental conflict do not mix. This assumption has been so widely taken for granted by educational thinkers that it has usually been left unstated. Effective education, it has gone without saying, depends on the existence of a consensus on what is to be taught and how. If teachers disagree about what the truth is, or about which truths are most important to teach, students will be confused, the curriculum will be incoherent, and educators will lose the confidence of the public. The eruption of fundamental philosophical conflict over education has therefore been a source of deep distress to educational institutions, whose response has typically been to try to deny these conflicts or to paper them over.

Thus when modern academic administration emerged at the end of the nineteenth century—and here the point is amply supported by educational historians, as we shall see—it seemed natural to conceive it as an art of circumventing or neutralizing conflict, usually by keeping warring professors isolated from one another. Otherwise, it was felt, clashing individuals and factions would endlessly bicker, wash their dirty linen in public, and embarrass the university in the eyes of outsiders.

This assumption that academic conflict is inherently destructive, and that a major function of academic administration must therefore be to prevent or muffle it, has continued to hold sway in American universities to the present day. For reasons to be examined here, however, this way of thinking about administration and conflict has increasingly reached a dead end. The unprecedented challenges higher education faces today make it imperative to develop a new idea of administrative conflict management, one that seeks to make productive use of academic conflicts instead of trying to shut them down.

Once upon a time, from the 17th to the late 19th centuries, American colleges were small, quasimonastic institutions bound together by a common religious and social creed. They were governed with a paternalistic hand by the faculty, the chaplain, and the college president. The faculty oversaw student life and dealt with discipline problems; the chaplain officiated at the compulsory daily services; and the president personally recruited the students, greeted them on arrival, and taught the senior year "Evidences of Christianity" course that was the culmination of the curriculum. The small size of the college, its marginal relation to the mainstream of American life, its commitment to a common religion, and its curricular emphasis on the ancient languages lent the institution a strong sense of unity. In such an organic community, there was no need yet for academic administration as it would later be conceived.

THE AMERICAN COLLEGE: THE 20TH CENTURY

These conditions began to change dramatically in the 1890s, when American higher education entered the first stages of the vast process of expansion that would eventually produce the multiversity of the late 20th century. In place of the communitarian *Gemeinschaft* of the college there was now the bureaucratic, departmentalized specialization of the university, with its sprawling campus, its organized and subsidized athletic teams, its close ties with business and the professions, its research facilities and laboratories organized on the scientific model, and its ambitious effort to encompass all the diverse branches of human knowledge. Some would never forgive the university for its loss of innocence, and many colleges resisted change to a greater or lesser extent. Yet the change was clearly a necessary response to the democratizing and industrializing forces of the modern world. The old college had achieved a tight community, but only by its exclusion of vast areas of modern thought and large sectors of the American population.

Administration grew exponentially as higher education became larger, more complex, and more closely integrated into the world of business, government, and professional life. As Clark Kerr writes in *The Uses of the University*, administrative expansion followed certain inexorable laws:

> As an institution becomes larger, administration becomes more formalized and separate as a distinct function; as the institution becomes more complex, the role of administration becomes more central in integrating it; as it becomes more related to the once external world, the administration assumes the burden of these relationships (Kerr, 1963).

Yet a fourth factor was implicit in the three that Kerr mentions here—that of increased conflict. It was not just the greater size, complexity, and degree of worldly involvement of the new university that demanded an expanded role for academic administration. Just as important was the potential for conflict that arose as the narrow religious uniformity of the old college gave way to a bewildering diversity of intellectual, cultural, and disciplinary specializations.

To be sure, from our present vantage point, the degree of diversity and conflict in the academic culture of the first half of the 20th century seems modest and limited. Until the early 1960s, the American university remained a relatively restricted institution both socially and intellectually, its culture still largely dominated by a white, Anglo-Saxon male elite which confidently shared many social and intellectual attitudes. As intense as the academic disputes in this period often became, they took place against a broad background of agreement and mutual respect that took for granted certain traditional gentlemanly norms of conduct. Rival schools of historiography, say, might fiercely attack each other's interpretations or their evidence, but their members remained bound together by common premises about the goals and methods of history and by their identification with a common ideal of the gentleman and scholar. It is just this tacit assumption of agreement and respect—this assumption that, however opposed they may be on intellectual issues, professional rivals are much the same kind of person—that would weaken or disappear in the conflicts that would rock the university from the mid-1960s to today's "culture wars" and has made our current battles between traditionalists and feminists or Marxists seem qualitatively different from earlier academic disputes. Nevertheless, though these recent conflicts make those of the pre-1960s university look relatively modest, they become more significant when the comparison is with the culture of the 19th century college, by contrast with which the American university of the early 20th century seemed a hotbed of conflict and intellectual diversity.

THE NEW UNIVERSITY

In place of a single spiritual mission that could be exemplified in the old college president, the new university proliferated a multiplicity of different missions. As vocational and scientific training were added to the traditional mission of transmitting moral and religious values, as conflicts arose between pure and applied research and between humanistic and scientific models of inquiry, and as each discipline and field developed its own distinctive perspectives, no single individual could any longer understand the whole, much less claim to embody it. Clearly such rapidly multiplying differences could only lead to chaos unless some powerful counterforce were developed to keep divisiveness in check. Academic administration became that counterforce.

Whereas the old college had been held together by a common set of beliefs, the new university was held together by bureaucratic administration (though there is a sense in which administration is itself a kind of belief system). Administration took the place of shared beliefs, filling the vacuum left by the waning of consensus on the academic mission. The ideal of a unitary educational mission remained prominent in academic rhetoric, especially on ceremonial occasions and in the college catalog, but it materialized less and less in institutional fact. Missionary presidents like Robert Maynard Hutchins arose periodically to reassert the ideal, but they inevitably turned out to be rearguard voices crying in the wilderness.

This link between the waning of consensus and the rise of administration has been recognized by historians. As Laurence R. Veysey puts it in *The Emergence of the American University* (1965), the new university, unlike the 19th century college, was an "institution beholden to no metaphysic." "Talk about the higher purposes of the university," Veysey adds, became "increasingly ritualistic." For "neither the Christian religion in any of its varieties, nor positive science, nor humane culture proved self-evidently capable of making sense of the entire range of knowledge and opinion." Administration, Veysey concludes, was "the structural device which made possible the new epoch of institutional empire-building without recourse to specific shared values." "Bureaucratic modes served as a low but tolerable common denominator, linking individuals, cliques, and factions who did not think in the same terms."

CONFLICT SUPPRESSION

Building academic empires without recourse to shared values meant playing down or avoiding conflict. As Veysey puts it, the tacit or explicit assumption of the new university was that "quarrelsome debate, including that based on conflicts among academic ideals, must be minimized or suppressed whenever it became threateningly serious" (Veysey, 1965), and "each academic group normally refrained from too rude or brutal an unmasking of the rest." Burton R. Bledstein in *The Culture of Professionalism* (1976) makes a similar point, observing that the new "universities quietly took divisive issues such as race, capitalism, labor, and deviant behavior out of the public domain and isolated these problems within the sphere of professionals—men who learned to know better than to air publicly their differences." And Frederick Rudolph, in his study of the college curriculum, observes that the modern bureaucratic university typically dealt with conflicts "by walking away" from the choices over which college authorities had agonized throughout the century: "practical or classical studies, old professions or new vocations, pure or applied science, training for culture and character or for jobs" (Rudolph, 1977).

In effect, the new university responded to such hard choices with a tolerant relativism that encouraged peaceful coexistence—or armed truce—rather than open debate. The tacit motto of the new institution was "I won't interfere with what you want to teach or study if you don't interfere with me." As Harvard philosopher George Santayana put it, the new academic professionalism gave lip service to the dogmas of traditional idealism that had characterized Santayana's "genteel tradition." Its real attitude, however, was "Plato, the Pope, and Mrs. Eddy shall have one vote each" (Santayana, 1921).

As Veysey and others suggest, the new form of administration maintained a state of academic detente by a tactic of dividing and isolating, separating potentially warring faculty members, departments, and intellectual perspectives so that their conflicts would not disrupt internal order or discredit the university to the outside world. The danger that one academic group would commit "too rude or brutal an unmasking of the rest," in Veysey's phrase, was minimized when the groups in question rarely came into contact. Bureaucratic methods kept the peace, in short, by encouraging a structure of "patterned isolation," as Veysey terms it, that kept potentially clashing factions safely insulated from each other. In a real sense, to quote Veysey (1965) one last time, the new university was driven by a "need to fail to communicate." "The university throve, as it were, on ignorance."

The assertion that the modern university thrives on ignorance may seem extravagant, but it contains an important grain of truth. As the modern university evolved into a scene of increasing conflict, protective structures evolved that enabled academics to tune out critics and rivals among their colleagues, though they could hardly fail to be aware of the existence of these threatening forces. The expanding topography of the campus minimized the chances of open conflict by making it increasingly unlikely that academics from different sectors of the scholarly world would come into contact. With the new science complex at one end of the campus and the humanities buildings at the other, years might elapse before a professor of classics encountered a particular colleague in physics or the social sciences, and when such contact did take place it usually would be mostly on social occasions in which serious discussions of intellectual issues would seem out of place. The patterned isolation of courses, departments, disciplines, and campus offices and buildings cushioned professors from having to confront the fact that their most cherished assumptions might be harshly disputed by the colleague in the next classroom or the building across the quad.

It was left to the student body, essentially, to bring together what the faculty had put asunder. The college curriculum, so often likened (justifiably, in my view) to a cafeteria counter in its proliferation of noncommunicating courses and subjects, became a mirror of the patterned isolation of the university at large. Like the American city, the American curriculum has developed by accretion and adding-on, paralleling the way the pressures of urban social conflict have been relieved by the movement of the more prosperous to suburbia. Whenever a threatening new academic topic or field appeared—secularized science, vocational education, creative writing, econometrics, psychohistory, deconstruction, feminism—the curriculum has assimilated it by adding a new "suburb"—a new course, a new chair, a new program—thereby allowing the established courses and programs to go on largely as before. Curricular conflicts were "resolved" in this fashion, by appeasing each of the established pressure groups and isolating them in their separate sectors of the curriculum where they would no longer get in each other's way. Such a strategy satisfied impatient insurgents, who now had the license to stir things up in their corner of the curriculum, but it also satisfied disgruntled conservatives, who could continue doing what they had always done in theirs. Eventually, the conflict itself would be forgotten as each group went its separate way.

For example, at the turn of the century, the emerging field of modern languages and literatures, which had already displaced the departments of classics, came into conflict with the study of rhetoric and oratory that had been a mainstay of the old college. When this conflict came to a head in the 1920s, schools of speech were established that terminated the hostilities by giving the rhetoricians and orators a new home. Within a short time the conflict would be forgotten, and departments of speech and English would coexist side by side, no longer needing to deal with the fact—though it might be confusing to students—that in many ways they represented competing approaches to the same subject matter.

Similarly, when rifts opened between quantitative and nonquantitative social scientists or psychologists, order was restored by another bifurcation and division of curricular spoils. The process was repeated once more when creative writers and artists challenged the domination of academic departments by literary and art historians after World War II, resulting in the now fully institutionalized divisions between art and art history and creative writing and literature, in which artists and critics are rarely in regular communication. In parallel fashion, freshman composition has evolved in isolation from the study of journalism (even though many of the models of writing in composition courses are journalistic) and from the study of literature.

Most recently, the process of change-by-accretion has been played out in the emergence of women's studies, black studies, ethnic studies, gay studies, and other programs that reflect the "identity politics" of post-1960s culture. These programs are often labeled "separatist" by their detractors, sometimes with justification, but what the label ignores is that such separatism only replicates the "respectable" separatism of the established academic fields, each of which achieved its autonomy by its own version of identity politics. When feminists or gay scholars form a separate enclave, they are only following the time-honored route to institutional success and prestige for academic subgroups, which has been to close ranks around one's inner circle and wall oneself off from threatening outsiders.

To give this system its due, it has made universities wonderfully receptive to innovation while avoiding paralyzing deadlocks over turf. By continually expanding the playing field, universities have been able to absorb and assimilate new ideas and research fields without displacing or inconveniencing established departments and fields, and it has enabled factions to coexist which would otherwise have been at one another's throats. Administrators have been able to take justifiable pride in the rich diversity of viewpoints in the modern research university and its achievement of a harmonious blend of the old and the new. Few could wish to return to the old college, which kept peace by shutting out innovation and incurring stagnation as a result.

The problem, however, is that sweeping conflicts under the rug has its costs, whether it comes about by excluding dissenting voices, as did the old college, or by incorporating dissenting voices but isolating them, as did the new university. When conflicts are not openly acknowledged and confronted, debates over fundamental matters of principle that are virtually at the center of intellectual life are avoided, creating temporary peace and quiet but draining academic culture of one of its most vital sources of energy. When conflicts are not channeled into productive debate, they can only fester and deepen, eventually erupting in explosive incidents that leave resentments and bad feelings in their wake. And when conflicts are evaded rather than engaged, courses remain disconnected and fragmented, and curricular incoherence deepens.

For a long time, however, as I noted earlier, these consequences of conflict-avoidance were prevented from becoming overly damaging by the persistence of that relatively large degree of inherited social and intellectual uniformity to which I have earlier referred. And as long as universities enjoyed an ever-increasing base of financial support, as they did for the most part throughout the first half of this century, they could relieve conflicting pressures by expanding the playing field. It is easy in retrospect to see that the "patterned isolation" that has allowed academic conflicts to be avoided for so long was a luxury made possible by rising affluence. Today, this base of financial support is eroding at the very moment when the old residue of social and intellectual uniformity has eroded as well. These and other factors have combined to make academic conflicts more difficult to disarm and sweep under the carpet today than they were a generation ago.

CONFLICT ERUPTION

It is not simply that these conflicts have become more antagonistic as academic culture has become more demographically diverse, and as many of the disciplines have turned reflexively inward to interrogate or problematize their traditional premises, and as the money has run out that once enabled administrators to buy off and appease clashing academic groups. Deepening the problem further is the fact that internal conflicts within and between academic disciplines have become increasingly difficult to disentangle from conflicts in the wider culture. Recent scholarly debates over the role of gender or ethnic identity in the arts, for example, tend to echo and merge with debates in the public sphere over issues of hate speech, affirmative action, sexual harassment, and gay rights.

In part, the new coincidence between academic disputes and larger public conflicts results from the greatly increased concern of the academic

disciplines over the last generation with the culture and politics of the present day. This increased involvement in the contemporary has been an
especially striking feature of the humanities, which before World War II
operated within an antiquarian assumption that modern and contemporary
culture had not yet passed that "test of time" that qualified subjects to be
studied academically. The more academics demand the right to set up as
commentators on contemporary culture, and often as commentators who
contest established social orthodoxies, the more chance they have of colliding ideologically with journalists as well as with politicians and lay people.
The increasingly public nature of academic controversy and the difficulty
of distinguishing academic and real politics goes hand in hand with the
increasingly overt politicization of scholarship and teaching. In equal part,
the new inseparability of academic and public conflicts is made possible by
the emergence of a college-educated middle class created by the vastly
expanded postwar access to higher education, a development that has created a new kind of journalistic audience that is eager to be kept up to date
about academic intellectual concerns. Controversies that would once have
remained esoteric are now widely reported in the journalistic media and
reach a broad audience. A case in point is the recent so-called Sokal Hoax,
in which a physicist satirized the epistemological theories of postmodern
science studies by getting what he subsequently declared to be a bogus article accepted by a leading postmodern journal. Other examples would
include the widely publicized disputes over political correctness touched off
by best-sellers like Allan Bloom's *The Closing of the American Mind* (1987),
Dinesh D'Souza's *Illiberal Education* (1991), Arthur Schlesinger, Jr.'s *The
Disuniting of America* (1992), and Christina Hoff Sommers' *Who Killed
Feminism?* (1994) as well as more local controversies aroused by books like
Martin Bernal's *Black Athena* (1991), which challenge traditional scholarly
assumptions about the homogeneity of Western culture.

     Here, then, are some of the factors that have made today's academic
conflicts far less exclusively academic, and consequently far less amenable to
traditional forms of administrative management, than such conflicts were as
recently as the fifties. And as these conflicts have deepened, the curriculum
at once reflects them and yet remains curiously unchanged. Having long
been notoriously fragmented and lacking in coherence and focus, the curriculum has lately become positively schizophrenic, fracturing at many institutions into two ideologically opposed curricula, one for traditionalists and
one for progressives, yet neither very coherent in its own terms. Thus at any
aspiring current institution, the curriculum tends to send out a set of wildly

mixed ideological messages that never engage one another out in the open and therefore add up to a kind of cognitive dissonance for the student. Thus it is possible for a student to go from one class in which it goes without saying (and therefore may not even be stated) that the Western tradition is an august heritage to be unproblematically passed on, to another class—possibly in the next hour—in which it goes without saying that this same tradition is deeply compromised by imperialism and domination.

To be sure, for a percentage of the student body—those who come to college with some already developed skill at synthesizing ideas on their own—such a do-it-yourself curriculum in which each student on his or her own connects what the professors themselves do not—is often intensely exciting and rewarding. The rest, however, are able to cope with the bombardment of mixed messages only by resorting to the familiar strategy of giving each instructor whatever he or she presumably wants even when it is contradictory. It is no wonder, perhaps, if current students tend to become relativists—as many critics of the university charge—when assumptions that are treated as axiomatic in one's morning class are dismissed as outmoded fallacies after lunch.

CONFLICT MANAGEMENT

Such an outline—admittedly schematic and oversimplified but in its essence accurate enough, I would hope—is the challenge the present situation presents to today's academic administrator, faced with an unprecedented degree of conflict that can no longer be papered over or shut down and therefore is no longer amenable to the time-honored ways of dealing with it. How is our beleaguered administrator to deal with such an unprecedented situation? As I suggested at the outset, the situation calls for a kind of Copernican revolution in the very concept of administration, which would reconceive administration as a practice of dealing with conflicts by nourishing and elevating them rather than trying to suppress or quiet them.

In *Beyond the Culture Wars: How Teaching the Conflicts Can Revitalize American Education* (Graff, 1992), I suggest a number of specific ways in which such a project could be carried out. Let me give a brief indication here by looking at several arenas of recent academic conflict that have proved to be notoriously resistant to traditional forms of academic conflict management.

Take the recent widely reported controversies over free speech, sexual harassment, and ethnic separatism that are tearing many campuses apart. Instead of waiting for such controversies to erupt on our campuses and then adopting a defensive crisis management—or media-management—

approach based on putting out fires, might not administrators begin heading off these controversies by encouraging faculty to develop a course or set of courses on the "fires" themselves? One could imagine a semester-long course on the hate speech controversy, with appropriate readings across several disciplines (several excellent readers on the issue are now in print), including the law school (if it is a university), the philosophy department, and the ethnic or gender studies program. A guest appearance principle would make such collaborative teaching feasible without the costliness of team-teaching. Such a course has actually been developed at UCLA, initiated with the encouragement of the vice provost, entitled "The History and Politics of Affirmative Action." *The New York Times* recently reported on the favorable student and faculty response to the course (Mydans, 1993).

Over the last decade, the emergence of multiculturalism as a social movement, combined with the more diverse demographics of the American campus, have exerted strong pressures to widen the canon of the academic humanities, and as a result of these pressures many universities and curriculum committees have been thrown onto a seemingly unresolvable collision course. Administrators have typically been caught in the middle between pressures for new courses and programs from multiculturalists, feminists, and gay scholars, on the one hand, and on the other, equally powerful counterpressures from more traditional sectors to hold the line against such insurgencies.

The standard administrative response to these pressures and counterpressures has been some version of patterned isolation, in which the warring factions are appeased and then safely isolated from one another in separate courses, course-tracks, and requirements. This outcome usually takes the form of a set of distribution requirements, in which students fulfill requirements in Western and in non-Western culture by choosing from a menu of courses designated in the catalog. In most cases, the number of courses on the menu is so large and diverse that no common experience joins them, and certainly no assurance that students will be asked seriously to engage with the question of what it might mean to call a culture Western or non-Western.

Even when some of the courses do attempt a serious engagement with such questions, however, the separation of Western and non-Western courses from one another prevents those comparisons and contrasts that differentially defined concepts such as Western and non-Western need in order to become intelligible. After all, when Western and non-Western cultures are isolated, students are deprived of the dialogue between cultures that they need in order to understand either. The irony in such curricular compromises is that though both sides in a sense win, both end up defeating their own educational purposes.

Again we see the disabling power of the assumption that without a consensus it is impossible to educate effectively. Consequently it does not occur to the parties in such curricular disputes that the clash of rival texts, traditions, and ideologies might itself provide a principle around which to organize such courses and requirements, one that would enable them to become more coherent and arguably more relevant to students' lives and futures than studying Western and non-Western cultures in isolation from each other. Instead of assigning Joseph Conrad's classic *Heart of Darkness* (1910), say, and the Nigerian Chinua Achebe's *Things Fall Apart* (1959), in separate general education courses, one could imagine building a new kind of course or course sequence around the pairing of these and other "rival" texts, supplementing such pairings with provocative critical texts (or excerpts from them) like Schlesinger's *The Disuniting of America* (1992) and Lawrence W. Levine's *The Opening of the American Mind* (1996)—a reply to critics of multiculturalism like Schlesinger. In this fashion, the framework provided by the culture war could help students make better sense of the texts than they could when reading them in isolation.

To be sure, some universities have responded to the multiculturalist challenge by infusing non-Western texts and materials into the traditional reading list, the tactic largely adopted by Stanford to resolve its widely reported skirmish in the early 1990s over its "Cultures, Ideas, Values" requirement. Even in such cases, however, the infusion tends not to be guided by a sense that the conflict of cultures and philosophies might themselves become a central part of the object of study. Though some mixing of texts and traditions occurs at the level of the reading list, traditionalist and progressive instructors remain quarantined in their separate sections or course tracks, so that their clashing philosophical ideas and ways of reading do not engage.

Another way to bring conflicts into productive engagement would be to begin tapping the vastly underutilized curricular and pedagogical potential of extracurricular academic symposia, public conferences, and other campus events. Over the past generation, with the advent of affordable jet travel, American campuses have generated such a rich culture of extracurricular symposia, readings, performances, panels, and other activities that no individual can possibly attend even a fraction of the events that occur on a given day. Though many of these events have an intimate bearing on texts and issues taken up in courses offered in the semester in which they take place, rarely is there any systematic effort to think ahead and synchronize the extracurricular event with the course or courses in which it could play a role. Thus at present in most cases the extracurricular culture *competes* with the curriculum—as well as with itself—instead of supplementing and enriching it.

One could imagine a number of possible symposia that could be organized around recent debates that would raise the level of academic public discourse while creating links between courses that now have no means of talking to one another. Students could be encouraged to write and present papers in such symposia as well as act as panel moderators and respondents, or indeed take over the organization of the symposium itself. Participation in professional conferences has for some time been a normal feature of graduate education. With proper adaptation, there is no reason such participation could not become an equally important part of undergraduate education at the home campus itself. In fact, I have observed very successful examples of such student symposia at several universities and have begun to experiment with them myself at the University of Chicago, where we have extended such events to include high school students.

A whole range of highly contested issues would present themselves for possible symposia. Take for example the recent debates over relativism and the competing claims of objectivist and social constructivist epistemologies. Students now are exposed to a crossfire between teachers who assure them that "everything is political," and who often treat anyone who does not recognize this fact as naive, and teachers who believe that such a notion of the omnipresence of politics spells the end of civilization, to say nothing of education. On the one hand, it is argued that if we deny the possibility of objective truths and values we accede in principle to a totalitarian world in which power is the only reality and Might Makes Right. On the other hand, it is argued that such authoritarian consequences follow if we affirm the possibility of objective truths and values. What makes these recent debates over the politics of truth confusing is that the same charges of authoritarian politics are hurled back and forth by both sides. A public symposium that was integrated into a course or used to connect several courses would enable campuses to start sorting out the confusing volley of accusations that circulate today around the question of the extent to which bad or good political consequences follow from a particular epistemological position. A text such as George Orwell's *Nineteen Eighty-four*—already widely assigned in courses across numerous different departments in the humanities and social sciences—could provide the focal point for discussion. A symposium on

"*Nineteen Eighty-four* and the Politics of Truth" could bring these courses and disciplines together and help a campus community begin working out its differences over such questions while drawing students into academic-intellectual issues.

With their present database capacities, administrators can quite readily identify those texts that, like Orwell's, happen to be assigned in several courses or disciplines in a given year and thereby provide encouragement to the instructors to develop thematic symposia around those texts. The great conflict between liberal arts and vocational ideals of education could become the subject of another symposium series, connecting courses in liberal arts with those in business or in practical writing. "The Arts in a Business Culture" would be a possible topic, or "Writing Across Different Worlds," or "The Social Uses of Writing," which would activate the perennial quarrel between practical and aesthetic conceptions of writing. The conflicts between traditional literary study and creative writing or between studio art and art history would also make good topics. The tensions between academic scholars and avant-garde artists and writers have a long and interesting history, but though these tensions are unwittingly acted out for students, they do not become the larger context of study that students need.

Electronic communication and other on-line technologies should make it much easier today than it was previously for any one course to become part of the context of other courses. They make possible a conversation that would cross not only course and department boundaries, but institutional and geographical ones as well.

If several courses can be put into dialogue by means of a symposium with a theme, one could go further and imagine an entire academic semester having a theme, intersecting with courses given that semester across a department, college, or university. A semester that was actually *about* something would give intellectual issues a chance to become a common topic of discussion on campus, as only the fortunes of the football or basketball teams usually are now. The theme could easily change from one semester to the next in order to satisfy conflicting constituencies, and not every course needs to be tied to the theme in order for the idea to work.

CONCLUSION

I have no illusions that persuading students and faculty to discuss their differences in such forums will be easy. But it this kind of difficult mediation that I believe is going to be the challenge for administrators of the future. All of us are going to have to retrain ourselves to be less frightened by conflict and less prone to run from it the moment it becomes hot and heavy. For if we can learn anything from the recent series of ugly and acrimonious battles we have been through, it is that such battles are here to stay, and that seeking to avoid them only guarantees that they will get worse.

REFERENCES

Achebe, C. (1959). *Things fall apart.* New York, NY: Astor-Honor.

Bernal, M. (1991). *Black Athena: The Afroasiatic roots of classical civilization.* New Brunswick, NJ: Rutgers University.

Bledstein, B. (1976). *The culture of professionalism: The middle class and the development of higher education in America.* New York, NY: Norton.

Bloom, A. (1987). *The closing of the American mind: How higher education has failed democracy and impoverished the souls of today's students.* New York, NY: Simon and Schuster.

Conrad, J. (1910). *Heart of darkness.* New York, NY: Harper.

D'Souza, D. (1991). *Illiberal education: The politics of race and sex on campus.* New York, NY: Free Press.

Graff, G. (1987). *Professing literature: An institutional history.* Chicago, IL: University of Chicago.

Graff, G. (1992). *Beyond the culture wars: How teaching the conflicts can revitalize American education.* New York, NY: Norton.

Kerr, C. (1963). *The uses of the university.* Cambridge, MA: Harvard University.

Kimbrough, R. (Ed.). (1963). *Heart of Darkness: An authoritative text, backgrounds and sources, essays and criticism.* New York, NY: Norton.

Levine, L. (1996). *The opening of the American mind: Canons, cultures, and history.* Boston, MA: Beacon.

Mydans, S. (1993, May 3). Class notes: A course at U.C.L.A. on the politics of affirmative action hits close to home. *New York Times*, B8.

Orwell, G. (1949). *Nineteen eighty-four.* New York, NY: Harcourt, Brace.

Rudolph, F. (1977). *Curriculum: A history of the American undergraduate course of study since 1636.* San Francisco, CA: Jossey-Bass.

Santayana, G. (1921). *Character and opinion in the United States.* New York, NY: Scribners.

Schlesinger, A. (1992). *The disuniting of America: Reflections on a multicultural society.* New York, NY: Norton.

Sommers, C. (1994). *Who stole feminism?: How women have betrayed women.* New York, NY: Simon and Schuster.

Veysey, L. (1965). *The emergence of the American university.* Chicago, IL: University of Chicago.

THE JANUS SYNDROME: MANAGING CONFLICT FROM THE MIDDLE

Benjamin Thomas, a world renowned biochemist, has served his discipline for the past 17 years, through the ranks of doctoral student to full professor. Now, at the peak of his distinguished research career, his faculty colleagues turn to him and ask that he run for the open position of department chair. Having a keen sense of service to his community and university, Thomas agrees to have his name on the ballot. Known for his trustworthiness and honesty, his colleagues unanimously elect him, and his dean assigns him a three-year term. Thomas enters his first day as chair not knowing what to expect from his new position. He had successfully managed large grants with support staff, faculty, and graduate assistants in the past, but he wasn't quite sure what would be expected of him from his dean and his colleagues. On his first day, a colleague walks into his office and said: "Well, Ben, congratulations, or should I say condolences, on your new assignment? I wish you well, but one thing I would like to know right now: Are you for us or against us? Are you going to side with the administration on the restructuring initiative, or are you still one of us, a faculty member?"

Higher education scholars propose that the chairperson hovers between faculty and administration. At best, the chair stands with one foot in each camp and shifts his or her weight from one foot to the other depending on the situation. With this role in mind, consider your sense of orientation on the continuum below, from faculty at 1 to administration at 7. Place a circle around the appropriate number.

Faculty   1   2   3   4   5   6   7   **Administration**

How did you respond to this continuum? When 800 department chairs responded, the majority found themselves somewhere in the middle (55% answered 3, 4, or 5) with only 6% administratively oriented (6 or 7) and 29% faculty oriented (1 or 2).

Caught between conflicting interests of faculty and administration, department chairs often don't know which way to turn. While mediating the concerns of administration and faculty, they try to champion the values of their faculty. As a result, they find themselves swiveling between their faculty colleagues and the administration (Gmelch, 1991). In essence, they are caught in the role of Janus, a Roman god with two faces looking in different directions at the same time. While chairs don't have to worry about being deified, they find themselves in a unique conflict position—between a rock and a hard place. Thus, the department chair is at the heart of the tension between two potentially different value systems and suffers from the conflict inherent in the position. Chairs must learn to swivel between administration and faculty without appearing dizzy, schizophrenic, or two-faced.

How can chairs find this balance and resolve the conflict that is so inherent in their position? Two strategies must be used: First, recognize the types of conflict chairs experience in departments; and second, devise appropriate responses to resolve that conflict. The next section of this chapter will identify the types of conflict in the chair's conflict molecule, followed by the conflict resolution continuum.

DEPARTMENT CONFLICT MOLECULE

Results are mixed on who within the academy suffers the most conflict. Our research leads us to conclude that department chairs, caught in the middle, constantly find themselves in conflict situations. Already viewed as neither fish nor fowl (faculty nor administration), the department chair, as represented in Figure 1, finds that demands from above typically conflict with those from below.

FIGURE 1

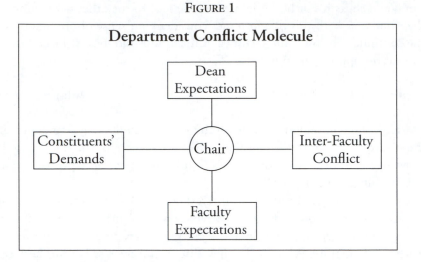

Department Conflict Molecule

The greater the differences between the expectations from above and below, the greater the potential for conflict. In one study, department chairs were asked to rank six decision areas in terms of the amount of role conflict (Carroll, 1974). As Table 1 portrays, faculty salary decisions and faculty promotions rank well above the other key areas as sources of conflicting expectations. It is not too difficult to discern how different points of view cause conflicting expectations among deans, chairs, and faculty regarding promotion and salary decisions—the important standards by which faculty productivity are measured. The other four conflict-ridden decision areas for chairs pertained to academic tenure, faculty firing, departmental budgets, and faculty time allocation.

TABLE 1

Department Chair Role Conflict	
Decision Area	*Weighted Composite Value**
Faculty salary decisions	530
Faculty promotion decisions	525
Academic tenure decisions	443
Faculty hiring decisions	391
Department budget decisions	360
Faculty time allocation decisions	348

* *Weighted composite value provides a relative ranking.*

Thus, department chairs find themselves with incompatible expectations and subjected to role conflict between the dean and faculty (see Higgerson, 1996; Gmelch & Sarros, 1996). For example, they must contend with expectations from the dean to cut costs, while they deal with faculty who demand more travel funds, instructional materials, and research dollars to maintain their expected productivity. As chairs look above and below to assess the expectations placed upon them, they must not forget to look to the sides, to their peers and outsiders.

Often department chairs find themselves trying to resolve inter-faculty conflicts that involve "bickering, whining, and feuding," and "ideological personal wars." In fact, most chairs' dissatisfaction with their jobs comes from faculty disagreeing with each other (Gmelch & Miskin, 1993). Ann Lucas points out: "By the very nature of their academic profession, faculty have been trained to be critical of other perspectives, to be skillful in defending their own professional and personal points of view, and to function most effectively in isolation. What many faculty members have not learned is how to make interpersonal conflict productive" (1994, p. 201).

On the other side of the molecule, chairs feel pressures from their constituents—students, agencies, and alumni. As a result, they may feel boxed in from all sides without enough time, resources, or reason to resolve the conflict. Although this chapter focuses on the resolution of chair-faculty related conflict, the conflict resolution techniques introduced are not unique to any one relationship in your conflict molecule.

CONFLICT MYTHS AND ILLUSIONS

To help clarify some of the illusions or misconceptions surrounding the conflict molecule, consider the following popularly accepted statements.

1. Conflict is destructive.

Conflict may have both positive as well as negative connotations. A certain amount of conflict, if related to professional concerns or academic issues rather than personalities, is healthy and part of the sense of debate of differences in the academy. As Bennis and his colleagues point out, "Elimination of conflict would mean the elimination of such differences" (Bennis, Benne, & Chen, 1969, p. 152). Most academics agree to disagree. Thus they view their disputes as not necessarily bad, abnormal, or dysfunctional, but as a fact of academic life.

2. Conflict should be avoided.

True, avoidance is at times an effective response to conflict, especially when the risk of intervention outweighs the gain, or when you need more information in order to understand and resolve the problem. But avoidance serves to restrict input and only provides a temporary solution to a heated situation. In academia, conflict is inevitable and will only increase with the growing diversity of populations in all sectors of the academic world (Holton, 1995).

3. Conflict is a personality problem.

Unfortunately, most people take conflict personally and believe that if they are involved in controversy, it must be due to their personality. Some chairs feel that for some reason conflict is their fault (Tucker, 1992). In complex organizations such as universities and colleges, conflict is sewn into the institutional fabric, regardless of the personalities residing there. It is easy to conclude that academies are plagued with conflict due to their many levels, rules and regulations, specialized disciplines, heterogeneous staff, participatory decision-making, segmented rewards, and tension between the academic and administrative core of faculty and administration (Gmelch, 1995).

4. Deans create the most conflict for department chairs.

A study conducted by the Center for the Study of the Department Chair concluded that chairs identified conflict with colleagues as their major source of stress. Over 40% of the chairs suffered from excessive stress from "making decisions affecting others, resolving collegial differences, and evaluating faculty performance" (Gmelch & Burns, 1994). In contrast, only 17% of the chairs complained of excessive stress from resolving differences with deans. Thus, chairs suffered more from interpersonal conflict with their colleagues than with their deans.

5. The conflict chairs experience is no different than any other administrator in education or industry.

In one sense, any academic leader, whether a central administrator or the dean of a college, is caught in the middle. However, the chair rests in a unique position, in a management role which has no parallel in business and industry, nor education for that matter. Its uniqueness stems from being at the heart of the tension between two opposite cores of the academy—the academic and administrative. Chairs must serve as a conduit between the department and the administrative structure in the university which are both organized differently. Whereas the academic core of teaching and research operates freely and independently in a loosely coupled system, the managerial core maintains the mechanistic qualities of a tightly coupled system.

6. There is one right way to handle conflict.

The strongest and most direct response many times is seen as the most decisive and durable, leaving little room for ambiguity and misinterpretation. However, disputes can be resolved by a variety of means. Chairs should consider a multitude of options, taking into consideration the formality of the process, the intended outcome, the role of the disputants, the faculty involved, the type of decision that will result, and the nature of the final settlement. The next section will consider the key characteristics of all these options and provide the chair with a continuum of options to resolve conflict.

THE CONFLICT RESOLUTION CONTINUUM

Department chairs and faculty often find themselves in disagreement over roles, procedures, resources, values, power, styles, and goals. Academic colleagues generally resolve their disputes by a variety of means. Table 2 illustrates some of these options that vary in terms of formality of the process, privacy of the discussion, and the parties involved (Eunson, 1997; Moore, 1996).

At the left end of the continuum, at Level 1, the majority of disagreements are handled through private, informal discussion and dialogue between the two parties. On the far right of the conflict continuum (Level 5), representing the more formal, regulated, public process involving third parties, lies the ground of litigation. In between the extremes of Level 1 and Level 5 (discussion resolution and legal resolution) are three of the most commonly used techniques in conflict situations—negotiation, mediation, and arbitration.

Chairs will be able to deal more effectively with conflict if they know the key characteristics and can use the strengths and weakness of these approaches. For example, negotiation, mediation, and arbitration can be used as separate or as complementary approaches. They are not mutually exclusive but in some circumstances can be seen as sequential phases in a conflict resolution process. Baden Eunson explains:

> Negotiation is a dispute resolution process between two parties, wherein both parties share sufficient communication and resources to reach a settlement without outside help. Mediation and arbitration involve third parties or outsiders. Mediation is a cooperative

TABLE 2

Conflict Resolution Continuum

Increased Use of Power and Less Control by Disputant

Levels	1. Discussion	2. Negotiation	3. Mediation	4. Arbitration	5. Litigation
KEY CHARACTERISTICS					
1. Formality	Informal/Voluntary	Semi-formal/Voluntary	Voluntary	Voluntary/Required	Formal/Required
2. Focus	Communicate Positions/Interests	Explore Issues/Interests	Explore Issues/Interests	Address Questions, Contested Issues	Legal Intervention on Standards
3. Flexibility of Procedures	Very High	Very High	Very High	Moderate	Low
4. Outcome	Develop Promises	Decision by Disputants	Guided Disputant Decision	Arbiter Decision	Authoritative Edict
ROLE OF DISPUTANTS					
5. Role of Individuals	Air Differences	Address Issues/Interests	Explore Solutions	Submit Evidence	Submit Evidence Through Attorney
6. Process	No Formal Procedures	Procedures Open	Develop Procedures	Procedures Pre-established	Legal Precedent Develop Procedure
7. Preservation of Relationships	Very High	Very High	High	Doubtful	Very Doubtful
8. Control by Disputants	Very High	Very high	High	Moderate	Low
9. People Involved	Discussants	Disputants	Use of Mediator	Use of Arbitrator or Advocate	Imposition
NATURE OF SETTLEMENT					
10. Type of Decision	Reduce Tension	Resolve Dispute	Mutual Gain (Win-Win)	Right vs. Wrong Rectification	Conformity to Case Law/Statutes
11. Amount of Authority/Coercion	Informal Agreement	Mutual Agreement	Mutual Agreement	Arbitrator Makes Final and Binding Decision	Decision Upheld by Legal Statutes

process wherein the mediator has little or no power to compel a final outcome. Arbitration involves a third party who has some power to compel the final outcome (Eunson, 1997, p. 126).

While early phases of disagreement are primarily based on informal discussion, if these processes prove inadequate, then the dispute moves into negotiation, mediation, arbitration, and ultimately litigation. This is not to say that lower levels represent weaker strategies in relation to mediation, arbitration, and litigation, but that some approaches are more appropriate under certain circumstances.

Level 1—Discussion: When Academics Agree to Disagree

Disagreements pitting faculty against the chair can arise in almost any department. However, they are usually resolved through the informal problem solving discussions by sharing ideas and perspectives in order to come to a common understanding. For example, in our department faculty had once demanded a reduction in their teaching load for the next academic year. At the same time, the department chair learned that the state legislature was demanding an increase in teaching loads. Through prudent discussion and creative problem solving, the faculty agreed with the chair that the time was not appropriate to force the issue and looked to alternative means to reduce overall faculty workloads. This is probably where the majority of academic disagreements end in academic life. Either they are resolved more or less to the satisfaction of both parties, die from debate or lack of interest, or remain unresolved due to lack of a reasonable conclusion.

Level 2—Negotiation: Escalation of Disagreement to Dispute

However, informal discussions could escalate into a dispute when "two parties are unable and/or unwilling to resolve their disagreement; that is, when one or both are not prepared to accept the status quo . . . or to accede to the demand or denial of demand by the other. A dispute is precipitated by a crisis in the relationship" (Gulliver, 1979, p. 75). At this point, the most common way to reach a mutually acceptable agreement is through negotiation.

Negotiation is a bargaining relationship between disputants who have a perceived or actual conflict of interest. As portrayed in Table 2, a faculty member and a department chair (or two faculty members) voluntarily join in a temporary relationship "designed to educate each other about their needs and interests, to exchange specific resources, or to resolve less tangible issues such as the form their relationship will take in the future or the procedure by which problems are to be resolved" (Moore, 1996, p. 8). The outcome of negotiations between academics depends on the approach they take, the distributive difference of power and resources, and the options available to them. Left unchecked or mediated, many times negotiation between unequal parties results in win-lose solutions. Ideally, negotiation produces a wise win-win agreement and preserves or improves the relationship between faculty.

This chapter may lead you to believe that your primary role in conflict situations with faculty is to negotiate an equitable settlement, protecting the interests of others and yourself at the same time. This assumes that you, personally, are in conflict with a fellow faculty member. Remember that most of the conflict in your department comes from inter-faculty relationships and that you may have to perform a role as the mediator, between faculty members, students and faculty, or even the faculty and the dean.

Level 3—Mediation: When Three Heads Are Better than Two

If your negotiation with or between faculty starts to break down and reaches an impasse, you may need to move to mediation. Mediation is initiated when both parties no longer have the ability to resolve the conflict on their own and resort to involving an impartial third party for assistance. At times this may be the dean, a faculty member, a chair from another department, or anyone who is mutually acceptable to both parties.

As evident from Table 2, the mediation process follows a different resolution pattern than the traditional negotiation session. Mediation extends the negotiation process by voluntarily involving a mutually acceptable third party (mediator) with limited or no authority to render a decision. The mediator tries to have both faculty members reach a mutually acceptable settlement of the issues and interests in the dispute, preserving the relationship between the participants.

The mediator facilitates the decision by listening, guiding, suggesting, and persuading the parties. The disputants do submit evidence to the mediator and participate in the decision-making process and outcomes.

In an attempt to prevent disputes turning into lawsuits, more and more colleges and universities are setting up mediation programs (Holton, 1995). The faculty senate at West Virginia University decided to explore using peer mediators to solve interpersonal problems among faculty members. Washington State University created a conflict resolution program to enhance the quality of life throughout the university system by adopting a comprehensive program model for students, faculty, and staff. The head of the public justice department at St. Mary's University in Texas and an officer with the National Association for Mediation Education (NAME) says, "Mediation is growing because of growing disputes and growing litigation. More and more people are looking for alternatives to formal grievance processes, arbitration, and litigation. Going to court is expensive and time consuming" (Staff, 1994).

Level 4—Arbitration: Last Chance Before the Attorneys Take Over

Arbitration is also a voluntary, but sometimes required, conflict resolution process whereby the disputants request the help of an impartial and neutral third party to make a final and binding decision regarding the contested issues. It is at this level of conflict resolution that your personal control of the dispute outcome decreases with the increased involvement of decision-makers outside the conflict relationship, such as the ombudsman, attorney general, or other objective parties within the university setting. The resolution also moves more toward a win-lose and either/or settlement.

In the arbitration process the disputants do submit evidence to the arbitrator but do not participate in the decision-making process and outcomes as is done by the parties in mediation. The arbitrator tries to decipher right from wrong. Unfortunately, if disagreements between academics escalate to arbitration, the preservation of their good relations is doubtful.

Level 5—Litigation: Legal Recourse and Conformity

Historically most deans and department chairs haven't worried about law suits from estranged faculty, but in today's age of legal reasoning a number of academic leaders face grievances annually—over tenure, promotion, discrimination, or other matters—that turn into lawsuits and require expensive and time-consuming litigation.

At this level the disputants have little control over the outcome as the final decision conforms to case law or legal statutes. The process is formal, and the outcome is upheld by the legal statutes. It is at this point that your once internal department issue becomes more public and your control over its outcome follows the win-lose (or lose-lose) pattern of the legal system. Once academic differences reach the litigation stage, preserving relationships becomes very difficult. Overall, while the academics lose control of the outcome they may gain from forceful advocacy of their points and action that reflects socially sanctioned norms such as due process rights and academic freedom.

SELECTING THE "RIGHT" RESOLUTION

Department chairs need to understand and be trained to take any one of these interventions. Academic disputes may escalate from the discussion level through to the litigation stages. The choice a chair makes among the five levels of resolution depends on a number of critical issues (Fisher & Ury, 1983; Moore, 1996; Raiffa, 1982):

1) The emotional intensity of faculty and its impact on preventing a private settlement

2) The skills and capability of the disagreeing faculty to resolve their own dispute

3) The timing of the chair's intervention in the disagreement

4) The pressure of deadlines and time constraints

5) The degree of interdependence faculty must achieve to meet their goals or satisfy their interests

6) The balance of power and resources between the faculty and possible ameliorating influence of a third party

7) The ability to identify key issues and basic interests of both parties

8) The perceived or actual value differences separating both parties

9) The clarity and complexity of the issues and interests

10) The availability on campus of alternative methods of resolution such as ombudsman, dispute resolution center, group counseling program, and/or skilled mediators

11) The power and ability to identify options to satisfy interests

12) The awareness and actuality of alternative solutions to the disagreement

To illustrate the importance of the above variables when dealing with a potentially difficult situation, consider the following simple scenario. Three weeks before the start of a new semester a key faculty member suddenly decides to retire, leaving two core classes without an instructor. What seems to be a simple management problem may be laced with multiple agendas, politics, and faculty self-interests. When faced with this scenario, one chair asked the program faculty to suggest a solution. The three remaining program faculty members discussed (Level 1) the problem (opportunity), but could not come to an agreement. At this point, the chair used the dozen points above to analyze the now escalating conflict scenario.

He found that the emotional intensity among the faculty had escalated to the point where they were not able to resolve it by themselves. Together they did not display nor possess the resolution skills needed to resolve their own dispute. Time was of the essence as the semester was starting in two weeks, and all three faculty members had multiple goals and different issues. An imbalance of power also existed among the three faculty members (a tenured associate professor, untenured assistant professor, and a visiting assistant professor). The key issues and basic interests of all parties were not evident, and the issues became more complex and politicized as the dean imposed his own solution. Although a dispute resolution center existed on campus, none of the parties involved wanted it to escalate to the use of an outside third party and lose control over the outcome and power to internally resolve their own issues. An impasse had taken place, and faculty were digging into their individual positions and not able to identify options to satisfy mutual interests. Faculty had lost sight of alternative solutions that may satisfy all parties to the greatest extent possible. Knowing these circumstances, what should the chair do? The chair felt it was time to intervene in the best interests of all parties.

How should the chair proceed? The chair decided on a three-step process. First, talk to each faculty member individually to collect the facts and separately explore their interests and possible solutions. Then, in the role as mediator, meet with the faculty collectively to try to resolve the problem. And, finally, seek the dean's concurrence with the proposed solution (since the dean had already become part of the solution and problem).

How would you conduct the confrontation meeting among the three faculty members? Here are some guidelines for conducting such a meeting where the chair acts as the neutral, third-party mediator.

CONFRONTATION STRATEGIES

Are certain faculty in your department frequently at odds with one another as these three faculty members were? Counterproductive, inter-faculty bickering hampers the productivity and morale of the department. If, as chair, you detect dysfunctional airing of differences where it is 1) not an isolated incident, 2) faculty members are engaging in unprofessional behavior, 3) personalities have superseded the issues, and 4) neither side is understanding the other's real interests, then it is time to take action and bring the faculty together to assist them in sorting out their differences. Here are some strategies you might use for conducting a confrontation meeting among differing faculty.

1) **Set the stage, and get the faculty close together.** Select a neutral location for the meeting such as a conference room or the chair's office. Parties should be seated close to each other at a round table or even no table

at all with chairs arranged in a circle or semicircle to equalize the perception of power.

2) **Leave your biases at the door.** Do not take sides with any of the faculty members during the meeting. Your role is to remain neutral, stay objective, and ask important questions.

3) **Act as the intermediary or mediator of the meeting.** As chair you may conduct one or a number of sessions with each or all disagreeing faculty together. As mediator you should be neutral and impartial, appropriately assertive, skilled in communication skills such as active listening, questioning, paraphrasing, and reframing, and knowledgeable enough to help generate options, alternative, and possible solutions.

4) **Establish ground rules or procedural guidelines.** Most departments have unwritten norms or rules of collegial behavior. Some departments already have established a set of beliefs about appropriate behaviors within the department such as:

   • We believe equity for all must be demonstrated by intolerance of acts of discrimination or belittlement.

   • We believe in the inherent value of each individual.

   • We believe mistakes are part of life, and we are able to learn from them.

   • We believe honesty is the foundation of respect and integrity.

Other belief statements are exhibited in Table 3. You may also wish to establish simple procedural guidelines, such as attack the problem, not the person; everything said is officially off the record; no written transcripts or tape recordings permitted; look for solutions that best meet the needs of all parties; parties may request a time-out period; and so forth.

5) **Get the facts, and nothing but the facts.** Ask each member to present their interpretation of the facts separately, without interruption by others. Make sure they focus on the problem, not the people or personalities. All the facts must be disclosed in order to generate adequate solutions.

6) **Clarify misunderstandings and miscommunications.** Let the parties air their differences. Venting allows them to openly express their feelings, frustrations, anger, and emotions which can lead to psychological satisfaction and the disclosure of possible latent interests. The chair must

TABLE 3

Department of Kinesiology and Leisure Studies

Beliefs

We believe a commitment to our students is fundamental to our mission.

We believe equity for all must be demonstrated by intolerance of acts of discrimination or belittlement.

We believe in direct and open communication.

We believe the strength of our department lies in our individual and collective contributions.

We believe in a participatory administration of strategies to achieve our departmental goals.

We believe in the inherent value of each individual.

We believe that each individual is accountable for his/her actions.

We believe mistakes are part of life, and we are able to learn from them.

We believe honesty is the foundation of respect and integrity.

---

make sure the process does not get out of control and create a breakdown in the communication. Agree that nothing will leave the room as far as feelings expressed out of frustration. Ask for clarification of information shared which may lead to understanding the real issues and interests of the parties.

7) **Don't reject options without trying to reframe and explore options.** Attempt to change the name of the game. Instead of allowing disputants to reject their opponents' positions, redirect the questioning to test whether the suggestion would meet the other party's true interests. In order to test the authenticity of the suggestion, ask: What if we were to...? Why is it that you want that? Why not? What would you suggest I do? (Ury, 1991).

8) **Do a reality check of the solutions suggested.** In this process, the chair assists faculty members to establish realistic expectations and offers of settlement. For example, ask: Will this solution work? Does it meet the needs of the other party? How practical is the suggestion? Can we deal with the consequences of this action?

9) **Be clear on consequences if a settlement can't be reached.** Remind the parties present that if a settlement cannot be reached, the dispute may

escalate to the next level. Educate your colleagues to the costs of not agreeing: The escalation of the dispute to higher levels of resolution results in increased power by third parties who may not understand the interests of all parties, loss of control by the disputants of the ultimate decision, greater formality and less privacy, erosion of professional relationships, and possibly legal and binding decisions mandating actions possibly unwanted by all parties.

THE GOAL: ACHIEVE THREE DOMAINS OF SETTLEMENT IN YOUR DEPARTMENT

A durable resolution among faculty or between chairs and faculty must be achieved at three levels of settlement: substantive, procedural, and psychological. This point is paramount in preserving the civility and credibility of expressing differences in the academy and needs elaboration to underscore its importance.

Regardless of the approach you use to resolve conflict in your department, whether you can settle it informally through discussion or have to escalate to negotiation, mediation, or arbitration, the key is in its durability and the preservation of academic relationships. The higher levels of resolution are based on more outside power and obligation of the parties to comply with someone else's solution and the less control both parties have over the outcome. The lower levels of conflict resolution are apt to explore and satisfy both parties' interests and establish a long-term, mutually acceptable solution. This long-term solution comes from each party's sense of satisfaction in three areas: substantive, procedural, and psychological (Gmelch & Miskin, 1993; Lincoln & O'Donnell, 1986; Moore, 1996). In order to avoid conflict aftermath as chair, you must make sure that you have worked toward all three levels of satisfaction.

Substantive satisfaction refers to the particular needs of all parties involved. All must feel a sense of equity and fairness which can only be achieved if a reasonable amount of interest satisfaction has been achieved on both sides.

Procedural satisfaction refers to how both the chair and faculty conduct themselves during the conflict resolution process: All parties have had an opportunity to express their points of view; are satisfied with where the meeting was held and how it was conducted; planning for implementation of the agreement has been worked out before the final settlement; and finally, civility and respect for each other's rights, free from personal attacks, has occurred before, during, and after the meeting. The ultimate test of procedural satisfaction is whether the department chair, dean, and the faculty leave with mutual respect and would be willing to engage in the same process again. This actually makes a stronger department with better morale.

Psychological satisfaction results when both parties believe that neither has won or lost but that a wise outcome has been achieved. Here, the question is whether the process has begun to establish and reinforce a long-term relationship. Did anyone engage in degrading tricky tactics during the conflict process? Did both parties maintain their self-esteem, respect, and dignity? This is critical for a group of tenured and relatively stable academics to achieve in order to build a true community of scholars and well-functioning team.

A psychologically satisfying resolution will provide extra benefits to both parties and the department:

1) Compliance with the agreement will be more likely.

2) Sabotage of the settlement will probably not occur.

3) Renewal of the dispute is less likely.

4) Anxiety of both the chair and faculty is relieved.

5) Healthier communication patterns are established for earlier resolution next time.

6) Both faculty and administration feel better after settlement, which adds to the spirit of a departmental team.

In the process of day-to-day interaction, all communities, universities, departments, and interpersonal relationships experience conflict at one time or another. The department environment, the diversity of faculty members, and the differences in chairs' preferred conflict resolution styles all limit the possibility of having collegial and civil academic colleagues who function as a team. The purpose of this chapter has been to expose department chairs to the types of conflict surrounding their conflict molecule and help organize a conflict resolution approach into a creative, usable framework—the continuum of conflict resolution. Five levels of conflict resolution were introduced; and while there is no best way to resolve conflict among academics, chairs should minimize their loss of control over the process and reduce the amount of power and coercion being used. As his or her ultimate goal, the chair needs to select the appropriate level of resolution given the existing conditions and seek the process that best preserves the relationships among colleagues in the academy.

REFERENCES

Bennis, W. G., Benne, K. D., & Chen, R. (1969). *The planning of change* (2nd ed.). New York, NY: Holt, Rhinehart, and Winston.

Carroll, A. B. (1974). Role conflict in academic organizations: An exploratory examination of the department chairman's experience. *Educational Administration Quarterly, 10* (2), 51-64.

Eunson, B. (1997). *Dealing with conflict.* Brisbane, Australia: John Wiley & Sons.

Fisher, R., & Ury, W. (1983). *Getting to yes: Negotiating agreement without giving in.* Ontario, Canada: Penguin Books.

Gmelch, W. H. (1995). Department chairs under siege: Resolving the web of conflict. In S. A Holton (Ed.), *Conflict Management in Higher Education.* San Francisco, CA: Jossey-Bass.

Gmelch, W. H. (1991). Paying the price for academic leadership: Department chair tradeoffs. *Educational Record, 72* (3),45-49.

Gmelch, W. H., & Burns, J. S. (1994). Sources of stress for academic department chairs. *Journal of Educational Administration, 32* (1), 79-94.

Gmelch, W. H., & Miskin, V. D. (1995). *Chairing an academic department.* Thousand Oaks, CA: Sage.

Gmelch, W. H., & Miskin, V. D. (1993). *Leadership skills for department chairs.* Bolton, MA: Anker.

Gmelch, W. H., & Sarros, J. C. (1996). How to work with your dean: Voices of American and Australian department chairs. *The Department Chair: A Newsletter for Academic Administrators, 6* (4), 1, 19-20.

Gulliver, P. H. (1979). *Disputes and negotiations.* San Diego, CA: Academic Press.

Higgerson, M. L. (1996). *Communication skills for department chairs.* Bolton, MA: Anker.

Holton, S. A (Ed.). (1995). *Conflict management in higher education.* San Francisco, CA: Jossey-Bass.

Lincoln, W., & O'Donnell, R. (1986). *The course for mediators and impartial hearing officers.* Tacoma, WA: National Center Associates.

Lucas, A. F. (1994). *Strengthening departmental leadership.* San Francisco, CA: Jossey-Bass.

Moore, C. W. (1996). *The mediation process: Practical strategies for resolving conflict.* San Francisco, CA: Jossey-Bass.

Raiffa, H. (1982). *The art and science of negotiation.* Cambridge, MA: The Belknap Press of Harvard University Press.

Staff. (1994, October). Mediation: Alternative to litigation. *Academic Leader,* 3-4.

Tucker, A. (1992). *Chairing the academic department: Leadership among peers* (3rd ed.). Phoenix, AZ: American Council on Education/Oryx.

Ury, W. (1991). *Getting past no: Negotiation with difficult people.* New York, NY: Bantam Books.

CHAIRS AS DEPARTMENT MANAGERS: WORKING WITH SUPPORT STAFF

B ob Alcott was deep in thought when he heard a knock at the door. "Excuse me, Dr. Alcott? I'm sorry to bother you, but I need to get the overhead transparency projector out of the equipment room." Standing in the doorway was Anna Cruz, the department's newest faculty hire.

"Can't Iris or Alice help you?" asked Dr. Alcott.

"I don't know where they are," replied Anna Cruz.

Reluctantly Dr. Alcott got up from his desk, fished out a set of master keys from his top desk drawer, and started toward the equipment room with Dr. Cruz. Lately, more of his time is spent handling duties that should be performed by Iris and Alice, the department secretaries.

Iris joined the department as head secretary seven years ago. She was a faithful and loyal employee until her husband was diagnosed with cancer. Iris is determined to nurse her now chronically ill husband at home. Even with a hired nurse helping during the day, Iris finds it impossible to make it to work by 8:00 a.m. because she is exhausted from having been up most of the night with her ailing husband. Iris always stays late to make up the time at the end of the day. Bob Alcott, the department chair, knows that Iris puts in her full work week even though she doesn't work the usual 8:00 a.m. to 5:00 p.m. hours.

Alice, the newest member of the office staff, is a single woman in her mid-twenties. When Bob Alcott hired Alice two years ago, he knew that she saw the secretarial position as a way to get a break on her college tuition. Alice is a conscientious worker even though her top priority is completing her baccalaureate degree. When Dr. Alcott hired Alice he agreed that she could take one course per semester during office hours. In previous semesters, Alice enrolled in a course that met during the noon hour when the office is closed, and she always consulted with Dr. Alcott about her plans for taking classes. This semester, without consulting Dr. Alcott, Alice registered for two daytime courses, one which meets on Tuesday and Thursday from 11:00 a.m. to 12:15 p.m. and another that meets at 8:00 a.m. on Monday, Wednesday, and Friday. Since Iris is seldom in before 9:00 a.m., the office is often unattended.

Now Bob Alcott finds that he is back-up for the secretarial staff when faculty need equipment, the phone rings, or students and other walk-in traffic need assistance. On some days, Bob Alcott finds that he spends more time at the secretaries' stations than he does at his own desk. Dr. Alcott likes both Iris and Alice. He wants to be supportive of Iris's need to nurse her husband at home and Alice's desire to complete her undergraduate degree. At the same time, he realizes that he must take some action to improve the overall functioning of the secretarial support staff.

IT's YOUR TURN

Place yourself in Bob Alcott's position. How would you manage this situation? While Iris and Alice have legitimate needs that conflict with their work schedule, both seem to take advantage of Dr. Alcott's generosity. More importantly, their tardiness and absenteeism creates a hardship on the chair and jeopardizes the operation of the department.

The department chair finds himself in a conflict with the support staff. Unless he successfully manages this situation, he will undoubtedly find himself in a conflict with faculty who need access to locked supply closets and other routine secretarial assistance. Since Alice's new behavior in taking classes during office hours occurred after Iris started coming to work late, the chair may also need to mediate conflict between Iris and Alice. We don't know if Alice is fully aware of Iris's home situation or the fact that Iris stays late to make up the hours missed. If not, Alice's behavior may be motivated by her belief that Iris receives preferential treatment.

Bob Alcott wants to be fair with both Iris and Alice. He intends to be supportive of their personal needs. Nevertheless, it is the department chair's responsibility to manage such conflict to preserve the efficient operation of the department. If you were Bob Alcott, what would you do to manage this conflict before it escalates further? What is your objective? What behavior must change to improve the situation? How would you approach Iris and Alice? Would you involve others in the management of this conflict, and if so, who would you include? Is there a way in which you can remain supportive of Iris and Alice without jeopardizing the office operation?

A WORD ABOUT CONFLICT

Conflict exists whenever two or more people disagree about some decision or action. Conflict is a natural outcome of human interaction because individuals do not always think alike. Indeed, individuals often disagree about what has happened or what should happen. Not all department members hold the same values or attitudes. Not all department members perceive and react to situations in the same way. Consequently, conflict is inevitable, and department chairs need to recognize this fact. It is also important to recognize that conflict can be positive. Conflict signals differences in how people think, and these differences of opinion are relevant to department dialog about important issues. Effective problem solving requires that we consider all viewpoints and possible alternatives. This cannot happen if all department members think alike. Hence some diversity in viewpoint is worthwhile, and department chairs need to remember that not all conflict is inherently bad or destructive. The chair's objective is to minimize destructive conflict that jeopardizes the welfare of the department.

RELEVANT COMMUNICATION CONCEPTS AND STRATEGIES

Support staff are very important to any academic department. Typically, support staff include all individuals who are not faculty appointments. Generally, support staff hold secretarial, administrative, and student work positions. The purpose of this chapter is to present a general framework for managing conflict among support staff. While the framework can also be used to manage conflict with faculty or the dean, the specific application in this chapter will be to instances involving support staff. The framework consists of three action steps that department chairs can take to more effectively manage conflict: minimize conflict potential; set the tone for airing disagreements; and make managing (not resolving) conflict the goal.

Step 1: Minimize Conflict Potential

Department chairs can do a lot to minimize the potential for destructive conflict by hiring the right staff, making performance expectations clear, making decisions affecting support staff in context, and evaluating performance on a regular basis. Let's consider each of these important administrative responsibilities and their direct relationship to conflict management.

Hire the right staff. The search process affords department chairs an opportunity to see how an applicant is likely to work with other department members. To accrue this benefit, the search process must include two important components. First, the applicant must understand all job performance expectations. Particularly in hiring civil service staff, applicants may only know the minimal position qualifications required for the general job classification. Yet one department's need for a civil service secretary III may be different from another department's need for a secretary with the same civil service job classification. It is the department chair's responsibility to clarify all of the job performance expectations for any support staff position. Applicants need to know what will be expected of them in the event they are hired to fill the position. This allows the applicant to ask questions and assess their own skills in relationship to the position needs.

Second, an effective search process allows applicants to meet all department members with whom they will work if hired. If, for example, the department is hiring a secretary who will service 15 department faculty by preparing final exams and instructional materials, then the applicants need to meet with these faculty. The meeting should be structured to allow the faculty and the applicant to discuss the type of work forwarded to the secretary, deadlines, and other matters needed in the performance of the open position. Similarly, if the department is hiring a new academic advisor on an administrative appointment, the applicants should meet with a representative sampling of students who will be served by the advisor that is hired. The chair can learn a lot of information about how an applicant will work in the position by observing how the applicant interacts with relevant parties during the interview.

It is important that other department members have a stake in the hiring of new support staff. This can only happen if department members are part of the search process. If the secretary to be hired must work in cooperation with other secretarial support staff, the applicants should spend time during the interview process with the existing secretarial support staff. If the theater department is hiring a box office manager, then all department members who must work with the box office manager should be permitted to meet with applicants. These individuals should be asked to forward their assessment of the applicants to the department chair before any final decision is made. In some instances, the department or groups of department members may want to meet with the department chair to discuss their individual reactions to the applicants. This is particularly helpful when team efforts are needed once the position is filled. This process assists the chair in making the best possible hire. It also helps the chair share the responsibility for making the best possible hire with other department members. By doing so, it is easier to gain the cooperation of other department members in helping the new hire succeed.

Too often, interview sessions become social events. It is insufficient to provide faculty an opportunity to meet applicants over lunch when they need an opportunity to discuss support needs with applicants in a more formal way. Similarly, it is also unacceptable to merely introduce applicants to department members with whom they will work if hired. If the secretary being hired will report to a department manager or head secretary, the department manager or head secretary needs an opportunity to interview the applicants individually. To the extent that the department chair creates a search process and interview protocol that mirrors department operation, the more likely the search process will yield an applicant that can work well with other department members.

Make performance expectations clear. Conflict is more likely to occur when individuals do not understand what is expected of them. As departments grow and evolve, the needs for individual performance can change. It is the responsibility of the department chair to make performance goals and expectations clear. It is imperative that the department chair help support staff translate department expectations into specific activities and achievements that will be valued and rewarded within the department. For example, the department may have a goal to increase the number of undergraduate majors. This goal may translate into a more courteous behavior on the part of the office receptionist when students have questions or need assistance. In the opening case study, Bob Alcott must make clear that the secretarial support staff must service department needs when the office is open between the hours of 8:00 a.m. and noon and 1:00 p.m. to 5:00 p.m. This does not necessarily mean that both secretaries must be present during these hours. Rather, Bob Alcott must assure that the office is staffed when open. With that minimum performance expectation as the standard, Iris and Alice can work with the department chair to determine flexible work schedules that accommodate their personal needs.

Department chairs have many opportunities for making performance expectations clear. Chairs can stress performance expectations during the search process, during formal performance evaluation, and any time that special conditions warrant a change in department policy or practice. It is, however, the department chair's responsibility to make certain that support staff understand what specific activities are needed to support department goals.

Make decisions affecting support staff in context. When support staff understand the logic for the department chair's decisions, those decisions appear less arbitrary. When support staff understand department goals and expectations, they have an underlying logic for many of the department chair's decisions and actions. For example, if Alice in the opening case study knew that Dr. Alcott believes that long-term employees with a consistent record of faithful service to the department earn the right to flexible work schedules during times of personal crisis, she would be less inclined to conclude that there is no expectation for holding regular office hours. Alice, however, may be unaware that Iris was a conscientious worker before her husband's illness. We're not certain that Alice knows that Iris stays late each day to make up the hours missed in the morning. Without this information, Alice may assume that Iris receives preferential treatment and, in fairness, she too should be able to set her own hours.

Often the department chair can minimize the potential for destructive conflict by helping department members learn the context for decisions and actions. Dr. Alcott, for example, may use his meeting with Alice to discuss her course schedule for the upcoming semester to remind her of the department expectation that the office be staffed when it is open and, at the same time, inform her of Iris's need to work a flexible schedule. Since Iris stays late to make up the hours missed, Dr. Alcott may want to suggest that Alice take a class that meets in the late afternoon. The discussion helps Alice learn that Iris does not receive preferential treatment in that she works a full day. If Alice wants to come early so she can work a full day before leaving for a late afternoon class, she can also work a flexible schedule. This would formalize the revised schedules of each secretary and better ensure that the office is staffed when open. By having this discussion sooner rather than later, the department chair can prevent destructive conflict from escalating.

Evaluate performance on a regular basis. The more often support staff hear constructive evaluative comments regarding their performance, the less anxious they are about formal performance evaluations that may be required by the campus personnel office. Chairs do not need an official evaluation form or a campus policy in order to offer evaluative comments on the work being done by support staff. Chairs do not need a formally scheduled meeting to make comments as to what is going right and what might be tried differently. As educators, we know that evaluative comments have more meaning if they are given in relation to the immediate and observable context. The chair who notices a secretary being short with a student seeking information will be more effective in altering that individual's behavior if the chair immediately reinforces the department's need to be courteous to students. This does not require the chair to issue a public reprimand. Depending on the personality of the support staff involved, the chair might make the point quite well by intervening in the situation with a, "perhaps I can help you?" directed toward the student.

When appropriate, chairs should involve support staff members in setting their own performance goals. This is particularly helpful if the support staff member is trying to change or improve a particular behavior. Take for example the technical director in a department of theater who is slow to submit receipts for set construction materials. The technical director's inefficiency can result in disrupting box office management and prevent the chair from determining whether a particular production run is over budget in time to remedy the fiscal problem. In this instance, the department chair may find it helpful to involve the technical director in a discussion about what might work to help get receipts submitted in a timely way. In some cases, this may involve setting a time frame for reviewing performance or evaluating the effectiveness of a particular strategy that the support staff member agrees to try.

Department chairs minimize the potential for destructive conflict by evaluating performance on a regular basis. When support staff expect the chair to offer praise and constructive comments regarding their work, they are generally less defensive about performance evaluation. Performance evaluation helps to build a relationship between chair and support staff that enables the chair to intervene as needed to defuse destructive conflict. Performance evaluation allows department chairs to demonstrate that they value good job performance and that they genuinely care about staff professional development. These conditions ease the task of managing conflict.

Step 2: Set the Tone for Airing Disagreements

The department climate and the chair's credibility are two components that help set the tone for airing disagreements. These factors are preconditions to the effective management of conflict with and among support staff. As preconditions, department chairs must work continuously to preserve the department climate and their credibility. The department climate and chair's credibility work against conflict management if they are not positive prior to a specific conflict.

Department climate. When a unit has a positive department climate, it has a healthy work environment that is characterized by open and effective communication. In a healthy work environment, department members can discuss differences of opinion in a candid and constructive manner without fear of retaliation. There is a high degree of mutual respect and trust among department members. This climate gives department chairs an advantage in managing conflict because it sets the tone for conflict and conflict management. If mutual respect and trust exists among support staff, and the chair can air differences openly and constructively with them, there is less opportunity for destructive conflict to escalate because support staff members are less prone to perceive differences of opinion as personal attacks.

Department chairs must realize that individual academic departments can have a climate that, though vulnerable to the total campus climate, can be very different from the campus environment. For example, a department with very low morale can exist on a campus that generally has high morale. It is also possible to have a department with an "everyone out for themselves" mentality on a campus that is characterized by a very caring and generous attitude. Chairs can influence the department climate through their own management of the department. For example, the chair can damage the department climate by appearing to give preferential treatment to some. In the opening case study, Alice may be reacting to what she perceives as Iris getting preferential treatment. From Alice's perspective, the chair permits Iris to come to work late whenever she wishes. The perception of unfairness damages the department climate and fuels destructive conflict.

Department chairs need to recognize how their own behavior influences the department climate and how the climate, in turn, facilitates or impedes their ability to manage conflict effectively. The climate influences whether or not support staff can air differences of opinion constructively. The climate determines whether individuals view the chair's action with suspicion and cynicism or trust. It is very difficult to build a positive department climate during conflict. For this reason, department chairs need to work continuously at building and maintaining a positive department climate that facilitates effective conflict management.

Chair's credibility. Credibility implies a trust that is essential to managing conflict. The more positive the chair's credibility, the more effective a chair can be in managing conflict. Without credibility, the department chair is virtually powerless in influencing how individuals perceive and interpret the attitudes and actions of the chair or other department members. Department chairs need to recognize the power and importance of credibility to their ability to effectively manage conflict.

Credibility does not come with the title of department chair, but is an earned attribute. Department members (and the dean) form assessments of the chair's credibility that influence how they interpret the chair's words and deeds. These are not simple assessments, but rather are evaluations that comprise three specific components:

- Perception of the chair's knowledge

- Perception of the chair's motive or intentions

- Perception of the chair's trustworthiness

All three components of the chair's credibility derive from perceptions by others. Credibility is an assigned attribute. In other words, a chair may be knowledgeable, have good intentions, and be trustworthy. That chair, however, is only credible if others perceive him or her as knowledgeable, well-intentioned, and trustworthy. Chairs need to give some thought to how department members form assessments of their credibility. In assessing the chair's knowledge, support staff consider if the chair knows how to do the job. Does the chair manage the office staff efficiently and fairly? The assessment of the chair's motives or intentions is more subjective. Support staff individually determine if the chair means well. Is the chair biased in his treatment of people or motivated by a personal agenda? The assessment of the chair's trustworthiness considers whether the chair is honest and reliable. Are the chair's decisions and actions predictable and consistent?

Department chairs can help protect their credibility if they think about how support staff are likely to perceive their language and actions. This does not mean that all support staff will form the same assessment of the chair's credibility. It is possible for two secretaries sitting at neighboring desks to form very different assessments of the same department chair. These differences may result from varying perceptions of what the department chair should do. Iris and Alice probably hold different assessments of their chair's credibility. Iris is likely to assign a higher credibility to Bob Alcott because, from her perspective, he trusts her to do her job and work a full day even if it isn't the typical 8:00 a.m. to 5:00 p.m. shift. Alice, on the other hand, is likely to perceive Bob Alcott as not managing the office well. From Alice's perspective, the department chair allows secretaries to come and go as they please without regard for the remaining support staff or the operation of the department.

Even though credibility is an assigned attribute derived from the perceptions held by others, department chairs can influence the credibility they have with department members. Credibility is not the result of doing what others want you to do as much as the result of doing what others expect you to do in carrying out the duties and responsibilities assigned to the department chair. In the case of Bob Alcott, both Iris and Alice will expect him to safeguard the effective operation of the department. Iris may not know that she is creating tension or jeopardizing the office operation by shifting her work hours as she wishes on a day-to-day basis. By focusing on the operation of the office, Bob Alcott can discuss the need to staff the office every hour that it is open without personalizing the conflict for either Iris or Alice. The task is to determine how to keep the office staffed during the workday and not who gets to do what they please. Department chairs can often improve their credibility and minimize the potential for destructive conflict by clarifying for others the roles and responsibilities associated with the chair's job. Iris and Alice cannot sense personal abuse if they understand that Dr. Alcott is simply doing what he must do for the department.

Unfortunately, it is easier to lose credibility than to acquire it. Chairs must continuously work to establish and preserve their credibility with support staff. If the department chair lacks credibility, it is virtually impossible to manage conflict because conflict participants will not perceive the chair as fair or unbiased. Chairs with high credibility, however, can more easily manage conflict because support staff trust them and believe that the department's welfare is the top priority.

Step 3: Make Managing (Not Resolving) Conflict Your Goal

Department chairs need to accept as their goal conflict management rather than conflict resolution. Conflict management, unlike conflict resolution, acknowledges that human interaction is dynamic and that people do not always think alike. Because conflict results from differences in attitudes, beliefs, and expectations, a conflict-free environment would be one that is so homogeneous that it could not be optimally innovative or productive. The department chair's goal then is to maximize constructive conflict and minimize destructive conflict. Conflict management includes three phases: early intervention, establishing ground rules for disagreement, and initiating conflict.

Intervene early. Sometimes department chairs can prevent or defuse a destructive conflict through early intervention. For example, the chair in the opening case study might have prevented the escalating conflict between Iris and Alice by informing Alice of the department's decision to support Iris in her time of family crisis. In this way, Dr. Alcott could let Alice know of Iris's long-term performance record and the department's desire to support a faithful employee through the arrangement of flex hours. This would let Alice know that Iris is working a full workweek even though she may not be working between the hours of 8:00 a.m. and 5:00 p.m. By not intervening early, Dr. Alcott allowed Alice to draw her own conclusions about Iris's work schedule and the priorities of the department.

Intervention is most effective in defusing conflict before conflict erupts. Successful early intervention requires that chairs notice and accurately interpret communication cues that signal a brewing conflict. There are three genre of cues to which chairs need to pay close attention: changes in behavior, changes in policy, and changes in the department. Noticeable changes in verbal and/or nonverbal behavior typically evidence changes in attitude. Such changes signal that the relationship among department members will be altered. Chairs need to note when a quiet person becomes vocal or a gregarious individual becomes silent and distant. Similarly, chairs need to be alert to changes in routine behavior (or dress). By noting such changes in behavior, department chairs can get an edge in managing conflict.

Changes in policy are a second category of activity that can fuel conflict. It doesn't matter if the policy change is imposed by central administration, an accrediting body, or by vote of the department. New or revised policy represents a change, and change is uncomfortable for most people. The anxiety can result in conflict. Finally, any significant change in the department can provide a fertile environment for destructive conflict. This might be a new chair, a new hire, a retirement, the integration of new computer equipment, office renovation, or a change in any aspect of the department that affects support staff. Even when such changes are recognized improvements, they can create discomfort and conflict among department members. By attending to the observable communication cues and intervening early, department chairs can defuse conflict before it escalates and becomes destructive.

Establish ground rules for disagreement. Conflict becomes less destructive if department members can air differences of opinion in a constructive manner. Department chairs can establish ground rules for airing disagreements in a way that prevents conflict from becoming destructive. The specific ground rules imposed in a particular department will, to some extent, be a product of the chair's personality and management style. Ground rules may also respond to the specific personalities within the department. While there is no standardized list of ground rules, some guidelines that the chair might establish include the following:

- Abusive language will not be tolerated.

- Derogatory comments that represent personal attacks on colleagues will not be tolerated.

- Differences of opinion will be discussed and everyone will be heard.

- Department members can express their views without interruption or fear of retaliation.

- Unsubstantiated assertions will not influence the vote or outcome.

- Issues, not personalities, are subject to debate.

- Tears or emotional outbursts do not derail discussion of substantive issues.

- Department issues will be discussed and decided at department meetings, not by any subgroup of department members (Higgerson, 1996).

Ground rules are most effective if they apply to all members of the department and are enforced across all situations. Chairs cannot expect to preserve a ground rule if it applies only to a few department members. Ground rules help a department chair keep the focus on the issue of disagreement, which is important to effective conflict management. For example, suppose Alice bursts into tears when Dr. Alcott approaches her about missing work to take classes that were unapproved. If at that moment Dr. Alcott responds to the tears, the issue of work performance is placed secondary to the need to make Alice feel better. If the chair, however, says, "Obviously you are not able to discuss this matter at this time," the chair makes clear that the matter will be discussed when the secretary can regain composure.

Know when to initiate conflict. Sometimes a conflict that remains below the surface can be destructive to department productivity and morale. Chairs can release potentially destructive tension by allowing the disagreement to be aired in a constructive and controlled manner. There are two instances when it is particularly useful to initiate conflict. The first is when the offender doesn't realize that his or her behavior is contributing to a department conflict. In the opening case study, Iris may not realize that coming late to work creates a problem. Even though Iris is conscientious about making up the missed time at the end of the day, she may be unaware that her tardiness poses a problem for anyone. By intervening and pointing out that a conflict does exist, the department chair can prevent the conflict from escalating. Dr. Alcott, for example, may suggest to Iris that she work a different schedule, coming in promptly at a specified starting time that is later than the 8:00 a.m. start of business and ending at a specified time. This would allow others to see that she is working regular hours even though they may not be between 8:00 a.m. and 5:00 p.m.

A second instance when a chair may need to initiate conflict is to help facilitate decision-making. In the case of Alice, the department chair may need to help her realize when she is likely to complete her baccalaureate if she wishes to remain a full-time employee. This may help Alice decide how important it is to hold the job or whether it would be preferable to seek a loan and finish her college education sooner. In helping Alice face the alternatives, the department chair reinforces performance expectations.

LET'S RECAP

Conflict with and among support staff is inevitable, but it need not be destructive. Department chairs can take specific action before conflict occurs to facilitate effective conflict management. By establishing and maintaining a positive department climate and high credibility, department chairs set the stage for effective conflict management. These tasks are continuous, but essential to the general health of the department as well as to the chair's ability to manage conflict effectively.

Department chairs are not powerless because they can minimize conflict potential through their decisions and actions when hiring new staff, making performance expectations clear, making decisions that affect support staff in context, and evaluating performance on a regular basis. These administrative tasks allow chairs to demonstrate their interest in professional development and the overall welfare of the department, two motives that good support staff will appreciate.

Finally, chairs need to remember that because conflict is inevitable, it is unrealistic to expect the goal of conflict resolution. Conflict management, unlike resolution, accepts that individuals will think and act differently. Conflict management acknowledges that conflict can be positive, even desirable. The department chair's objective is to manage conflict by minimizing destructive conflict and maximizing constructive conflict. This process unfolds through three specific phases. First, chairs need to be willing to intervene early to prevent destructive conflict from escalating. Second, chairs can establish ground rules for airing differences of opinion constructively. Third, chairs need to recognize when it is useful to initiate conflict in order to defuse destructive disagreements. Most of all, department chairs need to remember that they can manage conflict and do not need to be victims of destructive conflict.

REFERENCES

Higgerson, M. L. (1996). *Communication skills for department chairs.* Bolton, MA: Anker.

5   Ann F. Lucas

Spanning the Abyss: Managing Conflict Between Deans and Chairs

Factors Contributing to Conflict Between Deans and Chairs

Managing conflict so that it becomes a creative process and preventing dysfunctional conflict from tearing groups apart seem particularly difficult in higher education. One can speculate that this is because in academe being a team player has been neither required nor rewarded, and because the roles and responsibilities are often not clearly defined.

Increased stress levels in universities that have been triggered by extensive criticism of higher education for more than a decade, as well as the external demands for higher performance by faculty and students—to be accomplished on more limited budgets—raise the degree of anxiety and predispose individuals to respond to conflict in a dysfunctional way. Other stressors are the generational issues which seem to position some groups of faculty against others, such as when some junior people are brought in at higher salaries to reflect their market value and are given the latest upgrade of computer hardware and software not available to senior faculty. In turn, universities are demanding that younger colleagues publish more to earn tenure and promotion than was required of senior faculty who are making the tenure decisions. Conflict in higher education frequently fragments us into opposing groups that are not confronting and trying to resolve the issues that plague us.

Managing organizational conflict is usually viewed as the responsibility of leaders. The ability to handle conflict well requires that a leader be an individual of integrity who has a high level of interpersonal effectiveness and good communication skills. Capable leadership is also related to leadership style, understanding what motivates people, the knowledge and belief that a dysfunctional culture can be changed, as well as the understanding of how to do it, and the use of a collaborative style as a preferred approach in managing most conflict situations.

However, there are two other extremely important factors that determine how successfully conflict in a college can be handled. The first is the cultural climate of the institution, which includes the amount of, or lack of, support that deans and chairs receive from the provost and the president, the power that is given to deans and chairs, and whether a supportive or an adversarial climate exists between the deans and the academic departments. The second factor that is the source of many conflicts is the difference in perceptions that chairs and deans each have because of their positions in the organization.

Conflict is often rampant between deans and chairs. Deans and chairs frequently seem to be moving in different directions. In order to better understand such problems, I interviewed 35 chairs and deans from 15 different universities. They are not a stratified randomly selected group, but have come from comprehensive universities and liberal arts colleges and schools of business, engineering, and science. They are from unionized and nonunionized institutions, large state universities, and smaller private universities. This specific research was completed against a backdrop of conducting workshops and doing consulting for more than 6,500 chairs and about 100 deans at 160 different campuses across the country.

My interviews and consulting work with deans and chairs uncovered a number of issues that are sources of conflict and some creative ways that individuals have developed to manage these conflicts. Particular leadership styles, methods of solving problems and making decisions, and the level of trust within institutions emerged as key factors that contribute either to effective functioning of colleges and departments or to ongoing conflict and stagnation. A dysfunctional climate can make each decision and every inter-action between a dean and a chair a trigger for further escalation. How the different perspectives of deans and chairs, based on their unique positions in a university, create a potential source of conflict is another issue that surfaced frequently in my interviews. Each of these questions will be discussed in the following sections.

What will be presented first is a contrast between the leadership styles of two deans in universities with very different cultures. These deans use very different styles of communication, problem solving, and decision-making; have dissimilar levels of credibility; and are working in climates in which trust varies significantly. These factors are directly related to how effectively conflict is handled and how well the colleges are functioning.

TWO DEANS—TWO PERSPECTIVES

Dean Scott, who has been a dean at a university in a state system for about five years, wants his chairs to be leaders, not administrators. He believes chairs should involve faculty in handling strategic plans for the department, resolving faculty workload issues, and encouraging faculty development. Providing chairs with information on state budgets and foundation money that has come to the university, he even distributes money in the dean's fund directly to chairs so that there will be decentralized operating budgets. He uses a consultative decision-making style and then explains to chairs and faculty his rationale for the decisions he makes.

Dean Scott has a strong conviction that it is an important part of a dean's job to help chairs and faculty members think better of themselves. He is guided by a quotation from Goethe who said, "If you treat an individual as he is, he will stay as he is, but if you treat him as if he were what he ought to be and could be, he will become what he ought to be and could be." He believes a dean must grasp opportunities to create small wins for chairs and faculty. One example Dean Scott offered of how he made chairs and faculty know that they made a difference was to make public a very favorable alumni satisfaction survey whose findings were buried in a report. This document presented the results of a survey recently conducted by the system of higher education of 15,000 graduates of universities in the state. The survey included questions about how well the school prepared the student for the job market, or for graduate school, and whether, given the opportunity to do it over again, a student would go back to the same school he or she had attended.

Based on the alumni responses of how well their university had prepared them for the future, satisfaction of graduates ranked the university at which

Dean Scott served as third of 11 degree-granting institutions in the state. However, the results had not been circulated beyond top administration. The dean made this information public and promulgated it as an accomplishment for the chairs, faculty, and staff. By tying the outcome of the survey to the university and college mission, which was the development of educated persons through the interaction of competent, caring faculty and capable, motivated students, Dean Scott affirmed the value of their work. By emphasizing this accomplishment frequently at university senate meetings, college and chair meetings, in the college newsletter, on the university radio station, and on every other possible occasion, the dean reminded faculty and chairs of their goals and acknowledged their achievement of the university mission.

Reports requested by the provost and other administrators seem to fill a chair's day, affording him or her less time to address leadership responsibilities. Dean Scott tries to relieve chairs of report writing, and has it handled instead by assistant deans with the aid of graduate students. An example of a recent request by the provost is completion of workload audits. Since the dean was copied on this request, he stepped in and asked the assistant dean to collect the necessary information from the chairs, set up the report design, analyze the data, and write the final report. He then told the chairs that he was doing this to reduce their paperwork, and they appreciated it.

Dean Scott believes that almost all of his chairs can be trusted to make valid personnel decisions. When he disagrees with a recommendation made by a chair and feels he must oppose a faculty member's promotion, sabbatical, or released time for research, he calls in the chair and the college promotion and tenure committee and says, "I'm thinking of not recommending John Jones for promotion. Why shouldn't I do this?" He then provides the reasons for his decision. This is a very respectful discussion, and he listens carefully to any recommendations or any new information given to him. Then the dean goes with the chair to the office of each faculty member whose request for a personnel decision has been denied. He explains the rationale to the faculty member and what he or she will have to do in order to get a promotion in the future. This explanation is also given in writing. The approach usually works well, but, he says, there is one faculty member who has not spoken to him for four years.

Dean Scott believes the most significant area for potential problems between chairs and a dean is in the realm of communication. Since deans are frequently involved with an advisory council and other constituencies, they feel removed from chairs and faculty and have less time to spend with them.

Because he wants chairs to be the first to know whatever is going to affect them, the faculty, or the college, he sees chairs individually once a week and meets with all of his chairs as a group every two weeks. These meetings are usually conducted as problem solving meetings, not simply for passing along information that could be communicated in writing.

Dean Scott and his chairs function effectively as a team. The chairs defend his actions to their colleagues in the departments, and members of the entire college work well together to achieve their goals.

Dean Scott has created a climate of open communication by meeting frequently with his chairs, sharing information with them, both as a group and individually. He has created a climate of trust and respect by encouraging them to make their own decisions and not micromanaging. He is attentive to their problems and tries to ease the burden of excessive paperwork so they will have the time to be leaders. He lets them and the faculty know that they are valued. When he makes decisions, he shares his rationale with chairs and the faculty who are affected. When chairs and faculty members feel that a dean is fair and uses objective criteria in making decisions, they are more willing to accept the hard decisions, such as unfavorable personnel actions, or a negative decision on a budget request for equipment, as equitable instead of as a reason to take an adversarial position with the dean. When chairs and departments feel that a dean is playing favorites or is behaving in a capricious manner, conflict may go underground and surface at unpredictable moments, or it may simply make it difficult to accomplish anything that requires departmental commitment.

A leadership style in sharp contrast to the supportive approach just described is the use of power to get things done. When a leader concludes that conditions have gotten so bad that the use of power or mandates from the top is the only way left to get people to do what they should be doing, he or she often chooses an adversarial strategy.

Dean Hollinger, who works in a large state university system, says that chairs view the dean as their enemy and their mission is to prevent the dean from having any control over their departments. Dean Hollinger states that chairs have loyalty first to their discipline and the subdivision of that discipline, second to their professional associations, third to their department (when a department is made up of several disciplines), and last to the college. He complains that chairs have no carrots or sticks to use to motivate faculty—that there are across the board raises, little merit money, and a grievance system—and that if a dean or chair tries to punish people, grievances are filed.

When Dr. Hollinger was chosen through a national search and screen process to become dean three years ago, he felt he had come into a system in which things had gotten out of control. His description of these conditions was that faculty all had only a nine-hour teaching load, yet about two-thirds of them still were not publishing. He listed a number of other problems. Student evaluations of teaching were low for a number of faculty, and faculty rationalized the evaluations by saying that students were in no position to make judgments about their teaching. Despite the fact that faculty felt student ratings were unfair, they refused to develop any other way of evaluating teaching. Several chairs complained that they could not get faculty to do a fair share of work in the departments; faculty also refused to contribute other service to the university or to the external community. The faculty handbook described what was required of faculty in terms of minimal performance expected, and this was the standard cited when complaints were raised against faculty by any administrators. New productive faculty got turned off when they saw these conditions. The senior faculty intimidated the new faculty so that they did not feel free to recommend any changes. As administration viewed it, only about one-third of faculty were actually doing their jobs.

In an attempt to change what Dean Hollinger described as appalling conditions, one of his first actions as dean was to require chairs to assign unproductive faculty a Monday, Wednesday, Friday teaching schedule and 12 hours of teaching. He used the equity argument to assign a 12-hour load to those who had not published in ten years. Faculty who had published two articles in the preceding three years remained on a nine-hour teaching load. However, faculty also had to demonstrate significant teaching or service contributions. Those in the middle group, who had published something in the past decade, were continued on a nine-hour teaching load but were warned that their teaching loads would be elevated to 12 hours if they did not demonstrate an increase in productivity within the next two years.

Eighty percent of the chairs did assign unproductive faculty members 12-hour teaching loads as the dean had instructed. Grievances were filed, but they were not sustained by the grievance committee.

Dean Hollinger also experienced conflict with chairs and faculty when his actions on personnel decisions were unfavorable to faculty. In this university, chairs, department, and college promotion and tenure committees usually supported faculty in any personnel decisions. So it was the dean who had to make the difficult decisions. However, the dean's position on personnel actions was undermined by the president who promoted faculty not recommended by the deans. When the president was questioned by the deans, he gave them reassurances, but did not change his pattern of behavior.

Dean Hollinger tried to establish several positive initiatives, one of which was an international curriculum taught by knowledgeable people. He encouraged ten faculty to take sabbaticals in foreign countries, which he had arranged from grants through his own contacts. His attempts to launch a valuable and timely program were unsuccessful, he says, because the former dean had established a climate of resistance that maintained, "We already have too many foreign students and visiting professors from abroad." This made progress difficult, and it seemed like an ongoing struggle with limited payoff, so Dean Hollinger discontinued his efforts.

Dean Hollinger's conclusions are that, "The only way for a dean to be successful is to be obnoxious. Nice guys finish last," he said. After two years in office, he began to refer to faculty in writing as BUMs. When a grievance was filed against him for that, he said, "It's only an acronym for Bargaining Unit Member. Such abbreviations are part of the accelerated pace of modern life."

Finally, Dean Hollinger resigned from his position. He left feeling that the system was hopeless and that the culture made any kind of progress difficult. However, some of the changes he put in place, such as increased teaching loads for unproductive faculty were retained by chairs even after he resigned.

These two situations demonstrate how two organizational climates have created conditions in which conflict has been managed effectively in one college and has paralyzed a second institution. A positive, supportive culture creates a solid foundation for building teams of a dean and chairs working together towards shared goals. Much unhealthy conflict—the kind that creates personal animosity and drains psychic energy—is prevented. In a positive climate, when disagreement is real and remains focused on issues, more creative, comprehensive decisions are generated because all perspectives are listened to. In an adversarial, defensive climate, win-lose decisions are frequently made with no commitment to their implementation. In such an atmosphere, there are strong limits to what leaders can accomplish. Since the culture of an organization plays such a significant role in making conflict a creative force, the following section will look at ways of building a healthy organizational climate.

CHANGING DYSFUNCTIONAL CULTURES

In academe, as in most organizations, the way people function is a result of both formal and informal rules and procedures that their group follows. These rules and procedures are the norms that guide the behavior of faculty, chairs, and deans and have evolved over time from the department, college, and university culture. Schein (1992, p. 12), who has written extensively on organizational culture, defines this culture as "a pattern of shared basic assumptions that the group learned as it solved its problems of external adaptation and internal integration, that has worked well enough to be considered valid and, therefore, [is] to be taught to new members as the correct way to perceive, think, and feel in relation to those problems."

College and department norms, which have evolved from the culture, would include:

- What is expected of chairs and deans

- How much power they are given

- Whether they have information about the overall budget

- What the relationship has been between past deans and departments

- Whether the university is unionized

- What the role of the board of regents or board of trustees has been

- Whether there have been long or short periods of budgetary constraints

- How budget cuts have been handled, for example, if downsizing has been used, how it has been handled (Lucas, 1990)

- How decisions have been made in the university and whether decision-making has been participatory or top down

In the university at which Dean Hollinger was dean, the culture is toxic and full of conflict. This was partly a structural problem. Responsibility and accountability had not been built into the system. All faculty had been given reduced teaching assignments based on the expectation that they would be engaging in scholarly activity. However, there was no annual reporting to discover what a faculty member had accomplished with the prior year's release time. Since accountability was not built into the system, faculty thought release time was an entitlement. Other systemic problems included the lack of objective criteria for personnel decision-making, the lack of resolution meetings between the dean and the college promotion and tenure committee, which could have clarified criteria and made them more objective, and the president's telling the deans that he would support their recommendations, only to support the department's actions when the two were in conflict. All of these issues created high potential for conflict and an absence of readily available approaches for resolving disagreements, such as being able to refer to impartial, clearly written documents on how, when, and by whom evaluation of scholarly engagement would be evaluated.

Another basis for the conflict in this culture is the difference in perspective held by the dean and the departments. Dean Hollinger's point of view is that faculty were unproductive, did not care about teaching, were not doing research, and were not contributing service to the university or the community. The chair and faculty perspective was that they were teaching the way they had always taught, that that had always been good enough, and that there were no rewards for engaging in research or service. Since these differences in perspectives were never discussed, neither side could appreciate the other's point of view. However, as Martinko's recent summary of work on attributions (1994) has demonstrated, such differences in perception about what causes behavior are so predictable that they have been called the fundamental attribution error. This principle says that individuals explain their successes as the direct result of their own efforts and abilities, and their failures as caused by situational or external factors. Dean Hollinger's perception was that faculty had gotten lazy and were comfortable and felt no need to work hard because they were tenured; chairs and faculty felt they were doing fine and that further productivity was pointless since it wasn't expected and would not be rewarded. The dean felt that issuing mandates from the top was the only method of making faculty more productive. Since a fair number of universities find themselves in similar situations, where mandates from the top only exacerbate conflict, the question becomes are there other methods of motivating faculty and chairs, strategies that will not escalate conflict? And since organizational climates that are dysfunctional create a strong potential for conflict, how does one go about changing such a cultural climate?

Despite common beliefs, cultural change is the end product, not the beginning point of change. Because a toxic culture acts as a barrier to change, university administrators sometimes assume that they must first change the culture before initiating any other change. In reality, as current research indicates, one must begin by changing behavior and attitudes, and only after it becomes clear that new behaviors will lead to success, will they be anchored in the culture.

Moreover, institutional change ventures succeed when they are guided by an overall change plan, rather than undertaken in bits and pieces. Such an overarching plan includes eight distinct stages, according to John P. Kotter, who has had years of experience working with organizations involved in planned change. The change process proposed by Kotter (1996, p. 21) includes the following:

1) Create a sense of urgency.

2) Create a critical mass of individuals who will guide the change process.

3) Develop a vision and goals.

4) Communicate that vision simply and briefly.

5) Empower people to take action.

6) Build small successes.

7) Consolidate gains.

8) Anchor the new approaches in the culture.

The necessity of beginning change efforts by creating a sense of urgency has been demonstrated to me repeatedly in my own consulting work with universities. It is not enough that top administration be convinced that change is necessary. Unless chairs and faculty are also persuaded that the status quo is no longer working, there is no reason for them to buy into a change process. The most important barrier to change is individual resistance. When change is proposed, the first question people ask is, "How is this going to affect me?" After all, individuals know what they currently have. They don't know what they may lose if change occurs. And, if there is no sense of urgency, no reason to engage in change, people will simply dig in their heels and resist.

One way of increasing the sense of urgency is to bombard chairs and faculty with information about opportunities, the rewards that will come with those opportunities, and the fact that the institution as it currently operates cannot achieve those benefits. If there is other negative information about decline in enrollment; budget crunches; other nearby universities that have attracted students that would normally have attended your university because they have achieved disciplinary accreditation, such as accreditation by the American Assembly of Collegiate Schools of Business, or have developed new attractive programs; such information must be shared with faculty frequently and in small sound bites. Providing such a message once, even at an important college meeting, is never as effective as repeating it many times, at every meeting, in every newsletter, tying it to every goal.

In the account cited earlier, Dean Hollinger tried to mandate a culture change. However, because he attempted to do this by issuing edicts, faculty and chairs used every approach available to them to resist, including frequently filing grievances, using opportunities for small personal put-downs which led to retaliation by the dean, and speaking against what he was trying to do. If he had involved chairs and faculty in the change—both systemic change and attitudinal change based on an understanding of each others' perspectives—efforts might have been more successful.

The second stage in the change process is to organize a critical mass of individuals from different levels in the organization who will guide the change effort. People with power, such as deans and chairs, must guide the reins, and the president or provost must be kept informed. However, faculty members who are informal leaders must also be part of the coalition.

Creating a shared vision that will excite and stimulate chairs and faculty to change their dysfunctional behavior should be built into the third stage. A vision has to be simple, straightforward, and appealing. A good vision can be turned into an elevator speech; i.e., it can be communicated simply enough for another person to understand it if given in the time which exists between ascending or descending between two floors in an elevator. If there is no shared vision, change will be piecemeal, conflict will create barriers, and certainly no organizational transformation will occur.

Communicating that shared vision occurs in the fourth stage. When changes are being announced, deans need to explain how each change is tied to the mission and goals. At one university where I consulted, chairs and faculty told me they were angry and in ongoing conflict with their dean because he was constantly asking them to change for the sake of changing. When I interviewed the dean, it was clear that each change was related to the overall goals for the college. When I asked if he had told this to the chairs, he said yes, he had told them in the beginning what their mission and goals were and that achieving these goals would require change. However, he had not involved them in developing a shared vision, nor had he reminded them of the ways in which each change was related to the goals. They had, therefore, drawn the wrong conclusions, that he wanted to introduce change for the sake of change, and this was a constant source of friction.

The fifth stage involves empowering people to take action. Deans must allow chairs to make important decisions. Chairs need to know what the broad parameters are. Rarely should they have to check with the dean about routine decisions. They should, however, consult the dean about major decisions only when they have insufficient information to guide them.

Planning small wins is the sixth stage of change. Since major change takes time, individuals, particularly skeptics, need to see that change pays off. This is the time to reward those who are accomplishing the new goals and to make those rewards visible. Deans can do this by rewarding teaching, scholarship, or team efforts.

Consolidation of gains, the seventh stage in the change process, occurs when change efforts are incorporated into the culture, and are visibly moving the organization toward success. Yet a sense of urgency is maintained as new and higher goals are set.

Finally, gains are firmly anchored in the culture so that they become part of it. Such gains might include new cutting-edge programs that provide faculty exciting opportunities to develop untapped talents—programs that are also attractive to students and may increase enrollment. Ultimately, new approaches become embedded in the culture when it is clear that they work and are better than the old culture. This eight-stage change model provides a dean or a chair with guidelines on how to transform a department or college, particularly when improvement is essential, resistance high, and conflict is rampant so that the unit seems to be paralyzed and unable to move forward.

In the last decade higher education has engaged in change as a matter of necessity rather than choice. When increased emphasis on accountability is directed by those outside of academe, deans are the individuals who carry the message mandating achievement of higher performance measures. Thus deans are pitted against departments, which has added to the conflict. I would argue that we in the departments and colleges need to take charge of our own accountability, and thus establish our credibility by seizing the initiative, instead of having change imposed by external agents. Then we can determine the appropriate outcome measures and explain what we do in ways that make sense to others (Lucas, 1996). However, to avoid dysfunctional conflict, deans and chairs must lead such efforts together, thus functioning as partners rather than adversaries.

DIFFERENCES IN PERCEPTION BETWEEN DEANS AND CHAIRS

Up until this point, I have written about how the cultural climate of the university and the leadership style of the dean determine whether conflict becomes dysfunctional or actually improves decision-making in the college. I have also provided several suggestions about how a toxic culture can be changed and how deans and chairs can recognize and resolve conflicts that are caused by dissimilar perceptions. This section will extend the discussion of how the different perceptions of deans and chairs can be a significant source of conflict. Once this is understood, it is easier to 1) appreciate how apparently irreconcilable differences are often simply the result of individuals viewing issues based on their positions in a university, 2) identify common problems, and 3) engage in successful problem solving.

Deans and chairs view any given situation through very different windows. Because deans feel they must consider what is good for the college, their focus is how a department's goals fit the overall strategic plan of the college. Chairs, on the other hand, who have to live with faculty on a daily basis, tend to see themselves primarily as advocates for faculty, and that often means preserving the status quo of the department. One chair I interviewed commented:

> Chairs are first-line managers, first among equals, with responsibility but not enough authority to make decisions that would be good for their faculty and for the department. For example, when working on faculty development with each individual, a chair needs to prioritize among teaching, scholarship, and service. A faculty member may be an excellent teacher, be heavily involved in committee work and student advisement, but not do any publishing. The chair accepts this, but the dean wants everyone to publish. How can a chair let a faculty member know that his contributions as a quality teacher, his individual work with students, and his heavy service commitment to the department are appreciated, and yet tell him he has to publish if he is to achieve the goals set by the dean? The faculty member is more likely to stop doing all the things he has been doing because he feels such activities are not really valued.

Yet, a little later in the same interview, acknowledging the fact that there will be differences in perception between chairs and deans, this chair said:

> Chairs must learn to manage upward. Some deans do not have the necessary leadership and communication skills. Accept that and don't take it personally. In dealing with the dean, stay issue oriented and avoid defensiveness. The dean and the chair are both acting in role, so the task is to avoid becoming personal about things. Put issues on the table. Recognize that you would make the same decision if you were in that role. You want to find the best overall decision. But sometimes decisions involve sacrifices, that is, just taking a

solution that works, rather than the best one. Seeing the big picture is extremely important. Chairs must make decisions that are good for the quality and growth of the department, not just for an individual faculty member.

The deans' view of this difference in perspective is that some chairs won't make hard decisions if they think they will be unpopular in the department and will make the dean the bad guy by letting him or her resolve the issue. For example, in one college at a large university, steadily declining enrollment had resulted in a decision by the provost to reduce the number of faculty in the college. To avoid downsizing, the dean asked several chairs to develop some criteria that could be used as a basis for transferring some faculty to another college in the university which needed more full-time faculty. Several chairs refused to do this, so the dean had to make the decisions. The dean said he then became the bad guy with the faculty in those departments. In other departments, chairs explained to their faculty that this was the only way to avoid downsizing, so the chairs, with their faculty, developed criteria and accepted responsibility. The basic difference in how the chairs approached the problem was whether they exercised a leadership role by accepting responsibility. Those chairs who passed the decision up to the dean actually prevented their faculty from having input into decision-making. The chairs who called their faculty together to determine the criteria to be used, not only took an active role in decision-making with their colleagues, but also demonstrated effective leadership ability.

Effective deans recognize that chairs often feel they are the primary advocates for faculty and are aware that this perspective sometimes makes it difficult for them to support and implement administration decisions. However, there are times when a policy put in place by administration is irrevocable. At such moments, chairs need to consider carefully how they frame the policy they have been asked to implement, so that when they consult with their faculty members, they can use brainstorming creatively to generate action steps that serve both them and the college well. Poor framing of the issue can result in faculty rebellion so that they simply dig in their heels and refuse to become involved even though this sometimes means that they will have to live with consequences that hurt them and the department.

While acknowledging that many chairs do keep in mind what is best for the discipline—not just what is best for individual faculty members—deans believe that other chairs feel their primary task is to push the department's agenda forward, and that this difference in perception is one of the main sources of conflict between chairs and deans. However, effective deans manage the role conflict inherent in the position of chairs—to represent both faculty and upper administration—by creating a shared vision with all of the chairs in the college so that they develop a commitment to that vision. They feel that it is the dean's leadership responsibility to communicate the big picture of the college to the chairs, to remind them constantly of their common goals, and to reinforce them for achievement of these objectives. By creating a shared vision, by sharing information and resources, by assisting chairs and faculty to achieve their own goals, by helping them feel good about themselves so that they know they make a difference, deans support chairs in taking the administrative view, not just the faculty perspective.

DISCONTINUITY OF LEADERSHIP

While it is true that rotation of chairs is the norm in most universities, deans also move frequently, though their shift is from one university to another. Such discontinuity of leadership in colleges creates conflict because new leaders arrive with a different set of expectations that must be communicated, negotiated, tested for reality, revised, and finally turned into goals and implementation steps. This process causes a great deal of angst for chairs and faculty. As one chair said to me, "When a new dean takes over, you have to sell yourself all over again. There are senior faculty—the movers in the school who have committed their lives to the school—and a new leader comes in and doesn't value them. You need to prove yourself all over again to someone who has different biases."

Another chair complained about a new dean "who blew off senior faculty by giving them initiatives to handle, but then telling others they weren't performing well instead of talking to the individuals directly. When this word got out, people fell like dominoes. The fact that this dean did not give feedback directly undermined his leadership. Faculty members then began to do only what was required of them. One faculty member began conducting leadership training for his church and withdrew services from the university entirely."

Chairs interviewed were all in agreement about how new deans should behave to prevent dysfunctional conflict. As one said, "There is a big need for good communication skills, particularly good listening skills. When newcomers enter an established organization, they also need to affirm the good that's there and work with it instead of trying to change those things that are working well along with those things that aren't."

How Effective Leadership Styles
Can Improve Conflict Management

In addition to the cultural climate and the differences in perspective of deans and chairs, leadership styles have a significant effect on conflict and how successfully it is managed. This section enlarges the discussion of the impact that styles of leadership, decision-making, and conflict management have on making conflict a useful process rather than one that tears people apart.

A principle to be neglected at one's peril is that when leaders need commitment to a decision, they must involve those who are most affected by using a participative decision-making style. As one chair said, "Nobody ever washes a rental car. If the decision isn't mine, I'm not going to try to make it work." When making decisions, a leader has a choice of using one of four styles: unilateral, democratic (by voting), consensus, and consultative. Each of these styles is appropriate under certain circumstances. A unilateral style, one in which a leader makes the decision alone, is the right choice when a decision must be made quickly, as in an emergency, or when he or she is sure the decision is not important to others in the university, not always an easy matter to determine. Unilateral decision-making should rarely be used when strong commitment is needed from individuals who will be affected by the decision.

Decisions can also be made using a democratic approach such as voting. Although this sounds reasonable, the downside is that when a decision is made, those who voted against the decision will not support it and may even try to undermine it. This is often when conflict goes underground. People who voted against an issue may not talk about it openly, but will try to sabotage its implementation.

As a third option, a consensus style of decision-making can be used. Although quite time consuming, it is the method of choice when the commitment of all participants is needed. This approach requires a high level of trust, the perception that all individuals have had an opportunity to express their points of view, and that they have been listened to and understood by all of the others involved. At the end of the discussion, even though some may not agree with the final decision, they trust their colleagues enough to commit themselves to the direction taken.

Finally, a leader can use a consultative style, that is, ask those who will be most affected for input on the issue. This broadens the base of information and contributes to a more comprehensive decision. However, when this style is chosen, the rationale for the final decision must be made clear, and people must know why other options, perhaps some that they recommended, were not chosen. Otherwise, they will feel that their input was not taken seriously.

EXPLAINING THE RATIONALE FOR DECISION-MAKING

Conflict is often the result of misunderstanding or of not being given necessary information. At several universities at which I have consulted, chairs have told me they had serious conflict with their deans about the way that decisions were made. They said that the dean was insincere and was simply going through the motions of asking for their input. "After talking with us individually, the dean makes a completely different decision, one that ignores the advice we have given him." When I interviewed the deans in question, I found a dean was frequently using a consultative style of decision-making. He would ask a number of the chairs how particular situations should be handled. Then after getting all of their input, the dean would indeed make his own decisions because, after all, he was responsible, and had to account for his actions, to the provost. However, the dean had not explained his rationale to the chairs. Thus, his behavior had been interpreted as being disingenuous; that is, he was perceived to be insincere and lacking integrity.

This problem, which results in mistrust and loss of credibility, could have been prevented. When the dean announced his decision, he should have begun by thanking the chairs and faculty collectively for their valuable advice, then explained what he had learned from talking with them about the pros and cons of each option, and finally presented his reasons for choosing the alternative selected. In this way individuals who had been consulted would know that their opinions were respected and that they had been both heard and listened to.

This approach of explaining the rationale for decision-making is an open method of communicating and increases trust and a perception that individuals are being treated equitably. When open communication is not practiced, mistrust is pervasive. During one interview a chair confided, "There has been a state of strong financial retrenchment in this university for the past 15 years. We accept this, but there is also an unequal distribution of financial resources. We do not accept this. Chairs know that they are competing for scarce resources (budgets, faculty lines, computer equipment, lab equipment, office space), but one department is getting a stronger operating budget than others, and no justification is given. This creates strong dissatisfaction because of the injustice."

Being even-handed as a leader does not mean giving everyone the same amount of money; all it means is that when one department gets more, explanations need to be given. Such an explanation can also serve as a clear statement of what is valued and what will be rewarded. But if such a statement is not offered, the conclusion drawn will be that the dean is unjust.

Establishing credibility works both ways. Not only do deans have to establish trust by the way in which they behave, but chairs also have to establish credibility with the dean. Deans have told me that when a chair has established credibility, has good judgment, and has a history of putting careful thought into requests, the dean is very likely to approve a request without doing much investigating. However, when a chair has not yet established credibility, seems not to have put much thought into a request, or asks for anything his faculty wants without evaluating its validity or providing enough data, the dean typically refuses or routinely asks for more information.

CREATING TRUST SO THAT CONFLICTS CAN BE MANAGED EFFECTIVELY

Getting to know people as human beings, not just individuals who have a role in the university, helps to establish trust. Several deans talked with me about how an annual administrative council retreat for all chairs can be used to bring chairs on board. In addition to using a retreat to build relationships, reflect on accomplishments and what was learned from mistakes, and plan for the next year, deans say they create trust by being supportive and not expecting chairs to be able to handle any and all problems in the department simply because they are chairs. When the chairs have problems, the dean is available on an individual basis for assistance, discussion, and occasionally to present another perspective. They keep the lines of communication open so that any problems can be addressed immediately, instead of being pushed underground to fester.

Effective deans frequently conduct chair meetings as problem solving meetings which address the needs of the chairs. Such meetings are not used simply to convey information that could as easily be communicated in writing. Deans are valued by chairs when they allow all views to be heard at meetings and when they know when to summarize and ask if people are in agreement, rather than allow people to talk themselves out of a decision they have already made. In other words, deans who conduct effective meetings have credibility and are trusted.

Some deans do their best to avoid conflict. They may do this by mandating all decisions from above. Or they may quickly put down any divergent point of view at a meeting they are conducting by saying, "Let's not become fragmented. We need to stick together here." Although being willing to listen to and even encourage other points of view does make meetings longer and sometimes more uncomfortable, it also increases the probability that decisions made will be wiser, more comprehensive, and will generate commitment to their implementation.

CONFLICT RESULTING FROM LACK OF POSITION POWER FOR THE CHAIRS

Finally, in terms of the systemic factors that create conflict between chairs and deans, individuals interviewed from both groups agreed that because chairs don't have enough authority and power to be effective leaders of their departments, they are often unable to accomplish what deans ask them to do. Gene Rice has described how this came about:

> In the 1960s, in the democratizing spirit of the time, most academic departments instituted rotating chairs. Old curmudgeons who had ruled departments in authoritarian ways (or what passed for that) were summarily deposed, and the leadership—a word seldom used then because it smelled of power—of departments was passed among colleagues in a comfortably egalitarian manner. In many cases, secretaries took over. What could have been seen as a leadership opportunity was systematically transformed into what we disparagingly talked about as a "paper-shuffling chore" or a three-year sentence (Rice, 1994, p. xii).

Since many institutions have now used this system for three decades, chairs rotate every three, four, or five years. Much of the first year is spent learning what the responsibilities are. I would recommend a minimum of a four-year term, with intensive training given for at least a week before the chair begins a term, followed by an in-service program throughout the term of office. Senior chairs can then help new chairs, and newer chairs have a group of whom they can ask questions and with whom they can develop skills. In industrial, governmental, and medical organizations in-service training is ongoing. It is only in higher education that we have neglected, at our peril, the necessity of supporting our academic leadership.

There are considerable differences in the power that chairs have. In some state universities, in which chairs are often called department heads, those who lead large departments and who have been in position for many years are very powerful. Deans tread easily so as not to offend them. However, in many other places, chairs and deans agree that the position of chair must be taken more seriously by institutions, their job descriptions must be rewritten, they must be given some control over budgets, and chairs must be held accountable. Serious attention must also be given to the selection of chairs. When the goals of a department have been formulated by the faculty, with some input from the dean, a chair needs to be chosen who has the right set of leadership skills and values to gather the collective wisdom of colleagues in the achievement of those goals.

A chair also needs to have the courage to initiate discussion with the faculty about some of the tough issues related to faculty accountability in student learning and effective teaching, keeping the curriculum coherent and cutting-edge, and ongoing scholarly engagement of faculty. When a dean attempts to inaugurate change in these areas, chairs are not always responsive. They are uncertain about their loyalties, and while they need to have the boldness and determination to initiate change, they also need leadership development for their role in developing skills as change agents.

SUMMARY AND RECOMMENDATIONS

This chapter has considered several factors that are the source of conflict between chairs and deans and has made some recommendations about managing conflict more effectively. When the cultural climate in a university is toxic, there exists a potential for dysfunctional conflict that can be ignited rapidly. Some of the systemic issues that can create a destructive climate have been identified. Methods of changing the culture so that conflicts can be used constructively have been explored.

Discussion of the leadership styles of deans—how they generate trust through team building, create a climate which fosters open communication that spills down to the departmental level, solve problems and make decisions, communicate with chairs, manage conflict—have been followed by an examination of the impact these approaches have on chairs and departments with some recommendations for leading more effectively.

When the leadership roles of chairs are taken seriously, chairs have the power to participate fully in decision-making that affects their departments and have the courage to accept responsibility for many of the hard decisions that change agents must make.

Higher education is undergoing rapid change. In order to survive the stress that such change entails, chairs and deans need to work closely together as a team, understand the sources of conflict that separate them, and turn their differences into constructive, creative decision-making.

Putting into practice what we know about effective leadership, leading change, and managing conflict will not only improve the effectiveness of our colleges and universities, but will make them places in which high quality learning for our students and ongoing professional development and revitalization for our faculty will be the outcome.

REFERENCES

Kotter, J. P. (1996). *Leading change.* Boston, MA: Harvard Business School Press.

Lucas, A. F. (1994). *Strengthening departmental leadership: A team-building guide for chairs in colleges and universities.* San Francisco, CA: Jossey-Bass.

Lucas, A. F. (1996). Quality departments: Surveillance or accountability? *The Department Chair, 7*(1), 1, 20, 23.

Lucas, A. F. (1990). Redirecting faculty through organizational development: Fairleigh Dickinson University. In J. H. Schuster and D. W. Wheeler (Eds.), *Enhancing faculty careers.* San Francisco, CA: Jossey-Bass.

Martinko, M. (Ed). (1994). *Attribution theory: An organizational perspective.* Delray Beach, FL: St. Lucie Press.

Rice, R. E. (1994). Foreword. In A. Lucas, *Strengthening departmental leadership: A team-building guide for chairs in colleges and universities.* San Francisco, CA: Jossey-Bass.

Schein, E. H. (1992). *Organizational culture and leadership: A dynamic view* (2nd ed.). San Francisco, CA: Jossey-Bass.

6   Nancy L. Sorenson

THE CUTTING EDGE: THE DEAN AND CONFLICT

In its most idealized form, the university is about conflict. It is a setting where diversity of opinion and background are actively sought, where ideas are given full range, and where institutional health is judged by the vigor with which those ideas are defended. The role of the dean is largely defined by the need to mediate and manage the various manifestations of conflict that develop in this unique environment.

THE DEAN: ON THE CUTTING EDGE, OR IN THE MIDDLE?

A fellow dean once observed that though the president and provost say they want the dean to be a change agent, they will judge his or her effectiveness based on how quiet the halls are. My friend's observation hints at some of the structural conflicts you will face as a university dean. In many institutions, this is the first level of administration that is purely managerial. It is also the first level of administration where an external search is usual, and where the individual selected serves at the pleasure of the provost or president. This suggests more clarity about the role than probably exists in the minds of either faculty or senior administrators. Despite other evidence, department chairs and faculty may believe that you work for them and they expect you to promote the agendas they hold dear. However, promoting the faculty agenda is probably not the highest objective that senior administrators will hold for you. Walking the line between these sometimes conflicting expectations is a constant challenge.

Though dealing effectively with conflict won't assure your success as an administrator, inability to do so is likely to be the kiss of death. As in many lines of work, it is rarely technical incompetence that signals failure in the dean's position; more often it is lack of effectiveness in dealing with interpersonal issues. Even though these issues will have all the complexity and idiosyncrasy of the people involved with them, there are some general guidelines that can help you prepare for the kind of conflict that will be the substance of much of your work.

PREMISES AND PRINCIPLES ABOUT THE DEAN AND CONFLICT

Conflict Is Neutral

The comments and suggestions in this chapter are based on three premises about conflict. The first is that though it is ubiquitous, conflict is essentially neutral. It is how groups and individuals deal with conflict that gives it a value dimension. The dean who aims to create a conflict-free workplace is set on a fool's errand. A more realistic aim is to develop an environment where conflict is dealt with in straightforward and productive ways. At times this will require you to serve as a mediator of conflict. At other times you will find yourself managing conflict in more deliberate ways.

To mediate is to play a third-party role in disputes that arise between individuals or groups in the institution. It can be a particularly challenging role because parties to a conflict would often just as soon have blood as mediation. Furthermore, as dean, you will be called upon to mediate situations where your authority is limited, but where expectations for you to do something are high. Despite its difficulty, conflict mediation is an important function of any managerial position. It requires a reputation for integrity, knowledge of the particulars of a situation, understanding of how groups and individuals react to conflict, willingness to intervene, and—often—the wisdom of Solomon.

The most effective deans take an active hand in managing conflict. To manage suggests a level of action beyond mediation. Managing requires creating, predicting, orchestrating, and instructing. To be a manager of conflict you must be able to foresee points of stress, know who in the organization is most apt to react to that stress, and have creative ways of causing them to deal with it creatively.

There are times when you will need to take action with full awareness that it will precipitate active disagreement. However, most of us will go to great lengths to avoid conflict. From personal experience we know that having our ideas and ways of doing things challenged by others can feel like an attack on our value as individuals. In any one group of people, personal responses to conflict run the gamut. What one individual sees as a healthy interplay of ideas may be perceived by others as barbarous infighting. To deliberately generate anything so volatile as conflict takes a degree of personal courage. Nonetheless, in an organizational setting, conflict often signals opportunity. The juncture at which conflict occurs is like the zone of proximal development in theories of human development. The point at which things don't go quite right, where discomfort occurs, is often the point at which an organization and the people in it are ready to try something new. The creative leader will be alert for the ways that conflict signals potential for learning and change, and will be bold in capitalizing on it.

The Causes of Conflict Are Complex

Another premise about conflict is that its causes are generally more complex than we first credit. Our impulse is to define problem situations in terms of who's to blame. Assuming the complexity of causes will prevent you from adopting this blaming mentality. It can keep you from being prematurely identified with factions who are engaged in interpersonal battles. Your first response to any conflict should be to ask, "What is really happening here? Why is it happening now? Why are these people involved? Is it a problem that I should own? If so, what should be the level of my involvement?"

Working from the premise of complexity can provide a useful perspective on some common situations. Dealing with the local malcontent is a case in point. No one, not even an habitual malcontent, operates in a vacuum. Conflict that appears to be engineered by an individual unfolds within the system of roles and relationships that characterize the whole of a workplace. Pay attention. Despite what you see as that individual's personal deficiencies, the malcontent may be a bellwether for you. Someone who has a reputation for being a chronic complainer may serve the needs of a larger group that is unwilling to raise issues for themselves. When you can, disassociate the person from the issues that are raised and give attention to those. By turning the focus away from a person to the issues, you may succeed in putting the malcontent into perspective for others who are influenced by that person.

In times of institutional turmoil, it is particularly important to distinguish between what looks like localized conflict and what is symptomatic of more generalized stress. Relationships in an organization that is being impinged upon in some way are apt to be strained. You can be fairly certain that at some point in your career you will be called on to find ways to help individuals and groups deal with the stress and conflict that accompany organizational change. Identifying systemic origins of conflict, where they exist, is a necessary first step in helping people turn those situations into opportunities for personal and institutional growth.

Managing Conflict Is Largely about Managing Self

A third premise is that the central work of conflict management is the management of self. Conflict is ubiquitous, its causes complex, the choices for action confusing, the reactions of people unpredictable. Many times the only thing you can control with any degree of confidence is yourself. Self-management is grounded in careful reflection about principles you want to live by, your institutional roles and responsibilities, and your goals for the organization. The best preparation for dealing with conflict is to:

- Know what you want to stand for.

- Know the expectations that are inherent in your role.

- Know the core principles that will govern your action.

- Know where you want to take your unit.

- Know what you need to own and what you can let go.

Human beings seem to have a need to find fault, to assign blame, and to choose sides. Even your most considered action is apt to draw criticism and to be misinterpreted. Engaging in this personal reflection will do two things for you. It will establish a basis for consistent, predictable behavior, and it will establish broad parameters for decision-making that will allow you to have confidence in those decisions, even when ambiguities prevail.

Principles for Dealing with Conflict

From these three premises it is possible to set out some general guidelines for dealing with conflict.

1) Anticipate and prepare for conflict.

2) Look for underlying issues when conflict occurs.

3) Triangulate sources of information; hear all the players before making judgments or taking action.

4) Establish regularized procedures for responding to conflict: Gather information, identify the broad principles involved, solicit advice for action, plan a course of action, take action.

5) Strive for consistency of principle in how you deal with conflict; consistency of action is impossible.

6) Maintain even-handedness always, with everyone.

7) Monitor communication channels; communicate in multiple, alternative ways if traditional channels aren't working.

8) Understand people's basic needs and gauge your actions and responses with these in mind.

9) Articulate your mission; make it clear to others how it guides your decisions and actions.

10) Take responsibility and be willing to act decisively.

IDENTIFYING SOURCES OF CONFLICT

Each change you face, even those you initiate, will introduce the potential for conflict. Even the most seasoned dean will face some of the following situations that may spur conflict.

The Induction of New Faculty

Higher education has a curiously medieval approach to inducting new people. In the outside world, 30- to 40-year-olds are running multinational corporations worth billions of dollars. In higher education, we hire 30- to 40-year-old faculty members, call them "junior," and in the worst cases, deny them a voice for the first six or seven years of their service. Even where new faculty are treated with utmost dignity, the first year or two will be difficult for them. New course preparations, the need to establish a scholarly agenda, and service expectations can mean a crushing workload. Furthermore, senior faculty may be less than welcoming to newcomers. The newcomer's orientation to a different set of professional expectations, discrepancies in salary, and differences in workload can all be sources of conflict. If the new person is inducted into a highly politicized department, high levels of stress are likely. New people will be expected to become a part of one faction or another. These situations can be especially troubling because new faculty may be reluctant to speak openly about their discomfort to people within the department or to the department chair. Thus, you may intuit the conflict new faculty are facing.

Conflict over trivial things may be a sign of this kind of conflict. The senior faculty member who writes all over the single chalkboard in the classroom she uses and then writes "save" on it, making it impossible for the new faculty member who also teaches in the room to use it without provoking a fight; the person who lobbies the department to establish a complex set of rules about how furniture should be arranged in the classroom, in an effort to prevent newer faculty from arranging chairs in circles for discussion; the young female faculty member who reports that a senior male faculty member goes into her classroom and sweeps the lab equipment she has set up for her class onto the floor are examples. None of these situations have much to do with chalkboards or furniture. They have everything to do with who is in control. And they are situations that create anxiety and stress for the newcomer that may be difficult to articulate.

The new person needs to be able to put things in perspective and needs to find people both within and without the department who can provide personal and professional support. Though you will expect department chairs to address the situations, it is wise to be certain that they are doing so. Department chairs may have limited understanding of the newcomer's needs, and in some cases they may lack the personal wherewithal to take action. Encourage chairs to develop systematic mentoring plans. Familiarize them with the literature on the induction of new faculty into university life. Find ways to support new faculty in developing a focus to their work and an active scholarly agenda. Your active support in these areas will do much to spur achievement which in turn will help new people gain a sense of control over their professional lives and their options for the future.

Changes in Central Administration

Personnel changes at the president's or provost's level will often occasion several years of institutional stress as the community adjusts to new ways of operating. This is especially true during a change at the presidential level. This role has become much more public and political than in the past, and regents, trustees, governors, and legislators may actively seek to influence both the choice of the candidate and the agenda the candidate will pursue. Because new institutional directions may have personal and professional implications for you, it is wise to determine quickly how you will fit into any agenda a new president or provost may have.

It may become apparent that you are not a good fit with a new administration. A president with a charge to downsize or reorganize may see you as dispensable; you may not fit the profile of the team of loyalists that a president or provost wants to build. Though in most cases the lack of fit has nothing to do with your competence as an administrator, the ambiguity of situations like this has the potential to be personally and professionally damaging. It may be difficult to prioritize your responsibilities to the institution, to your unit, and to yourself. Having defined a mission for yourself that extends beyond the trappings of your job and title is essential, enabling you to work through the pride and anger that can cloud good decision-making. As in most things, if you can make deliberate choices for yourself, even if those choices are very difficult, you can minimize conflict for yourself and others. What are your choices? You can leave. You can step down gracefully. You can redefine yourself professionally. Kenny Rogers sang it: "Know when to hold 'em; know when to fold 'em." The dean's position is an unstable one, at best. Recognize that there may come a time when your best personal and professional choice is to step down and step away. By determining for yourself when that time has come, you can make your departure with grace and good feeling. More than one dean has ended a career in bitterness and defeat because they stayed too long.

Appointment of New Department Chairs

The appointment of a new department chair does to a department what the appointment of a new provost or president does to a dean. A new appointment, even when it is from the ranks, introduces uncertainty to department life. It is hard to predict ahead of time how certain personality characteristics or viewpoints will play out in actual practice. The chair who views his or her role as one of dispensing patronage, for example, will generate a set of conflicts in the unit that are quite different from those that were experienced with a chair who went by the rules in matters of decision-making. These conflicts may make their way to your office and may generate direct conflict between chair and dean.

It is easy to assume too much when a chair is appointed from inside the department. As a faculty member, the chair probably had little cause to attend to the details of university business, and thus may have an incomplete understanding of how particular decisions interconnect. By being explicit about your expectations and providing technical assistance where it is needed, you can help a new chair make a good start, and you establish the basis for future accountability.

Changing Student Body

More than a little conflict occurs on campus because we continue to deliver services to the ideal student who is seeking a liberal education for its own good sake. When we look carefully at the students who actually show up in our classrooms, we decry their shallow consumerism and rampant vocationalism. Our first inclination is to see them as deficient because the values they hold are so distant from our own. Our students are different, and they are making our institutions different, but it is a mistake to see differences as deficiencies. We may wish to move students beyond where they are, we may have an obligation to move them beyond, but we cannot do so unless we are willing to meet them where they are. It is only from a profound understanding of those we teach that we can help them make sense of another set of values. One of the challenges you will face is finding ways to respond to changing student needs.

Changes in Peer Group of Managers

Changes in your peer group can reorder the dynamics of the workplace in unexpected ways. Though your fellow deans are colleagues, to some extent they are also competitors. The degree to which your peers can be described as one or the other depends very much on the personalities of the members of the group and the relationships that the individuals establish with one another and with members of the central administration. Changes in the group may trigger readjustments of relationships with upper level administrators and within the group itself. As a group, the deans have a significant influence on the climate of the institution. Where they minimize competition and function as a team, they make the institution stronger.

Each shift in the organization introduces the potential for conflict. Though it will take new guises throughout your career, each of its instances will be a test of your values and your commitment to the institution and the people you serve.

STRATEGIES AND TACTICS FOR HANDLING CONFLICT

As a mediator and manager of conflict, you will need to be able to read situations and people. Every conflict is different. Each has a different history and involves different players. Your strategies will vary according to who the players are, your assessment of what motivates them, and what you want to achieve in a particular situation. The examples below describe some common kinds of conflict and illustrate the kind of analysis and strategy-setting you might use with them.

The Blocker

Blocking is a common tactic of individuals or groups who are engaged in maintaining a power base. To be a blocker, an individual must have some degree of influence in an organization. Blockers use their influence to prevent action or to divert or obstruct communication. It is not uncommon to find a department chair or one or more senior faculty consistently cast in this role.

Situation. A dean discovered that a department chair had failed to notify his faculty of a program that allowed them to submit proposals for funding of new computer equipment out of a central institutional account. The chair regularly submitted requests for new equipment, but had used the process to sustain a system of patronage within the department. By the time the dean realized what was happening, several faculty were experiencing such acute needs for updated equipment that they had resorted to using student labs to support their work.

Your objective. To unclog communication channels.

Strategies. From time to time, check the effectiveness of your communication channels. This is especially important if you rely on a limited number of people to communicate to the rest of the faculty and staff. If you find that the usual communication channels are ineffective, are being blocked or misused, ascertain whether your administrative group senses similar difficulties with communication. It may be that you need a complete overhaul in how you communicate internally.

In some instances you may be able to remove blocks to communication by being more explicit about what information you want passed along to faculty and staff and in what form you wish to have it communicated. If this fails to solve the problem, broaden the group with which you share information. For example, you might add program coordinators, or heads of significant college committees, or rotating faculty representatives, or students to a committee of chairs that isn't communicating adequately to others in the faculty. The broader the group with which you communicate, the less likely it is that communication can be blocked or misrepresented. On certain matters, it may be wise to communicate directly with everyone, so you avoid blockages of important or time-sensitive communiqués. The use of e-mail makes this an easy, inexpensive strategy to employ.

The Exploder

The exploder is someone who has learned to use explosive displays of anger to manipulate others. Unchecked, this behavior has a debilitating effect on the workplace. A little of it goes a long way; others in the setting will tiptoe around the exploder and engage in a variety of avoidance tactics to avoid scenes.

Situation. A committee worked for months to develop a project proposal that had required considerable compromise and careful crafting. In a final meeting of the committee, when it appeared that the project was coming together in a way that one member of the group didn't like, that person created a loud, ugly scene. One committee member immediately resigned, another threw up her hands and said, "All right, all right, we'll do whatever you want." The others simply sat in stunned silence. Not only did the exploder get his way, but the group reinforced his behavior by caving in. They can be sure that the scene will be repeated in the future.

Your objective. To prevent this behavior from influencing outcomes.

Strategies. When you know the exploder well, you can sometimes predict this behavior. You may then be able to orchestrate a situation to control the behavior. You can try precipitating discussion of an issue before the individual has a chance to gather steam, or you may involve people in the discussion who are skilled in dealing with the individual and his or her behavior. Sometimes changing a meeting venue can be helpful, as can spotlighting the individual's concerns by asking for his or her input early in the discussion.

If there is someone in your unit who has gotten away with explosive interactions in the past, you will have to find a way to signal to them and to others that this behavior will not be tolerated. One way to do that is through direct confrontation following an occurrence of the behavior. This should be done politely, calmly, simply. Without making judgments, state what you have been told about a situation, state what your expectations are for how people in the organization should work together, issue an invitation to come to you with concerns or assistance in the future. Plan the confrontation ahead of time. Get in, give your message, and get out. Your purpose is not to engage in a discussion about issues or personalities. It is simply to send the message that you will not put up with the behavior.

If you have an inkling that the explosive behavior may be triggered in a one-to-one meeting, plan for backup support. Arrange for a secretary to interrupt at some key point, or ask your associate dean to stand by. With extremely volatile people, you may need to alert security personnel. If a conversation begins to get out of control, or you begin to lose you composure, terminate it at once and reschedule. Don't let the exploder be the one to end the conversation.

The Complainer

The complainer is absorbed with feelings of dissatisfaction and resentment. Complainers express their unhappiness in criticism of others. What motivates the complaint or the complainer may be unclear. Personal problems can be a trigger, though jealously, insecurity, lack of attention, thwarting of personal ambitions, or burnout may be factors. Over time, chronic complaining can be both destructive to the individual and debilitating to other people in the organization.

Situation. A new associate dean was named from the faculty ranks. For years she had had a friendship with one of the only other women in her department. The change in their relative positions marked a dramatic change in their relations. The woman who remained in the department distanced herself from her friend and became obsessed with fault-finding. People respected the new associate dean's competence and discounted the complaints, so at first the behavior was merely annoying, though personally disappointing. The situation became more serious when several new people were hired into the department. The complainer befriended these people and used them as a sounding board for her grievances. Relations between this group and the associate dean became increasingly strained, and it became more and more difficult for the associate dean to work effectively with them.

Your objective. To minimize the effect of the complainer on the system and diminish the complainer's behavior.

Strategies. Before you do anything, you need to ascertain whether the complaints have any substance. It is important to address any issues that are real. In cases where you are the focus of complaints, you may need to determine whether individuals are feeling neglected or excluded because they have been left out of the communication loop. By soliciting input and being as explicit as possible about the rationale for actions you take, you can prevent many complaints.

With the chronic complainer, it is important to gain some understanding of underlying causes of the behavior. If personal problems are at its root, your options for intervention may be limited. Nonetheless, it is useful to understand what your options are, and it will make clear that your main objective must be to diminish the potential for development of a culture of complaint. Thus, though you will continue to look for ways to diminish the complainer's behavior, you will want to give equal attention to the audience for the complaints, in order to help them find more productive ways to deal with their concerns. Find out who is listening to the complainer and why. Set expectations for this group of people to surface their issues and to deal directly with them. Make it rewarding for them to do so; call them on it when they fail to do so.

Sometimes it may be helpful to involve the complainer in dealing with issues and problems that he or she raises. Another approach is to confront the complainer directly. You might say, "I understand you are unhappy about this situation. Can you tell me why? I appreciate having a chance to discuss this with you. In the future I would like you to come and talk to me directly about these kinds of things. It is helpful for me to hear first hand what you think." Avoid being overly solicitous of the complainer, or you could find that you have reinforced unwanted behaviors. The individual needs to be held accountable both for the complaining behavior and for helping to find solutions to any real problems.

The complainer may profit from a dose of reality therapy. If the individual is developing a reputation as a chronic complainer, someone may need to counsel the individual about the long-term effects of that reputation on his or her professional life. This could be done as a part of the individual's performance review, or it might be handled as part of a more personal counseling session.

The Sniper

The sniper is someone in the organization who feels powerless and who compensates by making secretive, surprise attacks that are intended to embarrass, undermine, and diminish the individuals who are under attack. The latter are usually perceived as contributing to the sniper's disempowerment.

Situation. Snipers may aim for a broad audience. For example, just before a large group meeting to discuss a new mission statement the dean and a faculty group had crafted, someone circulated a cartoon ridiculing mission statements as manifestations of the general incompetence and addled thinking of administrators. At other times the sniper's action will be more targeted. A member of a tenure and promotion committee who had a grudge against a candidate went through the promotion papers circling typos in red and putting question marks in the margin next to key pieces of evidence.

Your objective. To recapture the sniper's audience and diminish tension.

Strategies. You can usually ascertain the origin of a sniper attack, but even when you have absolute proof of who it is, confrontation is unlikely to be a useful strategy. The intent of a sniper attack is to discomfit someone, to make the person angry and defensive. It is best not to oblige. Instead, look for a way to deflect the attack or turn it to your advantage. In response to something like the cartoon episode, you might turn the tables by reading the cartoon at the faculty meeting and thanking the sender for reminding you about the pitfalls of writing mission statements. Where the sniping is more limited in scope, your action should focus on protecting the person under attack. In the case of the tenure packet, you might simply recopy the marked pages, and thus inhibit the intended effect of the attack.

The Bully

The bully is habitually overbearing, intimidating, and cruel. The behavior tends to be used selectively, however, in that only people who are in some way weaker than the bully will be subjected to his or her tactics. One result is that some people in the organization may underestimate the damage that is done by the bully to others. Not having been subjected to the assaults, they mistakenly think that the bully is just a strong personality and that they know how to get along with him or her. In truth, a bully is highly dysfunctional and can cause great distress to members of the organization.

Situation. A department chair discovered that a new faculty member had opposed his reappointment. He embarked on a campaign of harassment in retaliation. He was careful to follow the letter of the law, so it was difficult for the faculty member to make a public case of her treatment. He converted her office into a copy center and moved her across campus to an office far removed from her colleagues; he scheduled her classes so that she had both early morning and late evening assignments; he brought the quality of her teaching and research into question. He implied in private conversation that others thought she might not meet their standards for achieving tenure at the institution. It was all subtle, but the cumulative effect made the life of the new faculty member unbearable.

Your objective. To empower people to deal with the bully.

Strategies. The bully is an abuser. He or she often relies on the tactics we associate with other abusers: isolating the victim, undercutting the victim's self-image, creating dependency. A leader has special responsibility where someone is victimizing others in these ways. Your strategy should be to assist the individuals to recognize and act out of their own power. To a degree you can do that by example, showing your own willingness to stand up to the bully, firmly, consistently, and without anger. Bullies have as much power as individuals or a groups give them, but it may require outside intervention to help people resist victimization. If an organization has accommodated a bully for any length of time, it will take time and effort to find ways to restore a sense of community and self-reliance among its members.

The Saboteur

The saboteur, like the sniper, works out of a position of perceived weakness. However, instead of aiming to undercut someone with peers or subordinates, the saboteur aims his or her activity up and out at superiors and external constituents. Sabotage may be motivated by a desire for greater personal power, anger, revenge, or jealousy.

Situation. A faculty member had developed a guru-like relationship with a particular set of students. He was in the habit of encouraging them to take complaints about other professors, especially those he didn't like, to the dean. Upon meeting with these students, the dean began to suspect that some of them were involved in a campaign to discredit particular faculty members. The complaints had little to do with the teaching or professional capabilities of the faculty in question, and more to do with students' dislike of particular people or imagined wrongs that had been done to them. The students were uninterested in the dean's offer to mediate a dialogue with the faculty members in question. After awhile, the visits diminished and the dean put the series of incidents out of mind. Several months later, he learned that the faculty guru was advising students to bypass him altogether, to take their complaints directly to the provost, and to tell the provost that the dean wouldn't do anything about their concerns.

Your objective. To protect yourself and others.

Strategies. Dealing with the saboteur requires some careful investigation. To take any kind of action, you need to be fairly certain who is involved and why. Though you may never have enough evidence to deal with the saboteur straight on, you need to know enough so that you can take strategic action. You will need to decide how much to reveal to your superiors. You don't want to overreact, but at the same time you will want to supply enough information to your superiors so that they can have confidence in how you are dealing with the issues. Your best defense against sabotage is a reputation for integrity, a strong relationship with your boss, and a history of openness with subordinates. Especially in instances where there may be significant opposition to your actions, the reasons for those actions should be made clear to people both up and down within the organization.

The Dropout

The dropout gives minimal effort, sometimes to the whole range of professional expectations: teaching, scholarship, and service; and sometimes to selected areas of responsibility: the business of the department, or a joint project. The dropout is of concern for a number of reasons. People who are disengaged feel undervalued and unappreciated or feel that higher levels of engagement somehow put them at risk. First, he or she is resented by other people in the organization, especially when they have to fill the gap that the drop-out leaves. Second, it seems to be difficult for dropouts to recoup from this pattern of behavior once they become habituated to it. Work life becomes miserable for the individual and the misery can easily infect others.

Situation. An assistant dean for enrollment management was a highly effective administrator. He encountered a personal and professional dilemma when a new dean was appointed. The new dean was a competent enough administrator, but she was a rigid, vindictive person who made life miserable for most of her subordinates. Active efforts to have her removed from the position were underway within months of her appointment. The assistant dean was pulled in two directions. Though he had established a reasonable working relationship with the dean, he saw the effect she was having on others in the organization and was sympathetic with those who wanted her removed. At the same time, his stance was that as long as he held an administrative position he owed his loyalty and best effort to his boss, and that if he could no longer give that loyalty and effort, he was obligated to relinquish his position. His stance was neither understood nor appreciated by others in the organization, and his loyalty to the dean was taken as betrayal of others in the unit. Eventually the dean left the position. Though the assistant dean considered presenting himself as a candidate for the opening, in the end he elected to leave his administrative position and return to his home department to teach. There he essentially dropped out of sight. He came to campus to teach his classes and made little contact with colleagues beyond that.

Your objective. To deploy the dropout's talents.

Strategies. Personal attention can be a significant factor in effecting reengagement of the dropout. Spend some time reviewing the person's areas of expertise. Ask for a current curriculum vita and find some time to talk to him or her about past accomplishments and current interests.

Your interest must be authentic. People see surface expressions of interest for what they are: a form of manipulation. It will take an investment of your time, but the truth is that if you really make an effort to know someone, you will find the person is inherently interesting. As you gain a better understanding of the individual, you can often find ways of reconnecting him or her through a special project or a request to take on a responsibility. Don't minimize the importance of the small effort. By the time you notice the dropout's disengagement, he or she may have internalized a habit of mind that will take some time to remedy. Though it be considerable, any time and attention you spend in reengaging someone who has chosen to drop out will bring enormous benefit to the individual and to your organization.

CONCLUSION

We have a tendency to think that if there is conflict in our organizational unit, we are doing something wrong. Nothing could be further from the

truth. Conflict is a natural state. Anywhere that people have cause to interact with one another, conflict will exist. The more complex the organization in which that interaction takes place, the more tangled the causes and
the outcomes of conflict will be. The dean's role is not so much about preventing conflict as it is learning how to manage it and mediate its effects.
The role is a challenging one, requiring curiosity about why people behave
as they do, tolerance for a wide variation in human behavior, and dedication to making the institution a place where differences can be aired in
open and productive ways.

Judith A. Sturnick

AND NEVER
THE TWAIN SHALL MEET:
ADMINISTRATOR-FACULTY
CONFLICT

The wag who said, "The reason that campus politics are so brutal is because the stakes are so low" never worked with conflict management in higher education! Our disputes are not insignificant, and the wars we fight over them are often fierce. Unresolved conflict or mismanaged conflict, therefore, always has the potential of pulling the campus off course and away from strategic priorities. Because small fires can flare into major conflagrations, the importance of sound conflict management at all levels of the institution is critical, yet this is not something we do well.

RECOGNIZING CONFLICT EARLY

Conflict is managed best when it is addressed as soon as it occurs. This is not, however, our habit on campus. The protocol of academic culture, together with our patterns of avoidance and denial, frequently result in either ignoring the issues, hoping that they will disappear through benign neglect, or rushing to thoughtless judgment. While it is true that some conflicts do die a natural death, most of them do not. One measure of our effectiveness as leaders is the degree to which we can make sound judgment calls about the importance of the emergent conflict as well as the timing of actions to be taken.

There are questions we can ask ourselves in making these assessments, such as: Does this dispute have deep roots in the institution's culture? Is the scope greater than the sum of its parts? Does it impact on campus value systems? Is it systemic in nature? Does it affect campus direction, vision, goals, and priorities? Are people already choosing sides over it? Although these questions can have different responses, depending on whether they are viewed from an administrative or faculty perspective, they make up the context for determining the timing of actions around conflict.

These queries are too important to let pass without some additional observations. We have all witnessed sad histories where ancient or unresolved conflicts have held individuals, groups, and even the institution hostage for decades. A wounding slight grows into a scabrous sore as years go by; a perceived injustice becomes a major act of tyranny; a small feud erupts into grievous warfare in which there are many casualties and no victors. Remember that campus cultures are all too primed to become internecine, and provocations for that shift may be seemingly minor, as well as major, incidents. Remember too that all of us on campus, whether faculty or administrators, are historians by nature. We test the present by the past, linking separate incidents (ancient and new) into chains of meaning, connecting our personal and private angers with more public matters. In this fashion, institutional issues are contaminated by, and mingled with, old conflicts. Consequently, if you can answer "yes" to any one of the questions posed in the preceding paragraph, then that conflict deserves your immediate and wisest attention. Let me restate a point already made: The conflict soonest dealt with is usually the conflict soonest mended.

PRINCIPLES OF CONFLICT MANAGEMENT

The Great Divide between faculty and administration may be especially daunting for newly minted administrators, particularly green deans or chairs who are just realizing the amount of time they will spend on conflict management vis-à-vis "leadership." The majority of disputes can be managed, however, and there are workable principles which can be used to minimize the realities of "never the twain shall meet."

Three Initial Principles

I will begin with a simple statement of three initial principles:

Principle 1. Make a judgment about the breadth and seriousness of the situation in order to assess action timing.

Principle 2. Clearly define the issues and competing agendas—for your sake and for the sake of all parties involved—so that the focus of conflict management remains on the issues, not on personalities.

Principle 3. Remember that the institution's governance process must be honored and adhered to.

These principles are simple and direct, even though they are often complicated by that lurking division between administrators and faculty. It does not hurt to remind ourselves of that reality—especially since the resolution of any conflict may be perceived as having quite different ends by one group versus the other. As an illustration, let us take a look at one of my recent campus experiences which exemplifies the contrast between faculty and administration perspectives, while also giving us an opportunity to apply these first three principles of conflict management.

A Case of Conflict

I was asked to spend two days on a campus—in the aftermath of a vote of no confidence in the president—to assist the institution in its healing process. The special task force which requested my help was made up of faculty and professional staff and was chaired by a mid-level administrator. Their charge to me was quite crisp: "Help us acknowledge and name the major issues which divide the campus, define some strategic actions for moving forward, and emphasize to the president that he must deal with the issues." As I worked with the groups at this university, it also became obvious that campus constituencies were willing to give the upper administration one last chance to listen to them and take strategic actions to address their concerns.

In contrast, when the president took me to breakfast the morning of my first day there, his agenda was quite different. He did not want "old issues" to be "rehashed;" instead, he wanted to move forward as quickly as possible. There was merit in both points of view, of course, since both sets of actions were needed to create a healing climate, but the needs and realities of the organizational echelon were disparate. (A side comment can be made at this point, since this example is such a provocative illustration of unmanaged conflict: The vote of no confidence had been imminent for months prior to the action, simmering in the midst of numerous conflicts and governance processes which were ignored.)

Applying the Three Principles

Let's apply the three principles of conflict management to this situation. Because the viewpoints are so contradictory, effective resolutions cannot be reached without a clear articulation of the issues. In the case I am using, the basic issues were these: The president wanted radically to change the mission of the institution. Because (remember the Great Divide) he believed that if he raised the matter on campus before it was structured in his and the board of trustees' minds, the entrenched faculty would shoot it down, he chose to keep his plans undercover.

Essentially, the campus learned of the possible mission change in a newspaper article which appeared immediately after the board meeting at which the matter was discussed. At that point, the very conflicts which the president had hoped to defuse by not first taking the matter to the campus leadership burst into flames of anger, disbelief, and fear. The bypassing of the governance structure (long a sore point already at this institution, and a concern raised by the last accreditation visit) exacerbated the multiple conflicts around issues. In addition, the principle of timing of conflict management was sorely misjudged.

There are no villains in this plot, but there are many missteps by campus leadership, divided perceptions of the institutional mission, lack of communication, and little sense of common ground. A major mission change inevitably creates churning conflict, affecting as it does every facet of institutional life and organization. There is no way—given this scenario and the inattention to conflict management—that controversy could have been minimized.

On the other hand, using simply the three tenets of conflict resolution outlined thus far, a different set choices could have been made. Not unexpectedly, the deans and department chairs—closest to the trenches yet given no voice in the mission revisions—who could and should play a significant role in managing conflict were not consulted at all. The president should have given more thoughtful analysis to the controversies around mission change, realized that these issues (which would need to be resolved at all levels of the organization) had to surface so that conflicts could be aired, defined, and managed as soon as possible.

The issues and reasoning behind the mission change should have been thoroughly discussed with the deans and chairs (thus allowing conflict resolution to be worked through between upper- and mid-level leadership, as well as within the ranks of deans and chairs). In turn, the deans and chairs could have defined and translated the issues to members of the campus community. Rather than taking the position that such a sweeping initiative as major mission revision should be essentially outlined in secrecy by top administrators, campus input led by deans and chairs should have been sought much earlier in the process. These key matters should also have included an appropriate and timely role for campus governance.

By the time I visited the campus as a consultant, the most bitter elements of the dispute had gone underground and a surface niceness had been restored. This explains why the perspective of chairs, faculty, and staff was that the still-bitter concerns needed to be resurfaced before they could be managed (what we do not name, we do not deal with). This is also why the judgment of the upper administration was to take advantage of the quiet, disregard the issues or consider them already resolved, and distract the constituents with action planning.

Principle Four: Help Constituents Explore Potential Resolutions

Because it is almost impossible to manage hidden conflict, let's consider an effective facilitating role for the deans and chairs in this situation. Understanding all too well the underground hurt and rage on campus, they could have been given the latitude to acknowledge and trigger the conflicts, publicly define the issues, and articulate areas of both agreement and disagreement. Using their three conflict management skills (perhaps with a brush-up workshop), they could then have employed a fourth principle of conflict management: helping constituents explore potential resolutions. In many campus conflicts, the closer to the trenches that issues can be addressed, the more effective the dialogues around possible strategies. This requires a critical and responsible role for the deans and chairs in institutional leadership. At this point, the campus could begin considering action plans for the future. At its core, conflict management is a highly rational process.

Principle Five: Find Common Ground

Let's pursue the principle of mediating disputes at the grass roots of the institution (departments and units) as frequently as possible. In all conflict management, every effort should be made to keep the institution as a whole from becoming embroiled. When a conflict works its unresolved way up the organizational ladder, it hooks into more and more auxiliary issues, agendas, and turf concerns. It also becomes more difficult to find common ground on which disputing parties can stand. Finding that common ground and clarifying exactly what that is, becomes the fifth tool of conflict management.

Principle Six: Manage Your Own Emotions

In the illustration of the mission that I have been using so far in this discussion, there were strong emotions and self-interests that emerged which, in turn, made the issues stickier to deal with. This reality brings us to the sixth principle of conflict management: managing your own emotions and ego. In your leadership role, and in order to increase your effectiveness in conflict resolution, you must sort out your anger, fear, insecurity, prerogatives, competitiveness, ambition, desire to be liked or loved by your constituents, distrust of the motives of administrators above you, preference not to rock the boat, and so on. These feelings and matters of self-interest are natural. However, your position dictates that you moderate your own internal conflicts in addition to the external situational conflicts. This is easier said than done, of course.

How do we accomplish self-management? It may even help to find a trusted colleague or friend with whom you can discuss your emotions and personal agendas; explaining what you are experiencing is itself a way of self-clarification, and hearing the advice of your colleague also allows you to detach and gain perspective. As a dispute moderator, you are responsible for remaining reasonable, calm, open, fair, and courteous (even to those rascals who are fomenting mutiny in the ranks). The most effective conflict managers are those who are trustworthy, no matter what the issues, and who achieve credibility by consistent exercise of sound judgment—possible only when you have swept away your own emotional and ego-centered debris.

Principle Seven: Listen Attentively and Make No Assumptions

Detachment from your self-interests allows you to hear what the disputing parties are saying, be attentive to the hidden issues behind the stated issues, and understand what needs to be clarified. There are added advantages here for the effectiveness of your role as dean or chair: As you are able to refrain from personalizing the issues, you can also keep the conflict management focus on issues, not personalities.

Principle Eight: Focus on Issues, Not Personalities

As we have seen too often on our campuses, conflicts are frequently tangled around long histories of personal animosity. Ameliorating the animosity would be nice, but that is not your purpose in conflict resolution: Your purpose is to keep the issue(s) clear, to state and restate what they are, and to maintain the focus on them.

Principle Nine: Describe, Don't Judge

Principle nine is simple, but easier said than done as you are defining the issues, the areas of agreement and disagreement, and as you are summarizing and restating the issues during the resolution process. You can neither remain a neutral facilitator, nor maintain your credibility with all parties, once you show bias.

Principle Ten: Stay in a Problem Solving Mode

Problem solving is, after all, the purpose of the conflict management process. The greater the range of possibilities articulated, the more likely a resolution is possible. Adhering to a problem solving mind set also prevents the conflict from becoming entangled with extraneous past histories and personal attacks—no matter how strongly the disputants wish to indulge in these diversions.

Principle Eleven: Stay in the Specific Present

Past grievances are in the past. Acknowledge those grievances, but keep them out of the present conflict.

Principle Twelve: Stay Positive

Assist the parties to reframe language and issues. Shifting negative words and imagery to positive definitions and questions creates a different climate for the discussion. Sometimes it even adds enlightenment.

Principle Thirteen: Establish Formal Ground Rules for Behavior

No personal attacks, table-pounding, blaming, swearing, shouting, or other inappropriate behavior is allowed. Over the years in my administrative roles, I have witnessed more than one opportunity for resolution get washed away in the undertow of virulent emotions. When everyone knows the ground rules, however, there is less likelihood of resolution lost.

Principle Fourteen: Conflict Management Takes Time

Understand that in complicated or very intense conflict, more than one session or discussion may be necessary to manage the conflict. Often, people need time out to process information before they can proceed toward resolution. Avoid the temptation to create premature dispute conclusions; everything we know about conflict management underscores the fact that the process must be brought to completion—otherwise the conflict simply reemerges later, more intense than before.

Principle Fifteen: Plan the Follow-Up

Every conflict management session should conclude with a summary of the key discussion points and the components of agreement reached—as well as areas of disagreement not yet resolved. This summary assures that everyone leaves the meeting with the same understanding of what ensued, what was agreed to, and what was not agreed to. In addition, address these questions before ending the session: Who is responsible for what? By when? How will accountability be assured? How and when will follow-up occur to deal with the remaining issues and to assess progress?

Although these guidelines may seem idealistic or difficult to apply to organizational realities, the fact is that these are effective management and leadership tools in conflict management. Not only do they represent a standard for our behavior as facilitators, but keeping them in mind provides us with a frame of reference or a context for even the most heated conflicts. In addition, these principles can be taught across the institution. Campuses which set up training in conflict management for leaders from all constituencies provide both practical techniques and a supportive climate for dispute resolution. In fact, some campuses are now undertaking such training as a community-building activity.

Another Case in Conflict

Let's look at another case study to which you can apply the conflict management principles which have been outlined. The following narrative reminds us once again that real-life disputes are often sticky, messy, and enmeshed in contradictions. This particular case study is further complicated by adding race and gender issues—as well as homophobia. But even in messy situations, the more orderly the management approach, the stronger are the possibilities for reasonable resolutions.

The dean of a medium-sized public institution is faced with the need to mediate the following situation. During the past two years, one of the most visible institutional priorities has been campus diversification. With the strong support of the board, 11 minority faculty have been recruited for tenure track positions, and the percentage of women faculty has increased from five to eight percent. This has not occurred without opposition, however, some of which is overt and most of which is covert. A historically white, male administration and faculty is not easy to change. Despite the fact that the student population is essentially half female and half male, vestiges of the old hierarchy exist in fact and in attitude. To date, there are no key administrators of color, and only one department chair—of ethnic studies—is a minority. It is also rumored—somewhat to the uneasiness of many individuals on campus—that two of the "diversity hires" are homosexual.

In an attempt to create a just and equitable campus climate, the board and the president have also instituted a new sexual harassment policy. At an open forum prior to its implementation, there was heated discussion centered on the definition of sexual harassment, as well as fear—voiced by both faculty and staff—that persecutions will result from the new policy. Two members of the philosophy department also question whether the new guidelines are an infringement of academic freedom.

One of the recently hired women faculty members (Assistant Professor O'Neil), who teaches both literature and women's studies, has come forward with charges of sexual harassment against her department chair, Dr. Evans. For years, members of the campus community have heard rumors about his inappropriate behavior with students. However, since there have been few female faculty members on campus (and none in his department), there have been no allegations from his colleagues. The dean has personally heard him make overtly sexist and racist remarks, and on one occasion the dean orally—but informally—reprimanded him. His personnel file contains no record of this.

Professor O'Neil alleges that she was touched inappropriately and that her reappointment was mentioned as he stroked her long hair. Dr. Evans indignantly insists that he had merely offered himself as a mentor, that he has no recollection of any inappropriate gestures, and that he simply commented one day that she had lovely hair.

The dean has set up a committee, following the new procedures, to investigate the charges. Privately, President Ames has asked the dean to see if the situation can be resolved quietly, behind the scenes. Publicly, he has spoken in support of an open, fair, and apolitical process.

As the committee proceeds with its work, two students and one staff member come forward with similar complaints. At the same time, a number of other individuals request the opportunity to speak to the committee on behalf of Dr. Evans' gentlemanly behavior; they all express shock that he is now the target of harassment allegations.

While the dean is attempting to let the process take its procedural course, Dr. Evans' wife makes an appointment. Mrs. Evans informs the dean that her husband could never have done anything like this. Eight years ago, she informs Dean Handler, her husband admitted to consensual involvement with an older student. After breaking off the affair, he agreed to marriage counseling, which they undertook for 15 months. She knows that he would never put their marriage at risk again by misconduct, and she pleads with the dean to intervene in the process. As part of her evidence that the charges are trumped up, she states that Professor O'Neil is a lesbian who is living with her partner in a jointly owned home five miles from campus, and that the faculty member is a man-hater who is out to get the good and decent man whose only intent was to help her gain reappointment.

Mrs. Evans further points out that some faculty members are suggesting that the dean, as a woman herself, cannot be objective in the situation. A letter signed by all but one of the department chairs (Dr. Michaels) is on its way to the president protesting Dean Handler's role as the administrator overseeing the sexual harassment process. The letter requests that the president himself step in to mediate, out of deference to Dr. Evans' 30 years of loyal service to the college. As a parting shot, the wife throws out the comment that a vote of no confidence in the dean is being discussed within the senior, tenured faculty.

After Mrs. Evans leaves the office, Dean Handler ruminates on the messiness of conflict, the contradictory stories, the agendas beneath the surface of the public issues, the impact of the campus' old cultural history on the present moment, the ways in which change threatens people, the ambiguity surrounding the president's comments, the emotional distance which has always marked her working relationship with the president, and the insecurity of her own position. Fleetingly, she also thinks of her lifelong ambition to be a campus president—an aspiration that present circumstances may destroy.

Applying the Principles of Conflict Management

This case is marked by chaos and confusion about what is real—as conflict often is in real life. For starters, how can the issues—including personal fears—be defined? What are the potential resolutions? How can the facts be determined in the midst of so many contradictory stories? Although neither the case nor the remedies are simple, the clarity of both process and focus on issues—as is true in all conflicts—needs to be maintained.

Fifteen principles for dealing with conflict have been presented in this essay. Although you will use all of them in most conflict management, your initial step in the resolution will vary, depending on the situation and your own judgment of what the first steps should be. In the case just narrated, the dean decided that her first step needed to be that of managing herself. She realized how controversial, messy, and contradictory the situation was and acknowledged that there would be no perfect resolution (there seldom is). In addition, she knew that, for some members of the campus community, their emotional biases would carry the day, no matter what the outcome of an investigation might be. No matter how thoughtfully and fairly she worked through the elements of the case, both her decision and she herself were likely to be misjudged. At the same time, everything that occurred in the process and procedures of this situation was a test case of the university's sexual harassment policies; to some extent, the legitimacy of sexual harassment as a campus issue would be determined by the outcomes of this case.

In managing her own emotions, the dean first took the time to sort out her feelings and to name them to herself. This is not New Age jargon, but rather an effective technique for facing oneself. Her emotions were fear, confusion, insecurity about her job and her competence to handle this situation, concern for her professional reputation, a wish to avoid unpleasantness, and—as a woman and the first female dean on campus—she also felt anger at the ugliness of sexual harassment as a fact of professional life. As was her habit, she wrote down her feelings in her journal, describing their impact on her life and potentially on her judgment.

She then called three people whom she trusted: her mentor, a female colleague, and a male friend, all of whom were some distance away. In those conversations, she described her emotions as well as the outlines of the situations, and asked for their advice and counsel. She later said that one of the wisest suggestions she received was this: You are responsible for your decisions; you are not responsible for the outcomes. Her job was to weigh the evidence and the recommendations from a fact-gathering committee and to reach a fair conclusion; not only was there no way in which outcomes or reactions to outcomes in the case could be predicted, but to focus on outcomes would skew the process and her judgment.

The dean further had to determine the timing of this conflict resolution. Basically, she had to decide if it would be better to move the process along as expeditiously as possible, or to delay and stall the process in hopes that the individuals involved would give up from exhaustion, or that Professor O'Neil would resign in frustration. What was at stake for the institution and the individuals in the case in either scenario? In her best judgment, this case could shake the university to its roots and leave scars which would remain for decades. With that in mind, the dean set the sexual harassment procedures in motion at once, in a very public way.

Next, acknowledging to herself that the president appeared to wish to sweep this conflict under the rug (despite his public rhetoric), she informed him of her actions, gave him her reasons for choosing to implement the new policy, and promised to keep him informed appropriately. From his demeanor, she knew she was taking a risk with this decision and that he was not entirely pleased with her or the situation. She also knew that she had made the best decision she was capable of making.

The dean's fact-finding process occurred in two phases. The first consisted of her initial interviews with the complainant, the accused party, and the chairs of each department. On the basis of this information (still highly inflammatory and contradictory), she convened the sexual harassment committee as called for under the new policy. According to the procedures (which had earlier gone through the governance process on campus), the membership was to consist of three faculty, one student, one representative of the professional staff, and one department chair. The dean, by statute, appointed one of the faculty members and the chair; all others were elected.

In her charge to the committee, the dean defined the issues as clearly as she could: The central issue was sexual harassment. Did it or did it not occur? The committee's responsibility was to hold confidential hearings on the charges and countercharges, to interview as many people as they thought necessary, to sort out the evidence, and to make recommendations to the dean regarding the disposition of the case. The committee selected one of the faculty members as chairperson, and the dean gave them a timeline of six weeks in which to complete their task.

At the first meeting of the committee, the dean also outlined some of the principles that she had learned in a conflict management workshop taken several months ago. Urging them to maintain their focus on the issue, she reminded them that such matters as the state of Evans' marriage and O'Neil's alleged lesbianism were tangential. She also encouraged them to clearly state the ground rules for behavior at the beginning of each interview.

In agreeing to follow and enforce ground rules, the committee discussed at length with the dean the hard realities of trying to describe, rather than to judge, in their own debriefing sessions and in the report which would later be sent to her. This conversation was additionally helpful in maintaining focus and keeping the committee in a problem solving mode.

In this case, past grievances could not legitimately be kept out of the information-gathering, since several accusers had stepped forward with stories of past harassment. Since the past and the present incidents were all of one cloth, they needed to be dealt with as such.

Committee members asked the dean to define the common ground. Although there was disagreement about what it was, all finally agreed that the common ground was the protection of the reputation of the university and—at least until all the evidence had been gathered—all parties involved in the case. Given the common ground, how many resolutions were possible in this conflict? In some ways, answering this question was one of the most difficult tasks of the committee. As it went back and forth with the dean in that first committee meeting, committee members agreed that there were a range of possibilities:

- A public apology by Evans to O'Neil and an agreement that he would attend sexual harassment workshops as well as seek counseling around his gender attitudes

- O'Neil's public apology to Evans, followed by her resignation

- The termination of either party from his or her position

- The suspension of either party, with or without pay

- Written reprimands placed in personnel files

- Required community service on campus

Regardless of what the evidence revealed, there were indeed many options for dealing with both accuser and accused; these would be reviewed again when the committee was considering its recommendations to the dean. Because litigation is always a possibility, all recommendations would also be reviewed with the university's legal counsel prior to the dean's decision(s).

At the conclusion of the meeting, the dean suggested that the committee remain empathetic yet unbiased during the hearings. "This is an academic community," she advised, "and it would be helpful to everyone concerned to remain as objective as possible. Try to understand the sense of violation that each one has expressed, and continue to sort out those emotions from the facts and the central issue. Maintain your focus, and honor the process." She left the room knowing that she had given them sound guidelines; she hoped for a fair and effective fact-finding which could then also lead to fair decision-making on her part.

As the committee concluded its work, it forwarded a summary of findings and recommendations to Dean Handler. At this point, the dean had to remind herself again of the conflict management tools she had learned and shared with that group. The evidence indicated, with considerable congruence, that Evans had a long history of sexual harassment which had deleteriously affected the lives of several female students. In at least one case, his actions caused a female student to withdraw from the university. It was years later before she could resume her interrupted education, and then she did so at another campus which held no painful memories.

In coming to her decisions in this case, Dean Handler had to practice once again the tools of conflict management: reviewing all the accurate information available; maintaining a tight focus on the issues; managing her own ego and emotions; describing the facts to herself without emotion-laden language (whether or not Evans is good or evil is outside her purview as the decision-maker); detaching herself from the outcomes; staying in a problem solving mode rather than a punitive one; and selecting the most reasonable resolution from the variety of possibilities for action.

You might be interested in her decision here. She suspended Evans for a year without pay, mandating his attendance at a class in gender issues and two sexual harassment workshops; she also placed a letter of reprimand in his file, stating that termination would result if there were further instances of such behavior. In addition, she was able to transfer Professor O'Neil to another department where her credentials and academic discipline were appropriate.

To mitigate prospects for future conflict, the dean spent two hours with the president, briefing him in detail on the facts gathered by the committee and the bases for her decisions. Not only did he accept the fairness of her disposition of the case, but he used it in a presentation to the board to validate the sexual harassment policy and to enhance the reputation of "his" campus for moral courage. When Evans appealed the decision to the president (as was allowable under the policy), the president supported the dean's decisions.

Furthermore, understanding that another component of conflict management (albeit too seldom stated as such) is trouble-shooting, the dean, with the support of department chairs and the provost, instituted a two-year series of educational workshops on sexual harassment for all constituencies (including students). Although of course there were still faculty who deemed harassment a spurious issue, the majority of the campus community came to understand its reality, dynamics, and destructiveness. The chair of the board even sat in on one of the workshops to show board support for these campus efforts.

Needless to say, there was not a vote of no confidence in the dean. In keeping her head, following practical conflict management principles, and keeping her eye on the decision rather than the outcomes, she actually garnered greater respect on campus. Her actions legitimized the issue of harassment and minimized its occurrence on campus. By her behavior and principles, she set a standard for the entire community.

This case is a successful story of conflict management. Yet even imperfect and marginally satisfactory conflict resolutions—since they serve the purpose of deescalation and provide breathing space for the institution—can be effective management tools. It has been my experience that human beings are capable of remarkable resilience and creative problem solving, even under the most difficult circumstances, if they are given enough time, safety, process, and structure. Good conflict management structures can provide that.

The issue of sexual harassment, because of the breadth of its implications, is also worthy of comment. Although the conflict originated at the department level and moved from the chair's jurisdiction to the dean's, the matter was institutional in nature, affecting every level of the organization. The scope of sexual harassment as a concern could have easily exacerbated the divide between faculty and administration, as has been the case on some campuses. But as this case unfolded, the issue actually drew the university together, uniting them behind a common educational and ethical cause.

CONFLICT MANAGEMENT: NEEDS AND BENEFITS

As a former faculty member (25 years) and president (11 years), I have grown increasingly concerned about the warfare between faculty and administration. Sometimes we do have different perspectives and agendas—sometimes legitimately so, and sometimes not legitimately so. Since now the general public has become so skeptical of our motives and the quality of our educational programs, conflict is no longer isolated to our campus milieu. The greater our eagerness to burn each other up in internecine battles, the less our credibility off campus. It is in the best interests of everyone concerned within our institutions that we manage our internal conflicts with judgment and wisdom. We have done immense damage to our academic reputations by allowing mismanaged—or unmanaged—disputes to spill over into full-scale eruptions played out in the media, the public, and sometimes in the legislature as well.

One more observation about conflict management. There is a positive side to disputes, since appropriately managed conflict can encourage creative thinking, honest communication, clarification of issues, and the generation of many alternative actions. Although conflict for its own sake is fruitless, the tension of creative conflict can challenge individuals, as well as our organizational systems, to change.

Although I do not wish to minimize the difficulty of conflict management, the fact is that every organization is fraught with disputes and disagreements, some of them minor and some of them major. Leadership at every level requires that we deal with these realities with some semblance of form and substance. Through effective use of conflict resolution tools, we can strengthen our leadership capabilities and strengthen our campus communities as well.

8 Clara M. Lovett

MANAGING CONFLICT ON THE FRONT LINES: LESSONS FROM THE JOURNALS OF A FORMER DEAN AND PROVOST

While serving as provost and vice president for academic affairs at George Mason University in the 1980s, I had the good fortune of working with the faculty and staff of the renowned Institute for Conflict Analysis and Resolution (ICAR). The institute's distinguished scholars/practitioners contribute to the growing literature on the origins and nature of conflict and also travel throughout the United States and the world offering their services as analysts and mediators. As the academic officer to whom the institute reported, I found it intriguing that its world-class theorists and mediators seemed rather inept at managing conflict within their own group and between themselves and colleagues from other academic units. With the benefit of hindsight, I realize now that ICAR was a microcosm of attitudes and behaviors common throughout the academy.

The philosophers and social scientists who teach and write on our campuses have produced most of the scholarly theories on the origins and resolution of conflict. In fact, some scholars, such as Moss Kanter, have also written articles and books that synthesize the theoretical findings and apply them to real-world situations. Yet the impact of all that good work on the organizational behavior of academic institutions thus far has been negligible. Since the 1970s, individual scholars such as Ann Lucas and association-sponsored programs such as the American Association of State Colleges and Universities' seminars for deans and chairs and the American Council on Education's well-established fellows program have disseminated theoretical findings and practical applications. Help is not hard to find. The learning opportunities available through higher education associations are tailored specifically to the culture of the academy, and they tend to be relatively inexpensive. But other opportunities are available to campus leaders willing to invest time and effort in learning to identify and manage conflict. For instance, the popular Noel/Levitz problem solving seminars often address this topic. So does Stephen Covey, whose "Seven Habits" training sessions are available in several formats and price ranges all over the country. Yet most faculty leaders on our campuses and many vice presidents and deans lack the institutional support or the personal motivation, or both, to reach out for the opportunities. Like the proverbial physician who is unwilling to heal himself, the academy in the past 30 or 40 years has built a culture that is unwilling to internalize and apply to itself the advice it dispenses with authority to other sectors of society.

The most common explanation for this curiously unscholarly behavior is, of course, that universities are not organizations, that is, organisms whose components have to function well together, but rather loose federations of specialized interest groups. The overall health of the organization is of interest to the specialized groups only insofar as it provides predictable support for them and assures their autonomy. I believe, however, that this explanation does not go far enough.

A deeper reason for the academy's widespread reluctance to understand the origins of conflict and how to manage it lies in what might be called "academic exceptionalism." As a historian I wonder sometimes whether the idea of academic exceptionalism is somehow rooted in the historiographical tradition of American exceptionalism. There certainly is an interesting parallelism between the two ideas. Just as historians of the United States have argued at times that this country's political institutions and culture are too unique to be studied in a comparative perspective, so have scholars of higher education argued for the exceptionalism of academic culture. However, it seems to me that the proponents of academic exceptionalism have been more successful than the historians of American exceptionalism ever were. Academic exceptionalism shelters our institutions and culture from uncomfortable or unflattering comparisons with all other systems of higher education and also with all other sectors of our own society. Having proclaimed our uniqueness, we can proudly proclaim to be the best in the world. Perhaps more importantly for the purposes of this discussion about conflict in higher education, academic exceptionalism gives us license to study other systems or sectors of our own society while learning little from their triumphs and failures that we deem applicable to ourselves. The result? Proud independence combined with a propensity to reinvent the wheel in the management of our affairs.

Powerful myths have been built around the idea that universities are uniquely different from all other organizations, whether public or private, for profit or not-for-profit. Two overarching myths, in particular, govern the ways we think about and deal with internal conflict. The first myth is that within the university, consensus (defined as the absence of conflict) is the norm, conflict the rare exception. According to this myth, conflict arises when people who have power exercise that power in ways that is, or is perceived to be, illegitimate. In other words, conflict is synonymous with evil. To return to the normal state of consensus, it is enough to remove the evil doer, the abuser of power, the deviant from the culturally accepted behaviors. Not accidentally, universities that experience high levels of conflict; e.g., concerning mission or resource allocation or governance, also exhibit high turnover in leadership positions. Faculty leaders and administrators become scapegoats in collective attempts to return to normalcy.

This understanding of consensus as the natural order of things in the academy is fraught with problems. One problem is that the removal of real or alleged evil doers and abusers seldom addresses the underlying causes of institutional conflict. When deep-seated institutional problems go unexplored and alternative explanations and solutions are rejected, the result is not stability but gridlock. What passes for consensus ("You leave me alone, I'll leave you alone") is in fact an uneasy truce among groups that hold one another in check. Consensus understood in these terms may assure that no one group is powerful enough to impose its will on others. But it also assures that no one will take initiatives without endless rounds of consultation, discussions, report-writing, and so on.

Another, perhaps more serious problem is that the only leaders who can function, or even survive, under these conditions are the least likely to address the causes of institutional conflict and propose solutions. And here again, the academy mostly fails to practice what its scholars preach to other organizations. Contemporary organizational theory, case studies used in our business schools, and biographies of leaders illustrate the importance of visioning, risk-taking, and conflict management. But academic exceptionalism and its overarching myths lead our institutions in quite a different direction toward a minimalist and rhetorical definition of consensus, an avoidance or denial of conflict, and the choice of care-takers over risk-takers for leadership positions.

The stories that follow illustrate what happens when the overarching myths take hold of our institutions and their leaders. The situations are real, though names and circumstances have been altered to protect the identity of individuals. The first story is about a leader so committed to sheltering her department from conflict that she tried first to sweep a problem under the rug and then tried to manage the problem without the help of others.

YOU CAN'T WISH REAL PROBLEMS AWAY: THE NORA JOHNSON STORY

I remember Nora Johnson with respect and fondness. She stood out among her peers, the 20 department chairs in the College of Arts and Sciences, for her intelligence, strong values, and political and fiscal savvy. I appreciated her contributions and also admired her personal qualities, a rare combination of grace and strength. One Friday afternoon, at the end of an unusually hectic week, Nora called and asked if she might drop in for a chat. I welcomed the call, looking forward to a visit with a favorite colleague. Perhaps by design Nora arrived late, after my staff had left the office. She looked unusually stressed and ill at ease. She had a painful story to tell.

For nearly five years, Nora told me, she had known that Joe Rausch, a senior member of her department, had severe health problems brought on by excessive drinking. Nora and others had covered for Joe, taking his classes when he was ill, assigning him a lighter load than was customary for the department, trying to look after him especially after the death of his wife. But Joe was doing worse. Students were complaining to Nora that he had failed to show up for class on a few occasions; when he did meet class he appeared distracted and disoriented; he failed to return papers and exams in a timely manner. The news was shocking, of course, but I tried to reassure Nora that this kind of problem was not unusual. I asked if she had confronted Joe with this matter.

Nora started to cry, then went on with her story. I learned that Joe had been her undergraduate mentor. He had encouraged her to apply for admission to one of the country's top departments in their field, had helped her gain admission, and then had been instrumental in bringing her back to the department as a faculty member. Yes, she had spoken with Joe on many occasions but had been met with complete denial. Sympathetic to her personal dilemma, I offered to help by talking with Joe myself. I met with him twice and got nowhere. He was as experienced at denial as he was at manipulating those who tried to help him. I recognized the pattern and realized I was not doing any better than Nora at handling the situation. In fact, in the short term I made matters worse because Joe told tales inside and outside the department about "administrative interference with [his] academic freedom."

Another semester went by. Nora did not bring up the matter again, but I found out through the college grapevine that she had covered Joe's exams and turned in his grades. It was my turn to drop in on Nora for a chat. Had she spoken with other members of the department, I asked, and sought their counsel? Nora answered that most department members were aware of Joe's drinking problem and were tired of making excuses for his behavior. But they had also made it clear to her that Joe was her problem, not theirs. I felt frustrated by my inability to help Nora resolve the conflict between her personal loyalty to Joe and her responsibility to colleagues and students. Not long after our second conversation, Nora offered her resignation and asked me to meet with a colleague whom she thought could take over the chair's duties.

Reluctantly, I met with Tom Henderson. Our conversation took an unexpected turn. When I opened up to reveal my concern for Joe and Nora, Tom said he thought he knew just what to do. He did not want to be chair; however, as a recovering alcoholic himself, he was willing to tell his own story to his colleagues and by so doing shame them into action on behalf of the department and the university. Tom's proposed solution worked. In the end, we were unable to help Joe, who chose early retirement and continued drinking to his grave. But we did help the students and protect the good name of the university.

Nora and I learned two invaluable lessons. First, problems like Joe Rausch's addiction cannot be wished away; they only get worse over time. Second, lonely heroism does not get us very far in solving problems. Whatever our roles, we must be willing to share our burdens and find allies. Help can come in unexpected ways and from unlikely sources.

IF A FIRE BREAKS OUT, RUN TOWARD IT, NOT AWAY FROM IT: THE ALISTAIR MCMAHON STORY

The second story is about what happens when a leader with broad-based experience in managing conflict outside the academy encounters and—in this case—embraces the overarching myths about academic exceptionalism.

Alistair McMahon was in his sixties and pursuing his third career when I became his supervisor. In his youth he had excelled in the technical field in which he had earned his doctoral degree. In midlife he had founded and led a very successful research and development company, becoming a wealthy, highly respected business and civic leader. He began his third career as an academic dean to give back the gifts and opportunities he had received through education. Though his educational values, especially his view of the baccalaureate degree, were a bit old-fashioned, his personal commitment to the job and his desire to serve faculty and students burned brightly. I learned much from him and enjoyed his company. Yet for about four years I watched him struggle and ultimately give up. Long after he had retired and I had moved to another institution, Alistair still blamed himself for his failed deanship. And I, the old academic hand, to this day blame myself for my inability to help him succeed.

Common wisdom has it that leaders from outside the academy often fail as deans, vice presidents, or presidents because they are unable to understand and appreciate academic exceptionalism. From the unhappy experience of Alistair McMahon I have drawn the opposite conclusion. An eager novice seeking acceptance into the academic brotherhood, Alistair embraced the myth that consensus is the normal state of affairs in the academy and tried as hard as anyone I have known to become a consensus leader as defined by the academy. He set aside a lifetime of experience in corporate management in favor of a consultative, very accessible, and friendly style of leadership. However, his dedication to student learning and his commitment to continuous quality improvement in all aspects of his school's operation led him to ask questions about the nature of the curriculum, the evaluation of teaching and scholarship, and the management of school resources that intruded constantly into the comfort zones of his faculty.

Alistair took seriously the institutional rhetoric about excellence in teaching and scholarship and expected everyone else to do the same. He never understood that his own interpretation of consensus leadership, that is, shared values and a shared willingness to question the way things were, was quite at odds with the interpretation of his faculty. Their idea of a consensus leader was one who supported without reservations what they were already doing, one who brought home as much of the institutional bacon as possible, one who did not ask difficult questions about what was being taught and why; in short, one who did not make waves.

At times, Alistair made waves. There was the time, for instance, when he read all the textbooks used by his faculty in introductory courses and came to the conclusion that there was about a 40% duplication of content across three of his departments. He asked why the faculty in the three departments, each of which complained incessantly about understaffing, did not get together and share the teaching of common material instead of requiring students to repeat it in each department's courses. On another occasion he asked the faculty to explain why every minor action at the department or college level required a committee. What was wrong, he asked, about empowering just one or two people to do the job, holding them accountable for reporting outcomes to the departments or the entire college?

These questions, however, were not in themselves the reason for Alistair's failure as a dean. The main problem was that when Alistair was faced with ridicule ("You can't be serious about common core courses across departments; this isn't the way things work in a university") or resistance, he almost always chose to retreat. He was convinced that the questions were worth asking, yet he also wanted to conform to the academy's notion of the consensus leader. His pursuit of consensus as defined by the academy crippled his ability to get support for needed changes from the central administration of the university and even blunted the impact of personal qualities—integrity, dedication, earnestness—that his faculty generally admired.

Reluctant to move toward the metaphorical fires that his troubling questions had ignited, Alistair dropped one issue after another. It did not take long for his faculty to figure out that they could stall or defeat any of his proposals for changes in curriculum, promotion and tenure matters, or resource management. They could not easily attack his ideas or deny the relevance of his questions. But they could, and did, intimidate him with charges of administrative meddling, tyranny, and worse. Alistair learned the hard way that faculty, regardless of discipline, are skilled in the use of debate, hyperbole, and invective.

Mentoring this good man in the strange ways of the academy, I tried to reassure him that the tensions between himself and his faculty were not unusual, that the dichotomy between the rhetoric of academic excellence and the reality of departmental practices was not uncommon. He listened, but I don't think he ever believed me. Nor did he ever recognize that his eagerness to be accepted by the faculty on their own terms conflicted with his desire to be an agent of change in the programs and management of his school.

Alas, the only lesson Alistair learned from this unhappy experience was that no human being is immune to failure. I learned that the myths of academic exceptionalism and consensus as the natural order of things are very powerful indeed. In the hands of true believers or opportunists, those myths can be used to curtail debate about academic values and practices, to preclude comparisons with other sectors of society, to keep the barbarians—any barbarians—at the gates.

CONFLICT WILL HAPPEN—YOU MIGHT AS WELL LEARN TO MANAGE IT

Alistair McMahon, the outsider who tried to become an insider, agonized over conflict with his faculty, blamed himself for it, and regarded it as a lapse of academic ideals. But at least Alistair was aware of it. The next stories illustrate what happens when academic leaders fail to recognize the need to manage internal conflict either because they are too comfortable with the overarching myths that they do not detect the telling signs of trouble, or because they do not understand the importance of the myths in academic circles. I have known academic insiders who were simply oblivious to the reality of or potential for conflict. They could not be expected to manage something they did not even recognize. One such insider was Sandra Shelby, interim chair of a large department in the College of Health Professions. She was appointed to this position when the long-term chair of the department became too ill to serve. Sandra's peers recommended her to me as a competent, energetic, enthusiastic colleague. Indeed, she had the endearing qualities of a born cheerleader. After a few months, however, I became concerned about her performance. Assurances that this or that task would be done were not accompanied by commensurate or consistent results.

A strong believer in collegial governance, Sandra gladly shared authority and decisions with three section heads in her department. At meetings, the three pretended to agree with Sandra's proposals and accept assignments from her. But afterwards, each of the three went off in a different direction, doing pretty much as he or she pleased. Sandra lectured her colleagues on good governance, preached and practiced good stewardship, worked on a new mission statement for the department, and worried about professional development opportunities for the staff and good advising for students. She did not seem to notice, however, that the gamesmanship practiced by her section heads divided the department and undermined her efforts at moral leadership and good management.

When the time came for me to appoint a chair for a multiyear term, two senior members of the department who supported Sandra's leadership shared their observations about the behavior of the section heads. Discreetly, I probed into Sandra's relationship with the section heads. With her best cheerleader's smile she assured me that all three supported her desire for a full term as chair of the department. She was right about that, of course; but it never occurred to her to ask why her three colleagues supported her candidacy. With regret, because I appreciated her hard work and personal qualities, I declined to appoint her. It seemed most unlikely that someone so naive would be able to recognize potential conflict in the department, let alone manage conflict if and when it occurred.

I have known many people like Sandra; she is a common type in a culture that, for the right or wrong reasons, values consensus builders. Less frequently, I have run across the opposite type: men and women (but mostly men) so accepting of conflict as a part of life that they do not appreciate the need to manage it. Neither are they likely to hone conflict-management skills. Their preferred approach is to suppress potential sources of conflict or ignore them. Like Sandra, but for quite different reasons, such people are at risk in leadership positions.

Laurence Hurst comes to mind. An African-American educator of commanding presence and sharp wit, Laurence became a university administrator after many years of experience in management and policy positions with K-12 schools. As I reflect on my working relationship with Laurence, I find that his experience with faculty was roughly the opposite of Alistair McMahon's. Both men were outsiders to the academy. But while Alistair sought acceptance into the academic brotherhood, convinced as he was that it embodied universal and eternal values, Laurence remained aloof.

The president's and my choice of Laurence for the deanship did not generate controversy. There was consensus within the school and on campus that we needed an educator with K-12 experience and also that we badly needed leaders from minority communities. Conflict erupted, however, when Laurence began to assemble a new leadership team for his school. An associate dean who had served for more than a decade was replaced by a younger person with whom Laurence had worked at another institution. And a retirement package was negotiated for an executive assistant to the dean who, according to campus lore, had been "the power behind the throne" under Laurence's predecessors.

These personnel changes, not uncommon with a change in leadership, were executed correctly from a legal standpoint, and humanely. Thus, Laurence was stunned when I dropped by his office one day and informed him that trouble was brewing within the school and beyond. There was talk (and perhaps it was just that) of staff resignations in the dean's office. And some faculty were reported as complaining that they had wanted an academic dean, not a superintendent of schools.

Laurence reacted to the situation in two ways. First, he insisted on reviewing the process used to make the personnel changes, though he knew as well as I did that the process was not the problem. Second, he circulated a memo to faculty and staff explaining why he needed a new team and affirming his right to appoint one. It did not occur to Laurence to ask questions about the nature of our campus grapevine or the possible reasons why routine personnel changes were generating criticism of his leadership

He chose to sit in his office and bide his time, waiting for the criticism to die down, wondering what all the fuss was about. Had Laurence talked with more people, especially members of his faculty, he would have realized that the campus gossips were acting out their fears of larger, more significant changes in the direction of his school. Opposition to the administrative changes as well as snide comments about the new dean's style of leadership were, in fact, time-honored campus tactics to divert Laurence's attention from more important pursuits. Given Laurence's lack of experience in the ways of the academy, the tactics worked. His reluctance to manage the relatively minor issue of administrative changes by smoking out the critics and understanding their motives prolonged the controversy and distracted him through most of his first year in office.

There are two lessons to be learned from the Laurence Hurst story. One is that leaders who make sensible decisions according to good processes are not ipso facto sheltered from opposition or criticism. A second one is that leaders who fail, whether out of ignorance, indifference, or arrogance, to manage conflict end up paying the price. If they do not forfeit their positions in the process, they may suffer a worse fate. They may lose the ability to make the right decisions for their units and their institutions.

IT GETS WORSE UP THE LADDER: CONFLICT AMONG PEERS

Most of the stories told thus far deal with conflicts between chairs or deans and faculty. Different, often sharper conflicts, arise between peers at the level of dean or vice president. The organization of the contemporary university and the pattern of resource allocation that parallels the organization foster isolation and competition among senior academic administrators. In good times, deans and vice presidents measure their own success—and are evaluated by others—on the basis of how much they have strengthened and enlarged their silos. Success can be measured in dollars (how much has your budget grown this year?) or in positions (has your faculty or staff FTE grown this year?) or in reputation (how many external grants have you brought in this year?). Most presidents encourage this kind of competitive behavior. The common wisdom in the academy holds that competition for resources and influence among leaders at all levels is a good way of advancing an institution. Competition gives everyone a stake in advancement, usually defined as growth. Competition keeps leaders on their toes; it assures that only the most dedicated and energetic people occupy positions of leadership. In times of stress, however, when friendly competition becomes unlikely or impossible, presidents expect the very people who were groomed to compete and enlarge their silos to change their spots quickly. It is not surprising, therefore, that institutions frequently experience internal stress, even internecine warfare, at the same time as they endure stress from the outside.

In the early 1990s, a severe fiscal crisis hit the public system of higher education in Virginia. Due to faulty forecasts of state revenue, appropriations in support of operating budgets declined suddenly and dramatically. To convey the seriousness of the situation, the president I served at that time used the analogy of a night driver whose lights suddenly burn out. As provost, I was responsible for communicating to the deans and other senior academic leaders the need to reformulate plans and budgets, yet also the importance of maintaining momentum. None of us wanted to see a serious but temporary financial setback damage the long-term prospects of a dynamic and optimistic institution.

Fourteen senior administrators were directly involved in discussing the problems we faced and in recommending solutions. A few participants, among them our academically most distinguished deans, opined that a crisis due to the chicanery or incompetence of elected officials needed to be addressed by those officials, not by the universities or other affected agencies. This rhetorical position was duly applauded and seconded by the faculty senate and discussed in the media. It did not do any harm, but it did not address our problems either.

After a couple of meetings, more practical heads prevailed. Once we agreed that specific programmatic and budgetary measures were needed, the participants predictably split into two camps. One group advocated across-the-board budget reductions; another recommended preparing a selective list of programs and functions to be merged or eliminated. All of us knew that the former approach was totally out of step with the president's philosophy and that the latter approach, though useful, would trigger a civil war on campus. After hours of inconclusive discussion, two members of the group came up with a fresh idea. They proposed clustering academic programs and support functions in such a way that separate units could share what there was to be shared—faculty, technical and clerical personnel, operating dollars, equipment, and so on. A majority of participants recognized the wisdom of this approach, which was ultimately recommended to the president and implemented. But four diehards rejected it, among them two influential and powerful deans. They understood the need to do something to get over the crisis. But they were most uncomfortable with a management philosophy that deemphasized the separate identities and autonomy of the university's academic programs and support functions. Temporary tactical alliances were acceptable. A long-term commitment to a different way of doing business clearly was not. Presidential intervention persuaded one of the diehards to go along with the majority of his peers. But the second one chose to resign in protest.

This experience taught me useful lessons about peer culture and peer conflicts in the academy. The leaders with whom I shared information and responsibility were not timid bureaucrats. They knew that they and I were empowered to deal with the crisis and responsible collectively for keeping the university on track. They were not afraid to express their ideas and opinions; they were used to open and tough-minded debates. Yet they found it exceedingly difficult, perhaps painful, to recommend specific actions to the president in a situation in which the conventional academic definition of consensus did not apply.

Some participants were uncomfortable with the recommended course of action because they did not wish to weaken the bonds of collegiality. But for others the insistence on consensus became an excuse for avoiding scrutiny of their own programs and functions. In this instance, a fiscal crisis highlighted the gap between the rhetoric and the practice of peer decision-making. Every single member of the leadership group professed to believe in a culture of peers. But when the chips were down, some members of the group accepted the viewpoints of a majority of their peers while others did not. In the end, the president and I implemented the recommendations of the majority in the leadership group and accepted the inevitable consequences: One highly publicized resignation and a lot of grousing in some units. At several of our sister institutions, however, the leaders did not act until they had arrived at a consensus position. Conflict among peers was avoided by the only means possible: across-the-board budgets cuts that left all programs and functions in a weaker condition.

VICE PRESIDENTIAL LEADERSHIP
AND CONFLICT MANAGEMENT

A vice president, especially a vice president for academic affairs, can expect that conflict management and resolution will be a major part of the job. While chairs and deans, too, bear this responsibility, vice presidents are much more likely to experience the complexity, intensity, and importance of institutional conflict in all its aspects. I am not suggesting that this is unpleasant or unrewarding work. On the contrary, successful conflict management advances the institution and can generate wonderful psychological and practical benefits for the parties that come together. But conflict management is difficult work and calls for skills that are in short supply in academic circles.

At the vice presidential level, managing conflict is a lot like working on a puzzle, but knowing in advance that not all the pieces are on hand. A good puzzle solver starts from the desired outcome—the whole picture—and works backward to fit the pieces to the picture. Similarly, the vice president who wants to resolve conflicts with peers or subordinates must start with an outcome in mind. In most cases, he or she will start from a definition of the broad institutional interests at stake in a given situation. From there, he or she will proceed to identify and understand the particular interests of the individuals or groups in conflict. The story of Delia White and Sam Goodwin reminds me how this sort of exercise can be especially difficult in situations of conflict among peers.

Delia, the vice president for student affairs, and Sam, the vice president for external relations at a large comprehensive university, were experienced, loyal, and outspoken members of their president's cabinet. They tried hard to understand the big picture as he presented it at weekly cabinet meetings. And they gave a lot of thought to the implications of the big picture for the units and programs they supervised. But their interpretations of the presidential vision were very different and so were the messages they conveyed to their respective staffs.

Delia heard the president talk about a student-centered institution and filtered that message through her own professional experiences as a former dean for undergraduate studies and residence hall counselor. She urged her staff to focus their efforts on undergraduate residential students, although these students were only 25% of the total enrollment. Sam's idea of a student-centered institution, on the other hand, was one that treated the students as valued customers, providing conveniently packaged, accessible, and affordable goods and services. He lectured Delia and others about the need to win the loyalty of older and commuting students who put a high value on convenience and affordability.

These honestly held and passionately argued interpretations of the institutional big picture gave rise to conflict not just between the two vice presidents, but also among members of their staffs. At budget preparation time, when interpretations had to be translated into initiatives, and values into programmatic priorities, Delia and Sam requested a meeting with the president and admitted that they could not reconcile their differences. Reluctantly, the president made the decisions that his lieutenants were unable to make. But a year later, when Delia resigned to move with her family to another state, the president chose a successor whose approach to the management of students affairs was more compatible with Sam's approach to the management of external relations.

Delia and Sam worked at a complex institution with a multidimensional mission. But the difficulties they experienced occur frequently among vice presidential peers even at the most stable institutions, for instance, well-established liberal arts colleges, church-related colleges, or the older research universities, that are generally clear about their mission. Where the institutional big picture is clear, where there is little opportunity for or risk of conflicting interpretations of the institutional mission, conflict among vice presidential peers may erupt for other reasons. For instance, two or more vice presidents may be competing for the role of the president's chief confidant or the internal president.

At a time in higher education when most presidents are expected to be, and generally want to be, focused externally on politics, fundraising, public relations and such, there certainly is a need for strong and effective internal leadership. At most institutions the role of internal president is performed by the chief academic officer, traditionally *primus/a inter pares* among the vice presidents. But nowadays many presidents realize that the traditional primacy of the chief academic officer (CAO) in internal matters is a mixed blessing. Although a capable and trustworthy CAO is a great asset, the times demand teamwork among senior officers with very different backgrounds and abilities. For instance, effective chief information officers or chief financial officers may have acquired their expertise in industry, government, or the military. Their leadership styles do not blend easily with those of CAOs who have worked within the academy their entire lives. Diversity in leadership teams has never been more important to the well-being of our institutions than it is now. Yet diversity of perspectives and leadership styles, as much or more than ethnic or gender diversity, is a potential source of conflict. Presidents who recognize this reality and know how to manage conflict when it occurs have the opportunity to build unusually strong leadership teams. Those who do not are experiencing new kinds of institutional tensions that start at the top, among the vice presidents, and reverberate throughout the organization. The institutional puzzles are becoming larger and more complicated, the pieces more difficult to fit, and the big picture more difficult to bear in mind. But the rewards for presidents who become skilled at putting the puzzles together have never been greater.

| **Lynn Willett**

STUDENT AFFAIRS AND ACADEMIC AFFAIRS: PARTNERS IN CONFLICT RESOLUTION

A colleague of mine once described the birth of student affairs as a direct consequence of the death of Mr. Chips. The Mr. Chips analogy is a useful way to reminisce about 19th century relationships between faculty and students and merits some elaboration before pursuing the types of conflict on campus that are often addressed by student affairs staff.

Mr. Chips and his colleagues lived, ate, and socialized with their students. They were available through the evenings and on weekends for wide-ranging conversations and group activities that provided adult role models for students who were developing in both intellectual and personal ways. As 20th century society became more complicated, so did academic life, and Mr. Chips had more and more demands placed on him. He got married, became a commuter, was assigned to a search committee, was elected to a seat on the faculty senate, jumped on the publish or perish treadmill, volunteered to develop a new course for majors in his department, served on a task force to integrate technology with his discipline, edited the academic program chapter for the institution's accreditation report, and ... well, you get the idea. But, to Mr. Chip's surprise, few, if any, of these add-ons to his faculty role involved direct contact with students. And, to his great consternation, if there were opportunities for direct student contact outside the classroom—advising the student newspaper and traveling with a student club—there was no recognition or reward for those endeavors from his colleagues, who, coincidentally, made the tenure decisions that sealed his career fate. So, as Mr. Chips traded in his counseling sessions and his advising opportunities for the contractually defined teaching, research, and service activities, the student affairs profession was born.

Mr. Chips had conflicting feelings about the evolution of the student affairs profession. These sometime colleagues, sometime interlopers were a mixed blessing. On many days, Mr. Chips was relieved to have a network of colleagues who were responsible for the variety of problems that he saw in the classroom—alcohol, depression, learning disabilities. He knew that students' personal lives affected their ability to learn, but he also recognized that the demands on his time and the limits of his education precluded getting involved in more than a superficial way with students who needed support.

But there was certainly a downside to this so-called new breed of educators. First of all, what are they actually doing? Secondly, how many of them do we really need on our campus? And third, couldn't the money be better spent on more faculty positions? Mr. Chips also saw that students seemed much more appreciative of the support services on campus than they appreciated the challenges that the faculty provided in the classroom. This observation raised the possibility that student affairs was working at cross purposes with the faculty. Thus, the conflict between student affairs and academic affairs was born and has been nurtured ever since the appointment of the first college registrar. If, in fact, Mr. Chips has died or, at least, has evolved over the past century into a new type of faculty member, let's examine the characteristics of a student affairs staff and how it has evolved during that same time period.

As colleges and universities broadened both their mission and their student population, the narrow purpose of preparing young men for the ministry became outdated and inadequate. The doors of these changed institutions opened first to young men who were interested in professions other than the ministry, then to young women who were eager to pursue an intellectual life and prepare for professions. The doors became floodgates after World War II when the GI Bill brought a new kind of student from the battlefields of Europe. American campuses experienced enormous expansion in preparation for the arrival of the upwardly mobile baby boomers in the

1960s. During these growth years in higher education, student affairs moved through its own growth stages, from the original lonely registrar to the dean of women/dean of men structure, which was essentially a gender-specific Mr. Chips with reduced or nonexistent teaching loads, to a specialized set of departments providing services and programs for an increasingly diverse student body.

The modern dean and department chair have goals similar to their colleagues in student affairs: to encourage and support student learning. We know that our students spend only 25% of their time in the classroom and in classroom-related activities. We know that learning does not stop at the classroom door. We also know that educators with a background in academic affairs have different perspectives from those with a student affairs background. And, finally, we know that both groups of professionals—academic affairs and student affairs—are essential for students to have successful learning experiences. But, regardless of what we know, we set up camp professionally in either academic or student affairs, and our actions tend to be organizational chart-centered, rather than student-centered. We make assumptions about our colleagues in other areas of the institution based on stereotypes, not real information. We need to develop an understanding of what both academic affairs and student affairs bring to the work of educating students if we are going to solve problems and conflicts on campus.

Elizabeth Blake says it best:

> ... faculty members [are] accustomed to intellectual independence ... [and] want to cultivate a similarly independent originality in their students. Student affairs administrators, on the other hand, know that the campus must have a sense of community and a modicum of structure in order to function. [For faculty] the goal of formal learning is highly individual, even idiosyncratic; bachelor's degree recipients should in theory be intellectually *less* alike when they graduate than when they entered college. In contrast, a good campus student affairs program fosters cooperation and helps students develop community-building skills that they can apply in their personal lives (Blake, 1996, p. 1).

We need to celebrate that yin and yang and instead of bemoan it, figure out how to collaborate to benefit our students.

For deans or department chairs to collaborate with student affairs staff, they must first have a picture of what work student affairs is expected to do. The content of student affairs work is generally divided into two sections: programs and services for students and programs and services for the institution. The programs and services that are focused on students address the conditions that promote student access to education, set the stage for learning, provide a physically and emotionally healthy environment, develop life skills, and move students toward successful careers. The programs and services that are focused on the institution's needs emphasize the role of student affairs in resource allocation, policy development, and providing useful information about students to faculty and staff. Each campus has its own culture, and the work will vary depending upon the history of the campus and the particular staff. But, in general, Tables 8.1 and 8.2 describe the work of most student affairs organizations.

TABLE 8.1

Student Affairs Programs and Services for Students

Assist students in successful transition to college

Help students explore and clarify values

Encourage development of friendships among students and a sense of community within the institution

Help students acquire adequate financial resources to support their education

Create opportunities for students to expand their aesthetic and cultural appreciation

Teach students how to resolve individual and group conflicts

Provide programs and services for students who have learning difficulties

Help students understand and appreciate racial, ethnic, gender, and other differences

Design opportunities for leadership development

Establish programs that encourage healthy living and confront abusive behaviors

Provide opportunities for recreation and leisure-time activities

Help students clarify career objectives, explore options for further study, and secure employment

---

(from *Perspectives on Student Affairs*, NASPA, 1987)

Table 8.2

Student Affairs Programs and Services for Institutions

Support and explain the values, mission, and policies of the institution

Participate in the governance of the institution and share responsibility for decisions

Assess the educational and social experiences of students to improve institutional programs

Provide and interpret information about students during the development and modification of institutional policies, services, and practices

Establish policies and programs that contribute to a safe and secure campus

Effectively manage the human and fiscal resources for which student affairs is responsible

Support and advance institutional values by developing and enforcing behavioral standards for students

Advocate student participation in institutional governance

Provide essential services which contribute to the institutional mission and goals

Serve as a resource to faculty in their work with individual students and student groups

Encourage faculty-student interaction in programs and activities

Advocate and help create ethnically diverse and culturally rich environments for students

Assume leadership for the institution's responses to student crises

Be intellectually and professionally active

Establish and maintain effective working relationships with the local community

Coordinate student affairs programs and services with academic affairs, business affairs, development, and other major components of the institution

(from *Perspectives on Student Affairs,* NASPA, 1987)

Partnerships between student affairs and academic affairs increase the likelihood for student learning to occur. Let's look at four conflict situations that have potential for collaboration between academic affairs and student affairs.

SITUATION #1: PUT ME IN, COACH

In student affairs, we hear student complaints about classroom management practices that preclude student involvement in other campus experiences. To follow is an example of conflict between a student's cocurricular activities and an instructor's class rules.

Mark Time was thrilled to be a student at State University. He had to work hard for his grades, but he knew he could make it academically and was determined to remain both in school and eligible to play soccer. Soccer was his life, and he excelled at it. While his work in class had always been a chore, his ability on the soccer field came naturally and was a major source of self-esteem. The conditioning and skill development were hard work, but Mark achieved results and rewards for that work to a much greater extent than he was ever able to achieve in the classroom.

Mark was conscientious about talking to each of his instructors at the beginning of each semester about the soccer schedule. While each practice was important, especially in a team sport, Mark knew that a class session, study group, or special assignment was always a higher priority than practice. The flip side of that implicit deal was that with early notice, his instructors always accommodated the occasional game that overlapped with a class meeting time. That is, until he met Dr. Nochoice.

Dr. Nochoice was regarded as one of the best professors at the college. He was fascinated by sociology and conveyed that fascination to his students each semester. His lectures and the class discussions that followed were rich with examples and elaboration that made the subject matter relevant to the lives of his students and lasting in their memories. Because of Nochoice's teaching style, students rarely missed class; in fact, they sometimes brought their friends—and there were no attendance requirements. Also, there were no acceptable excuses for late papers or missed exams.

Mark was very worried about his meeting with Dr. Nochoice during the first week of the semester. He could see the conflict between the scheduled midterm and the regional tournament that would determine the soccer championship. And his worry was not misplaced. Dr. Nochoice explained to Mark that since he had refused to reschedule exams for students who had had a death in the family, he certainly was not going to make a separate exam because of a soccer game. Mark's choices were to stay in the course, knowing that the best grade he could get was a C, or drop the course. For Dr. Nochoice, there was no conflict.

Mark was very frustrated with Nochoice and talked to his coach for advice. The coach reminded Mark that the classroom was Nochoice's domain, and only Nochoice could change the rules. But Mark was frustrated by the rigidity of this instructor and met with Dean Between about the situation. He told the dean that he could not understand why a faculty member would make such unyielding rules with no consideration for very real human lives and situations. Did the dean believe that Nochoice's rules were reasonable, Mark asked, and couldn't he talk to Nochoice?

Discussion

Faculty members can, and must, set the rules for acceptable conduct in their classrooms. Students can, and will, make personal decisions about which of those rules they will abide by and then deal with the consequences. Conflicts can be avoided if the rules are perceived as fair and are connected to the goals of the educational experience.

For students who request exceptions, the issues are advance planning, limited requests for exceptions, a willingness to complete work prior to deadlines, and an understanding that each class and instructor will have different demands. For faculty it is important to develop classroom policies that are perceived as fair and reasonable, to give advance notice of all policies, and to be willing to consider exceptions to policies without the fear of setting precedents. When we work with human beings, exceptions may be the only way to be truly fair.

Dean Between may be tempted to explain Dr. Nochoice's prerogatives to Mark and end the conflict there. Certainly, the benefit to the dean for avoiding a confrontation with a faculty colleague would be greater than investigating the possible merits of a student complaint. But Dean Between has clear memories of how important his own college basketball experiences were to his perseverance in class and the development of life skills such as team play and standards of fairness.

Dean Between considers his options. If he chooses to discuss with Dr. Nochoice their opinions about fair and appropriate class rules, he better be sure that the trigger situation is a deserving one. What does he actually know about this Mark Time and his credibility? Also, what does he know about the instructions that student athletes are given by their coaches regarding class responsibilities?

The dean could answer these questions by calling the athletics director and discussing with the director some of Mark's personal characteristics that may affect the extent to which the dean may want to pursue Mark's concern. The director could also explain the position of the athletics department on conflicts between team obligations and class obligations. With this information and his own good judgment and experience, Dean Between can decide whether to discuss with Dr. Nochoice the barriers for students and the credibility problems for himself that he may be creating with his rigid classroom rules.

SITUATION #2: TAKE ME TO YOUR LEADER (OR WHO'S IN CHARGE HERE?)

Student affairs is sometimes saddled with the label of "keeper of the campus virtue," a daunting task indeed. But the origin of this stereotype has, as always, some element of truth. The judicial system (or some means of rules enforcement) is usually located in student affairs. Consequently, when students do something we don't like, the judicial office is a good resource, whether the behavior occurs inside or outside the classroom. Classroom conflict—as illustrated in this case—can be viewed in two ways: as a shortcoming of a faculty member's teaching skills or as an opportunity to apply student affairs' expertise to individual and group problems.

Dr. Michelle Angelo's art history class was widely known on campus as both interesting and demanding. She was very knowledgeable in her discipline and was always prepared for class. She expected her students to learn quickly in the first class meeting that she expected them to meet her high academic standards and that her extensive vocabulary combined with a penchant for sarcasm was the cornerstone of her classroom management style. After years of successful teaching, Dr. Angelo was both stunned and stymied by the arrival of "the clique."

Half of the class, five men and three women, was in the clique. They knew each other well and were, from the first day, enthralled by each other's every move, word, gesture, etc. And each move, word, and gesture was calculated to entertain, resulting in a type of miniseries in the back of the room that ran parallel to Dr. Angelo's best efforts to conduct an interesting and productive class. The activities early in the semester included late arrivals who provided elaborate, creative, and entertaining explanations for being late. As the semester progressed, the distractions included requests to use the restrooms with details of the stomach upset that made the request necessary; predictable book slamming related to the mention of a particular agreed-upon word; loud and detailed conversations at the beginning of each class about the previous night's sexual activities; and questions about the subject matter that were carefully constructed to distract Dr. Angelo. As the midterm approached, Dr. Angelo was increasingly frustrated with the excellent work that the clique produced in their papers and quizzes, the variety of disruptions that they were able to create, the helplessness that she felt regarding classroom control, and the offer of her department chair to sit in on one of the classes. She was loathe to signal to this group of students that she was having problems with them and, consequently, was opposed to her department head's offer. But if she did not permit him to help, how would she manage this situation on her own?

Discussion

In Dr. Angelo's mind, the conflict is one of control—a zero sum game between her and her students. From the student point of view there may be no conflict at all, only an effort to entertain themselves and each other—with no regard for the impact of their actions on Dr. Angelo or the other class members.

Faculty rarely take courses in pedagogy and even more rarely take courses in classroom management. One assumes that something magical happens in the process of writing doctoral dissertations and that the newly minted faculty member emerges with a complete understanding of textbook selection, syllabus design, and an innate talent for developing and describing clear and challenging assignments. Classroom management skills have much in common with group facilitation skills and, thus, Dr. Angelo could benefit from advice from someone who specializes in managing group discussions.

Her department head is faced with the problem of how to help Dr. Angelo without making her look or feel helpless. Rather than inserting himself directly into the situation, he might suggest that Dr. Angelo contact the judicial affairs coordinator for advice. The coordinator often has education and experience in conflict mediation and may be able to help Dr. Angelo brainstorm options that she had not considered. She could talk individually with persons who are part of the problem; enlist the support (perhaps through anonymous class evaluations) of those students who are not part of the problem; and single out leaders, in private, who are given a chance to hear her concerns, but are also given clear limits and a preview of the consequences if those limits are violated.

SITUATION #3: POISON OAK NOW COVERS THE IVORY TOWER

The dean's role often includes responsibility for making decisions to academically dismiss students from the institution. These decisions can pose conflicts between negatively and unfairly impacting a student's life or undermining the academic standards of the institution. Some decision-makers are uncomfortable with their authority and proclaim "no exceptions," "no appeals," "no excuses!" While this approach may seem, initially, very fair because of the rigid standard, the realities of being human also require intelligent exceptions to those standards. How to decide what is an intelligent exception is the question posed in this situation.

One of the most stressful times of the year for Dr. Integrity, the dean of the College of Arts and Sciences, was the two-week period after fall semester grades were mailed and before decisions about spring semester enrollment had to be made. He was inundated with pleas from remorseful students, desperate parents, proud grandparents, surprised neighbors, sympathetic physicians, newly hired psychotherapists, relentless employers, etc., all of whom believed that a 1.2 GPA is not that bad, a blip on the screen, insufficient reason to send the student home, or someone else's fault, etc. Jason Oblivious was no exception.

Jason, a first semester sophomore, explained his unfortunate situation to Dr. Integrity in excruciating detail, including pictures of his roommates and their friends busy at their favorite pastime, Dungeons and Dragons. Dr. Integrity listened patiently to the realities of Jason's life in a triple (room built for two, but housing three), the difficulty of studying not only in his room, but anywhere in the residence hall, and the distracting activities of his roommates. While the circumstances were less than ideal, Dr. Integrity knew that many students had to contend with problems in order to maintain satisfactory grade point averages.

But as Jason continued to detail his semester-long saga, Dr. Integrity was surprised to hear about an incident that consumed much of this student's semester. It seems that Jason was the prime support system for his friend, Karen, who lived in another building. Karen was in a constant state of fear. Her off-campus boyfriend was a violent type who often used his considerable bulk to threaten and intimidate her. Consequently, Jason served as an unofficial bodyguard for Karen, using much of his time and energy to be available to her. Jason missed many classes because of Karen's frightened telephone calls in the middle of the night and her pleas for Jason to sleep on the floor of her room.

As Dr. Integrity deliberated over Jason's academic future, he could not ignore the reports—from Jason and other students—about the living conditions in the residence halls that distracted them from their studies.

Discussion

Dr. Integrity faces at least two questions in this situation: Is Jason's personal account of his fall semester accurate? If true, how much should these events affect the decision about his continued enrollment? The dean has the responsibility to make these important decisions, but is not precluded from consulting others for information and/or advice. Many institutions use faculty committees with student affairs staff as full members or in an advisory capacity. But regardless of the particular structure, the dean could get a clearer picture of a student's personal experiences by contacting the director of residence life and asking for information from the staff members who had daily contact with Jason. With access to more complete information, the dean can make a more informed decision and advise the student in ways that promote student learning from the experience. The dean is in an influential position and, with a clear perspective of a student, can use that influence to maintain academic standards and hold students accountable for their actions or inactions.

SITUATION #4: A MAN'S CLASS IS HIS CASTLE

Over the past two decades, higher education has been subjected to increased scrutiny from the public-at-large and state and federal agencies. Consequently, many laws have been and continue to be passed that affect campus operations. Large institutions have full-time legal counsel to interpret regulations and advise the institution on practices that could be problematic. Smaller institutions usually do not have legal offices and often rely on student affairs for prevention in the form of advance notice and interpretation of legal requirements, so that expensive cures, such as court cases, bad press, and penalties are not necessary. This example illustrates the effect of legal constraints on educational practices.

In 23 years, Dr. Blindspot had never taught a student who had a learning disability—at least not one that he knew of. He questioned, if a student has a learning disability, why in heaven's name would the admissions staff allow that student to enroll in our college? Now, physical disabilities were a different story. Several times, the registrar had relocated Dr. Blindspot's class so that it would be accessible to a student in a wheelchair. But learning disabilities? Sounds to him like an excuse to avoid classwork.

So, his advice to Marsha Milestone, the ADA compliance officer for the college, was that she should convince this dyslexic freshman who kept asking for an appointment with him, to drop his course. He had standards for academic achievement in his classes that he was not going to compromise. He knew from his colleagues that once Milestone got her hooks into him, she would have him dancing to all kinds of requests: tape recorders in his lectures, oral exams, extended time tests, and on and on. Who knows where it would end. Well, for Dr. Blindspot, it would end before it ever got started, because he wasn't lowering his expectations one iota.

Milestone knew she was getting nowhere with Blindspot. She had received many complaints from students with documented disabilities about Blindspot's refusal to make the reasonable accommodations required by the law. She also knew that it was only a matter of time before a student would take their complaint to the court system. In desperation she turned to Blindspot's department head, Dr. Juggler, to help her deal with this intractable faculty member and protect the college from a lawsuit that they would definitely lose.

Discussion

Conflict that occurs internal to an institution—between staff and faculty or between faculty and students—can be annoying to colleagues and/or damaging to specific individuals. But breaking the law opens up the potential for serious consequences which may be as extreme as jeopardizing an institution's federal financial aid. Consequently, all employees of the institution must understand the difference between a request and a requirement. We are accustomed to debating our differences on campus and are not necessarily prepared to respond to changes in the classroom that are not debatable.

Juggler could prevent conflicts related to state and federal laws by providing information to the faculty. By using Milestone's expertise to bring faculty up-to-date about the letter and the spirit of the Americans with Disabilities Act, he protects his faculty from making uninformed decisions. As department head, he can use campus resources to keep his faculty current with information that affects their work.

The 1990 Americans with Disabilities Act is only one of many federal and state laws that affect our campus operations. For example, we are required by the Buckley Amendment to protect the privacy of some personal information, and, at the same time, are required by Sunshine Laws to release other information. Under the Student Right to Know Law, we must publicize certain campus crime statistics and, at the same time, protect the identity of certain victims. And all of our decision-making processes, including academic misconduct, are affected by the due process requirements of the law. Under due process, students are guaranteed the right to know what they are accused of, have an opportunity to respond to those accusations, and be able to appeal a decision that is made regarding those accusations.

Deans and department chairs can use their colleagues in student affairs to educate faculty about the law. Many conflicts that occur regarding these laws could be cut short with good information that is widely distributed, thoroughly discussed, and sensibly interpreted.

SUMMARY

Conflict in higher education often crosses the boundaries for decision-making that are established by job descriptions and organizational charts. Our students are well served by curricular decisions that are made in academic affairs and cocurricular decisions that are made in student affairs. But the examples in this chapter illustrate areas where the boundaries of the organization can detract from the quality of decisions that are made about students and their lives. By sharing information and perspectives across the reporting lines of academic affairs and student affairs, we can assist each other and improve the quality of the educational experience for our students.

On many of our campuses, the descendants of Mr. Chips are alive and well and contributing endless hours to the education of students. Also, on many campuses, those descendants are joined by student affairs staff who are engaged in teaching life skills to students, managing group activities as learning experiences, and interpreting the laws that affect our campus operations. The communication between these two groups can only make us each more effective in our primary roles and of greater benefit and service to the population that is most important to us all . . . our students.

REFERENCES

Blake, E. (1996, September/October). The yin and yang of student learning in college. *About Campus, 1* (4), 4.

National Association for Student Personnel Administrators (NASPA) (1987). *Perspectives on student affairs.* [Brochure]. Washington, DC.

10 Cynthia Berryman-Fink

CAN WE AGREE TO DISAGREE? FACULTY-FACULTY CONFLICT

You are the department chair of basic studies at Anywhere University. Professor Yee just informed you that Professor Borden is making disparaging remarks to students about Yee's teaching style and is advising students not to enroll in Yee's courses. Professor Yee demands that you get Professor Borden to stop this behavior or he will file a grievance against Borden and the department. Yesterday, the head of the curriculum committee in your department informed you that the intractable divisions between the research-oriented and the teaching-oriented faculty have brought the work of the committee to a halt. You are expected to solve the problem. Your secretary reminds you of the afternoon meeting you have with a junior faculty member who has serious complaints about biases among some faculty on the tenure committee who have voted against her tenure.

Could this be a description of your administrative responsibilities? For many department chairs, faculty conflicts seem to take ever-increasing amounts of administrative time and energy. A similar scenario of faculty conflict problems could be presented for deans. Managing faculty conflicts is one of the least pleasant aspects of an administrator's job, yet it is a role they cannot avoid. Chairs and deans must be skilled in handling faculty conflicts and can use many strategies and resources for effective conflict management.

This chapter examines the unique nature of the academic culture and the changes in higher education which fuel faculty conflict. It discusses the general nature of interpersonal conflict and the dangers of avoiding the conflict management role. Finally, it presents six strategies for managing faculty conflict, each with a mini-case study to show the application of these conflict-management techniques.

While interpersonal conflict is an inevitable part of any group or workplace organization, the unique culture of academic institutions makes conflict a particularly prevalent part of higher educational institutions (Bergquist, 1992). Since culture helps to define the nature of reality and of relationships for those who are a part of the culture, it is important that we examine how typical academic cultures shape interpersonal interaction. Let us look at some of the features of university life which can fuel faculty-faculty conflict.

THE UNIQUE NATURE OF THE ACADEMIC CULTURE

First, it is important to emphasize that colleges and universities operate on the principle of democratic decision-making. Virtually all decisions are based, in principle, upon collective thinking and widespread faculty input. Unlike the private sector which may solicit employee input or use team-based approaches to change, higher education follows the principle of shared governance, where administrators and faculty have equal input into the formulation of policy, procedures, and operating decisions. While not all university decisions actually occur through democratic decision-making, the ideal of shared governance permeates academic thinking. Whicker & Kronenfeld (1994) describe universities as peer-regulated, like legislatures, where the potential for conflict is rampant.

Secondly, faculty probably have more autonomy in doing their jobs than do many other types of employees. Indeed, many faculty resist even considering themselves as employees. Most faculty have some degree of control over what they teach, how they teach it, and when they teach it. They can decide what programs of research to pursue and what internal committees on which to serve. Faculty, for the most part, shape the direction of their careers and control their daily work schedules. When giving advice to deans and provosts on managing academic enterprises, Ehrle and Bennett (1988) describe faculty as independent-minded people who view themselves mostly in individualistic terms. This sense of independence can fuel and complicate conflict in the academy. Imagine two faculty members, each with a strong sense of self-control and autonomy, who need to arrive at a joint decision. Should their viewpoints differ, the possibility for forcing one's position and resisting another's position is great.

Next, add to this culture the notion of job security and longevity within an institution. Educational institutions are one of the few workplace environments which grant an employee a job for life. The tenure system can exacerbate faculty-faculty conflict in at least two ways. A tenured faculty member can resist organizational goals or refuse to cooperate with colleagues, and few organizational sanctions can be used to change that person's behavior. Performance reviews tied to real job consequences or possible termination provide little incentive in academe for faculty to work cooperatively. Also, upon receiving tenure, faculty are unlikely to seek positions elsewhere and thereby lose tenure. Thus, in many colleges and universities, faculty longevity places the same people working in the same department for decades. Personality conflicts, personal feuds, and group factions can exist for a lifetime.

A fourth feature of the academic culture relevant to conflict between faculty members is the value placed on free thought. Open discussion, free thought, and critical thinking as hallmarks of the academy are precursors to conflict (Holton, 1995). Faculty openly engage in debate, are trained to be adamantly and vocally critical of ideas, and value the clash of positions as an intellectual endeavor. It is not uncommon, then, for two or more faculty to forcefully pursue opposing arguments and refuse to compromise on intellectual or philosophical grounds. It is easy for faculty who debate different schools of thought about a subject matter to debate each other on everything else.

Another factor in higher education is the common isolation and competition among departments. Faculty members in departments of biology, English, or history may reside in the same academic division or college, but they will define their identity through their disciplinary departments and not their college affiliation. In departments such as electrical engineering, nursing, or special education which cross colleges, faculty may have even less in common. Departments within and across colleges often find themselves in competition for resources. Thus, instead of a spirit of teamwork or collaboration among faculty, there is often the protection of individual turf, antagonism, and competition among departmentally based faculty.

A sixth element fueling conflict in academe relates to the nature of faculty roles and performance expectations. In many institutions, faculty perform multiple roles. They teach, advise students, revise curriculum, do research, publish books and articles, and serve on university governance committees. They may seek external research or training grants, serve as speakers, trainers, or consultants to community organizations, act as leaders in professional organizations, run student internship programs, and advise student organizations. Such a diversity of roles can lead to conflict between faculty about the priorities of tasks. A teaching-oriented faculty member may find himself in conflict with a research-oriented faculty member when they must work together to formulate department goals or policy. Likewise, there can be much internal conflict about balancing roles, establishing priorities, and meshing individual goals with departmental goals.

Finally, unlike the situation in private companies, faculty often rotate through management and nonmanagement jobs. A faculty member may serve a term as department chair and then return to the faculty while another colleague becomes the department head. So the administrator can have as subordinates individuals who previously were his superiors. For example, in one academic department, the current department head has two former department chairs, a former vice provost, and her newly elected successor as members of the faculty. Imagine the possible power dynamics and the potential for interpersonal conflict! The ever-changing authority relationships clearly can create tension fueling conflict in institutions of higher education.

So we see that shared governance, faculty independence, employment longevity, the predisposition toward critical thinking, interdepartmental competition, multiple role expectations, and changing authority relationships can contribute to conflict among faculty.

When eccentric behavior, hidden agendas, and individual suspicions are added to the mix (Ehrle & Bennett, 1988), we can see that the academic culture is conflict-prone. This is not to imply that the cultural elements of the educational workplace always lead to conflict among faculty. Certainly, all of these features can have positive outcomes for the individual, the organization, and those served by academe. But taken collectively, the features of an academic culture make interpersonal conflict inevitable.

THE CHANGING NATURE OF HIGHER EDUCATION

Higher education has recently been presented with a number of changes and challenges which are sources of stress and disagreement among faculty. Kennedy (1995) describes a revolution in higher education, with great changes on the horizon, despite academe's tendency to resist change. By examining the various changes facing higher education, we can see additional sources of conflict among faculty.

Anyone working in a college or university is aware of the widespread budget reductions of the last decade. The pressures of financial constraint and continually diminishing resources have significantly hindered faculty morale and caused increased competition among faculty and departments. Where there may not have been as much conflict before, faculty now compete with each other for permanent positions, tenure, merit raises, students, classrooms, equipment, and supplies. Inevitably, when resources are scarce, those wanting the resources will find themselves in conflict.

Another change which has taken many faculty by surprise is the increased accountability regarding faculty workload. Previously, faculty did not have to document how many hours they worked per week or explain why they put their efforts into some activities rather than into others. Because of financial constraints, public scrutiny, and government intervention, faculty increasingly have to work harder and must justify their productivity. In such a climate, tensions run high and individuals are prone to protect themselves by criticizing others. Conflicts arise over who is and is not carrying their weight and how the work of a department will get done.

A third element in the higher education revolution is the perceived or actual threat to tenure and job security. Because of financial pressures, academic programs are being reviewed in record numbers, and some programs and faculty positions are being abolished. Some colleges and universities have instituted or begun discussing procedures for post-tenure review. So where tenure once provided absolute job security for faculty, the situation is more tenuous today. Faculty, worried about their jobs and disgruntled about the loss of public esteem previously accorded to the professoriate, will inevitably become cranky, contentious, and prone to conflict.

Jandt and Kaufman (1992) assert that another change is the evolution in academe from a community of scholars to a bureaucracy in which faculty must deal with increasing amounts of red tape and inflexibility. Such bureaucracy is altering the relationships between faculty and between faculty and their chairs. Conflicts may arise out of policy inflexibility, become escalated quickly, and lead to a reliance on formal mechanisms for handling conflict. They cite the influence of unionization and collective bargaining agreements on interpersonal relationships and conflict behavior in academe. The increase in litigation and fear of litigation in academe additionally creates a changing environment with implications for faculty-faculty conflict.

Other elements of change facing faculty include changing demographics of the student population and student preparedness, shifting values regarding research and scholarship, renewed attention to teaching effectiveness, and increasing involvement of higher education in the economy (Ehrle & Bennett, 1988; Fairweather, 1996). Many institutions serve a broader range of students than in the past, including nontraditionally aged students, part-time students, ethnic students, international students, and students with physical and learning disabilities. Such diversity can present challenges and stresses to faculty. Many faculty lament that students increasingly lack basic skills of reading, writing, oral communication, critical thinking, and library literacy, making the college faculty member's task more difficult. Faculty increasingly find themselves uncertain about their institution's mission related to their own career direction. Undergraduate institutions may be expecting more of an emphasis on research in addition to the teaching role. In some cases, the publish or perish concept is affecting even community college faculty. Concurrently, research universities are experiencing less funding opportunities and heightened expectations for teaching. And virtually all institutions of higher education demand innovations and excellence in teaching. Many state legislatures are expecting public institutions to embrace roles in advancing the state's economy.

Because of immense changes in higher education, faculty have lost the predictability about their jobs they once had. With a loss of predictability comes uncertainty, stress, and the potential for interpersonal conflict. It is imperative, then, that department chairs and deans be competent in conflict management. They must understand the general nature of conflict in the academy, identify their roles in managing faculty-faculty conflict, and use a wide range of institutional and individual strategies for dealing with conflict among faculty.

THE GENERAL NATURE OF CONFLICT

Mini-Case

Imagine that Professors Jensen and Popovitch of the curriculum and instruction department are serving as the coadvisors for the thesis of a student in their master's degree program, Ms. Nichols. Jensen's research training and experience is in quantitative methods, experiments with statistical analyses of information. Popovitch's research background and expertise is in qualitative methods, case studies, and narrative accounts with creative interpretations of information. Because they are both experts in the field of adult literacy, the subject of Ms. Nichols' thesis, it is natural that they be the coadvisors of her project. All master's level research in this department requires supervision by coadvisors. After three unsuccessful attempts to get her advisors' approval for her specific research project, Ms. Nichols appeals to you, chair of the department, to intervene on her behalf. She is exasperated because each faculty member insists that the project use the research method of his choice and neither is willing to compromise. She is angry about the additional time and tuition expense this conflict has caused her and insists that the department must assure her a means of completing her graduate degree.

By examining the specific features of this case, we can see elements that are common in most definitions of conflict. For the purposes of this chapter, let us define conflict as the situation arising when interdependent individuals who perceive incompatible goals interact in order to gain something of value to them (Anderson, Foster-Kuehn, & McKinney, 1996). Virtually all definitions of conflict refer to people having incompatible goals. Clearly, Jensen and Popovitch have opposing goals for how research ought to be conducted. While conflict can involve real differences of interest between people, they may also emerge because of perceptions of incompatible goals. Similarly, conflict emerges only when people need each other in some way. If people with incompatible goals were not dependent on each other for some outcome, then their incompatible goals could simultaneously coexist without conflict emerging. In our case, because graduate student research projects must be supervised by coadvisors, both faculty need each the other's cooperation if the project is to be completed.

Conflict manifests itself through communication. Thus the definition includes the notion of people interacting over salient issues. Presumably, in our case, Ms. Nichols designed a research project with methods which were satisfactory to one, but not both, of the coadvisors. Whether she served as the communication linkage between the disputing faculty or whether the faculty communicated to each other directly about preferred research methods, it was interaction over important issues that triggered the conflict. Notice how a clash in schools of thought fuels this conflict as an intellectual endeavor, yet the conflict presents serious practical consequences to the student and to the department.

While conflict can take many forms and be based on many different issues, there are some predictable factors in how conflicts typically transpire. First, it is human nature to blame others as the cause of conflict. Perhaps as a psychological self-defense mechanism, people punctuate a series of events by claiming that the other person started the problem, and they are merely reacting to the other's provocation. When department chairs or deans hear about a conflict situation, therefore, they should realize that the faculty member describing the incident will naturally slant the story to his or her advantage. Secondly, most people in conflict situations have a strong need to be right. This may be especially true for faculty who are accustomed to the role of expert or purveyor of what is correct and accurate. Department chairs and deans may want to find ways to help conflicting faculty members save face or preserve some of the feeling of being right. Thirdly, listening problems are inherent in conflict interaction. All parties in a conflict will lose listening effectiveness. They will hear what they want to hear, assume motive, make incorrect interpretations, and interrupt others. Administrators dealing with faculty conflicts may want to set some procedures by which the parties focus on listening to each other.

Likewise, effective conflict managers should be clear, specific, and redundant in communicating their points. Another common factor in conflict situations is people's belief in the primacy of rational thinking. Faculty especially think that rationality and reasoned discourse should prevail and is the best means of influencing others. Administrators who need to intervene in conflicts can capitalize on faculty's belief in rationality by creating conflict management procedures based on rational thinking. Department chairs and deans should be aware of the academic tendency to suppress emotion in favor of reason.

Many conflict management theorists have articulated common predispositions for handing conflict. People are predisposed to use a preferred style for dealing with conflict. Certainly alternate styles can be learned and strategic choices can be made about how to behave in conflict situations. Nevertheless, by realizing some typical conflict management modes, department chairs and deans can identify faculty members' response styles to conflict and intervene if stylistic differences seem to impede the satisfactory management of the conflict. Deutsch (1992) identifies six dimensions of conflict response. Though individuals habitually prefer a particular mode, they can modify behavior to embrace other styles.

1) *Conflict avoidance/conflict involvement.* Some people deny, suppress, or postpone conflict while others seek it out, enjoy it, or focus on disputes and disagreements.

2) *Hard/soft.* This dimension encompasses the continuum from aggressive, unyielding approaches to conflict on one end to gentle and unassertive styles on the other end.

3) *Rigid/loose.* The rigid approach seeks to establish rules by which conflict interaction will transpire while the loose style emphasizes improvisation and flexibility of communication in a conflict.

4) *Intellectual/emotional.* Some people are calm and detached in a conflict while others are emotionally intense.

5) *Escalating/minimizing.* This dimension refers to the tendency to perceive the conflict issues as large and to tie one's ego to the outcome or the tendency to lessen the seriousness of a conflict episode.

6) *Compulsively revealing/compulsively concealing.* In conflicts, people may be open and blunt about their feelings and attitudes, or they may avoid revealing feelings and thoughts.

While disputants may fall at the extremes or at the midpoint on any of these dimensions, it is clear to see some styles are incompatible. By knowing the dimensions underlying conflict management styles, department chairs and deans can help faculty understand variances in styles and perhaps try to negotiate the use of styles which have a greater success for effective resolution of conflicts.

DANGERS OF SUPPRESSED OR UNMANAGED CONFLICT

Mini-Case

Imagine the foreign languages department of 25 faculty who are polite but somewhat distant with each other. Their relationships with each other are impersonal and nonemotional. Each faculty member routinely teaches a set of courses which are not taught by anyone else. Each person has a small but private office. There are few department meetings, and when a meeting is scheduled, fewer than half of the faculty attend. Rarely do the faculty eat lunch together or socialize together off campus. There are not open displays of conflict, but the faculty seem dispirited and make occasional snide remarks about other faculty, administrators, and the college as a whole.

This case shows that not all conflicts surface as explicit disputes in which the parties divulge their grievances and interact to seek agreement. In some cases, conflict festers below the surface, suppressed or unmanaged for years. This hypothetical department, though not outwardly conflicting or hostile, may be experiencing repressed conflict or faculty avoidance of conflict. Each faculty member working in isolation on individual goals without collaboration to work on departmentally based tasks can signal suppressed conflict. While one might be inclined to leave well enough alone in such a nonhostile situation, there are many potential dangers of conflict avoidance. A lack of trust may underlie the isolating and impersonal style of behavior. Where there is a lack of trust, there is often withholding of information, the subtle sabotage of ideas and projects, as well as political undermining and behind-the-scenes coalition building.

Other signs of suppressed conflict among faculty include frequent complaints, low morale, poor attendance at academic functions, competition, and lessening productivity. As illustrated in our case, when conflict festers below the surface, it may leak out in mildly dysfunctional behavior, such as sarcasm and absenteeism. Certainly administrators need not look for conflict where it does not exist. On the other hand, the lack of visible disagreements does not mean that conflict is absent from the faculty group. When faculty are truly functioning as a team with department, division, or college goals coexisting with individual goals, there will be conflicts surfacing from time to time. Effective faculty groups will embrace conflict, not avoid it, in order to deal with differences directly and effectively. Where conflict ceases to emerge at all in ongoing faculty groups, administrators should question whether suppressed conflict festers within the group and whether some interventions are necessary to get the group functioning more authentically. In the hypothetical example of the foreign languages department, the chair or dean surely would want to investigate whether suppressed conflict is one of the causes of this department's gross lack of cohesiveness.

THE ROLE OF DEPARTMENT CHAIRS AND DEANS IN MANAGING FACULTY CONFLICT

Administrators play crucial roles in managing faculty-faculty conflict, though they do not always perceive or embrace such roles. Probably the most important task for chairs and deans relative to faculty conflict is to influence the culture of the academic enterprise over which they lead, be it a department, division, school, or college. Through their leadership, chairs and deans can help to shape an environment where destructive conflict is absent or rare. In other words, the administrator's role in conflict frequently is a preventive one. Chairs and deans, through their legitimate power, personal persuasion, as well as the ability to reward and coerce, should expect teamwork and cooperation from the faculty in their units (Gmelch, 1995). In such an atmosphere, incompatible goals may surface, but they will be resolved through discussion, and the best interests of the unit will take precedence over individual interests. Administrators should send clear messages that destructive conflict will not be tolerated. By exerting leadership to influence faculty behavior in the academic unit, chairs and deans can play an important role in conflict management.

Another way for administrators to affect conflict among their faculty is to apply policy consistently. When administrators are arbitrary or capricious in the application of policy, competition among departments or among faculty becomes greater. For example, imagine that some faculty refuse to report days when they are sick, thereby avoiding using their sick leave benefits. Though the college policy requires that any absence due to illness must be reported, some faculty believe that sick leave should not be used if they arrange for a substitute to teach their classes or if they hold a make-up session with students at a later date. Some chairs or deans may think it a waste of their time to provide oversight to ensure the consistent application of this policy. For pragmatic administrators, some battles are worth fighting and some are not. However, if some faculty follow the policy and some do not, then over time, the seeds of conflict—envy, resentment, and hostility—surface. The perception will quickly emerge that administrators have their favorites who can bend the rules. No visible conflict may result, but the foundation for repressed conflict has been laid. If some faculty can ignore one policy, then other faculty may think they have the right to ignore other policy. The fair, consistent, and predictable application of policy will go a long way to reduce feuds, resentment, and discontent among faculty.

Strong leadership and the consistent application of policy will not prevent all faculty conflict, however. Faculty will still disagree over ideology, priorities, and procedures. When conflicts emerge, chairs and deans must decide when to intervene and when not to. Ideally, in most cases the faculty will possess the skills to resolve their own disputes, so administrative intervention becomes unnecessary. Indeed, one of the strategies of the administrator might be to equip faculty with the requisite conflict management skills. An effective intervention a chair or dean might make is to plan conflict management workshops for the faculty. Systematic attention by the chair or dean to the process by which faculty manage their disagreements should save much administrative effort in eliminating the need for case-by-case interventions later.

It will sometimes be necessary for administrators to involve themselves directly in the disputes among their faculty. This is especially true for chairs, who often are naturally drawn into departmental disputes. Gmelch (1995) indicates that chairs are expected to resolve collegial differences and that dealing with interfaculty conflict represents a major source of stress and dissatisfaction for chairs. Socialized as scholars first, chairs often have little training in any aspects of departmental management, especially the management of personnel disputes. It is understandable why they may resist intervening in others' conflicts. But chairs and deans commonly are drawn into faculty conflicts by one or more of the disputants. While the next section of this chapter presents specific strategies for conflict management, let it suffice here to say that administrators can perform important functions of information seeking, clarification, and communication in interfaculty conflicts. To avoid those roles when conflict presents itself is to shirk administrative duties.

There is not always a clear answer about whether to intervene in faculty disputes. If the disputants do not seem able to manage the conflict themselves, if the conflict is affecting the morale of others, if students are being harmed in some way by the conflict, or if the issues have potential litigious consequences, then the administrator should intervene early in the faculty conflict. An objective but firm intervention by the dean especially can serve to remind the conflicting parties of the need for professional behavior and for speedy resolution.

CONFLICT MANAGEMENT STRATEGIES

What follows is a range of informal to formal strategies which can be used alone or in combination for managing faculty conflict. Some are individual tactics which an administrator can use while others require systemic institutional implementation. Ideally, an institution should have all of these options in place for dealing with faculty conflict. Each strategy is explained briefly and a mini-case application of that strategy is presented. This chapter seeks to provide an overview of a variety of conflict management strategies rather than a detailed explanation of any one tactic. On the more formal mechanisms, such as ombuds offices, mediation, arbitration, and grievance hearings, administrators would benefit from additional information, training, or consultation on the subject before attempting to use those strategies.

Informal Facilitation

By using some standard interpersonal communication skills, chairs and deans can help faculty to effectively manage their disputes. Such communication competencies help administrators not only in the realm of conflict, but in many other aspects of their leadership role. Several basic communication skills are necessary when the administrator hears the complaint from each person separately as well as when the administrator gets the parties together to discuss issues. First, effective listening is crucial for resolving conflict. The chair or dean must be a patient and careful listener and should expect the same from the conflicting parties. The faculty disputants as well as the administrator-as-facilitator should paraphrase statements made. Each person should objectively and specifically describe behaviors being manifested and desired behaviors. Assertiveness in stating one's goals and questioning others directly and diplomatically are additional tools to be used in conflict communication. Finally, all parties (the disputants and the facilitator) should show empathy for others' goals and feelings. People in conflicts often are willing to compromise or to put the conflict to rest merely because they felt listened to, had the opportunity to express themselves, and believed that someone understood their view.

Slaikeu (1996) describes interpersonal peacemaking, a process of informal facilitation which relies heavily on these interpersonal communication skills. Chairs and deans can use this process to encourage individual faculty to recognize ways they have contributed to conflicts. First, each party identifies the offense or hurt from his or her perspective. The facilitator encourages objective, concrete descriptions and careful listening. Secondly, the parties clarify their intentions. This helps to distinguish between intentions and outcomes. Faculty can often see that their colleagues did not intend to hurt them. Nevertheless, good intentions can still result in hurtful behavior. Next, each person discusses what they wish had happened. This sets the stage for stating desired behaviors or requesting change. Then, the facilitator helps the parties focus on resolution options and invites concrete offers for resolution. If each person offers a personal contribution for ending the conflict, conflict management has occurred. Finally, the administrator should summarize agreements and provide oversight to make sure that the faculty carry out the options to which they agreed.

Many faculty conflicts can be managed through this simple process. If disputing faculty come to know the process their chair or dean uses for helping them work through conflict, they can learn to apply effective communication techniques and interpersonal peacemaking strategies to their own disagreements.

Mini-Case

Imagine a situation where a dean has provided funds to two departments, history and English, to jointly purchase and share some instructional technology equipment. The two departments, located on adjacent floors of the same building, agreed on the purchase of a laptop computer, data projector, and instructional software. Now the departments cannot agree on the schedule of usage, shared maintenance costs, and security procedures relative to the equipment. Both department chairs have brought their respective complaints to the dean, who is faced with the task of informal facilitation of this conflict. First the dean must listen carefully to the complaint from each department head, paraphrasing key points to check understanding. Likewise, each department head must be encouraged to listen to each other's concerns in the presence of the dean and to paraphrase key points in each other's story. Both chairs should be coached to objectively and specifically describe problem behaviors from each of their perspectives. Perhaps the English chair says that history faculty are frequently late in returning the equipment. Perhaps the history chair indicates that English faculty frequently leave the equipment unattended in the classroom. The dean's job would be to get the disputants to clarify what is meant by "frequently late" and "frequently unattended." How often do these behaviors occur? To what extent is the equipment returned late—several minutes, hours, days? To what extent is the equipment left unattended—several minutes, hours, days? The dean, as informal facilitator, can get the parties to empathize with each other's concerns by soliciting their feelings about late or stolen equipment interfering with their class objectives. Both parties likely would have similar feelings, which the informal facilitator should point out. A discussion of why the equipment is late or unattended, coupled with an examination of intentions versus outcomes, would move the parties toward peacemaking. Perhaps the parties do not intend to inconvenience each other or do not realize they are jeopardizing the equipment. Nevertheless, their behaviors lead to such outcomes. Next, the dean must move the parties to the solution step. Each person could diplomatically state desired changes. The dean should encourage the chairs to consider additional options and could suggest options as well. Suppose the chairs discovered that moving the equipment back and forth between departments throughout the day was causing the schedule and security problems, and they agreed that the equipment should be bolted to a movable cart and transported only once a day. The history faculty would use the equipment on Mondays, Wednesdays, and Fridays, and the English faculty would use it on Tuesdays and Thursdays during the first semester of each year, and the schedule would reverse during the second semester. The dean should secure this agreement in writing and check periodically to see how the arrangement is working. By using key communication strategies, the dean as informal facilitator can help the disputants solve this conflict in a short amount of time. Effective informal facilitation precludes the need to use more formal, contentious, and time-consuming conflict management strategies. Some persistent conflicts may require the next intervention on the continuum of conflict management tactics—negotiation.

Negotiation

By helping faculty to see themselves as friendly rivals with the goal of reaching an agreement through mutual concessions, chairs and deans can additionally help faculty manage their conflicts. Negotiation for conflict management purposes is a slightly more structured and formal process than informal facilitation, yet it is not as structured as a labor negotiation, for example. Here the emphasis is on the exchange of proposals and counter-proposals as a means of reaching a mutually satisfactory settlement of the conflict.

First, the administrator-as-negotiator must help the faculty to see that they are involved in joint decision-making. The disagreement must be reframed from that of a conflict with winners and losers to a decision-making activity where disparate interests must be coordinated into an outcome. Faculty should be encouraged to use "we" language rather than terms like "me vs. you" or "us vs. them." By linguistically encouraging cooperation, the administrator helps the opposing parties to see themselves in relationship to each other or as one unit with a common task. The chair, who is helping faculty to negotiate a solution to conflict, should point out common interests and help the participants to see common ground. Each person must focus on interests or goals, not on positions.

Mini-Case

Imagine that two faculty hold different positions about curriculum requirements in the department of mechanical engineering. Professor Hernandez believes that students should take a full year of basic math and physics courses before taking any engineering courses. Professor Schwartz believes that principles of math and physics should be integrated into the engineering curriculum which students should begin as freshmen. Their positions are mutually exclusive, so they face conflict.

The department chair can assist in negotiation by getting each faculty member to see that they have the common interest of a rigorous, challenging, relevant curriculum for students. By acknowledging common interests rather than fighting for opposing positions, the faculty can pursue a variety of means for creating the curriculum. Perhaps neither of their original positions becomes the final outcome.

Once faculty agree on common goals, they should be encouraged to submit their respective proposals for achieving that goal. Professor Schwartz may propose an intensive, required summer tutorial in math and physics for all incoming freshmen engineering students. Professor Hernandez may offer a counterproposal or may amend the first proposal. Perhaps he suggests a year-long math and physics recitation course during the academic year to accompany the engineering coursework. Numerous proposals should emerge with no one quite sure who proposed what. Lots of ideas should be put on the table for consideration. It is the negotiator's role to encourage brainstorming and a problem/solution orientation rather than a win/lose orientation to the conflict. The chair should ask each person to consider the merits of each other's proposals. At some point in the discussion, the merits of ideas should supersede the identification of which person proposed the idea. Defensiveness around the ownership of ideas lessens when there is agreement about the goal, and multiple parties contribute to the plan for achieving that goal. Where disagreements persist about the means to a common goal, the faculty should seek to persuade, not coerce, each other into making concessions. The chair should ask the disputants to analyze together the advantages and disadvantages of the various proposals. Collectively, they should build the best solution without regard to their individual, original positions.

Let's assume that Hernandez and Schwartz agree to setting higher admission standards in math and physics for incoming freshmen, requiring an intensive summer tutorial for selected students, and mandating a one-credit math and physics recitation course to be taken by all students in conjunction with their engineering coursework. This outcome would be superior to the initial proposals of the two faculty members in conflict. Through a process of negotiation, the solution is satisfactory to both parties, and neither feels a sense of having lost in the conflict. The same interpersonal communication skills described with informal facilitation can be used in negotiation.

Mediation

Should face-to-face negotiation fail to resolve conflict, the next step on the continuum of strategies is mediation. In this technique, an acceptable, impartial, and neutral third party who has no authoritative decision-making power assists disputants in reaching a voluntary settlement. This strategy is an extension of the previous two methods in that the same communication skills and decision-making processes are used, but the chair or dean does not serve as mediator. The administrator can assist the faculty in deciding to use mediators, identify qualified mediators, and can help the faculty agree on the selection of a particular individual as mediator.

Mediation as a conflict management process is somewhat more formal than the methods discussed previously. Those individuals serving as mediators should receive training in the mediation process. They need to be aware of typical stages of mediation, mediation techniques, notetaking, and the use of written materials, and a range of communication styles and behavioral techniques that can be employed. Keltner (1994) describes mediation as a self-empowering process whereby participants take responsibility for making decisions, while using a third party to help them explore issues, identify alternatives, select outcomes, and implement decisions. Mediators can simultaneously help conflicting faculty examine their relationship issues, establish a process of resolving conflict, and explore the substance of the conflict. A full explication of the mediation process cannot be given within this chapter. Suffice it to say that chairs and deans should consider implementing a mediation process in their units. A range of legal, governmental, and community resources are available in most geographic areas to assist administrators in establishing mediation programs in colleges and universities.

Mini-Case

Imagine that a long-standing feud exists between Professor Georgiou of the fashion design program and Professor Latif of the graphic design program in the department of art at a small college. Each person routinely makes disparaging remarks about the other. Students are subjected to negative comments about each faculty member's professional expertise, teaching methods, and ethics. In desperation, a group of students has asked the department chair to put an end to this faculty feud which is affecting their attitudes and performance in the department of art. Because of the personal nature of this conflict and the need for the head to be perceived as absolutely impartial, using a mediator might be the best strategy for conflict management in this case.

The department chair should develop a short list of faculty from outside of the department of art who might serve as mediators. It is important that none of the possible mediators have any professional or personal connection to the disputants. Professors Latif and Georgiou should agree on the selection of a mediator. If this proves difficult, a name can be selected at random after each disputant has had the opportunity to eliminate one name from the list. The person serving as mediator should have had formal training in the mediation processes. The mediator's role is to help the disputants reach a voluntary agreement. The mediator would likely meet separately with each faculty member to learn the issues and explore possible solutions. At some point, the mediator would probably bring the disputants face-to-face for discussions. In this example, various relationship issues would need to be explored. The disputants would need to agree that the students' welfare supersedes their personal animosities. Eventually, both people would need to agree in writing to a plan of civil behavior and would need to state their intentions to follow the plan. While a mediator is not likely to get the disputants to end the long-standing feud, he can get agreement on a plan of action for managing the conflict.

Ombuds Programs

Some colleges and universities have an ombudsperson who essentially serves as informal facilitator, negotiator, and mediator combined. Warters (1995) has labeled the college ombudsperson as perhaps the most enduring and successful multiple-constituency model of resolving campus conflicts. The ombudsperson is an independent, high-level person who receives complaints, pursues inquiries into the matters involved, and makes recommendations for suitable action (Lupton, 1984). This person deals with complaints from all constituencies in the institution including students, faculty, and staff. The ombudsperson has no vested interest in the outcome and no decision-making authority but merely seeks to serve justice. The ombudsperson raises questions, discovers facts, helps disputants to see others' perspectives on the situation, suggests options to the parties, and makes recommendations. An ombuds system has the value of existing in a formal organizational structure, but the methods of conflict resolution used in ombuds programs are informal ones. All of the elements of effective interpersonal communication, peacemaking, mutual concessions, common interests, and voluntary settlements relative to other conflict management strategies are used in ombuds programs.

Mini-Case

Imagine that two faculty members, who are specialists in human genetics, have collaborated to obtain a grant from the National Institutes of Health. Professor Garrett, from the department of biology in the College of Arts and Sciences, insists that laboratory experiments for the project follow a certain set of procedures. Professor Perkins, from the department of cell biophysics in the College of Medicine, insists on a different set of procedures for laboratory experiments. The two researchers must cooperate for the project to be completed and the final year of funding to be obtained. Since this conflict crosses college jurisdictions, there is not one chair or even one dean who can take on a conflict-management role.

The services of a university ombudsperson may prove useful in this case. This is another informal strategy for managing conflict where the disputants must agree to participate and must agree to the settlement. The ombudsperson would question both parties about the necessity for certain laboratory procedures, inquire about the importance of their agreement to project completion, may suggest the consequences of their lack of agreement, and help them generate options. Initially, fact-finding is an important role for the ombudsperson. From both of their perspectives: What are the facts of the genetics research experiments which require certain lab procedures? What requirements might be set by the granting agency? The ombudsperson asks many questions, asks the disputants to look at the conflict from many perspectives, helps to generate options, makes concrete recommendations, and works diligently with the disputants for as long as it takes to solve the problem. The ombudsperson uses all of the techniques of informal peacemaking, negotiation, and mediation.

By being an employee of the university, she may bring knowledge, contacts, and resources of the university to the conflict-management task. But by being independent of the formal structure—not reporting to the deans of either the Arts and Sciences or Medical Colleges at the university, she can be blunt and assertive in working with the disputants. Since her job is conflict-management, she can devote more time to this situation than can a faculty-volunteer mediator. The ombudsperson would use all of the communication strategies we have discussed thus far to help the disputants reach a settlement.

Arbitration

This is a quasijudicial process in which a neutral third party makes a decision in a dispute when the parties in conflict cannot reach resolution. It is more formal than any of the procedures discussed previously, yet less formal than an actual court proceeding. There are two types of arbitration. In binding arbitration, both the institution and faculty member must accept the finding of the arbiter. In advisory arbitration, the arbiter makes a recommendation which may or may not be accepted. Arbiters typically are attorneys hired by the university.

The administrator's role in arbitration is to seek agreement from the disputants regarding arbitration and to either select the arbiter or help the disputants reach agreement in the selection of an arbiter. Once these decisions have been made, in the case of binding arbitration, the only remaining role for the chair or dean is to ensure that the arbiter's decision is implemented. Most of the work of an arbitration falls on the faculty disputants to prepare their cases, gather supporting data and evidence, and present information at the hearing. Since arbiters typically are attorneys not in the employ of the university, the administration incurs the costs of arbitration.

While not used frequently in higher education, arbitration can be useful when all other internal mechanisms for conflict management have failed. The disputants typically feel they have been given a fair hearing, whatever the outcome, because they willingly participate in the process and realize the objectivity of a trained, external arbiter.

Mini-Case

Imagine that the board of trustees of the university has mandated that, as a cost-saving strategy, the department of computer science will merge with the department of computer engineering. The departments have two years to develop a combined curriculum and admission standards; create a common set of reappointment, promotion, and tenure requirements; and select a department head. At the end of two years, the departments have agreed on all of the tasks except the selection of a chair. The former chairs of the separate departments each have applied, as has one senior faculty member from each formerly separate department. With a pool of four candidates for department head, the faculty have reached a roadblock. They cannot agree on one candidate, and the dean fears alienating half of the newly formed department with whatever candidate she endorses. The dean might be well-advised to take this conflict to arbitration, thereby having an outside party ostensibly make the decision. An outside arbiter, not employed by the university but knowledgeable about university culture and leadership, would be hired to review the credentials of all candidates; interview candidates; assess faculty, student, staff, and alumni opinion; assess the dean's sentiments; and either make a recommendation in the case of nonbinding arbitration or select the new department chair in the case of binding arbitration.

While using an arbiter can be costly and can potentially embarrass an institution, in this case, the long-term benefits of having an external person make this sensitive decision may preclude hostilities and conflicts for years to come. If the arbiter seeks input from all relevant parties and makes a careful, informed decision, then all parties are likely to accept that decision, and the new department can proceed with its business unhampered by resentments and animosities.

Grievances

Most colleges and universities, whether or not the faculty is unionized, have a grievance policy. It specifies what types of disputes are grievable and the process and timetable by which a grievance hearing occurs. The procedural steps in grievance systems typically include an attempt at informal resolution and a formal hearing process. If the dispute cannot be resolved informally, an ad hoc committee hears the evidence and makes a recommendation, often to the college president.

While most faculty-initiated grievances are brought against administrators, there are circumstances in which one faculty member may grieve the actions of another. For instance, faculty may charge their colleagues with sexual harassment, discriminatory behavior, or violation of their academic freedom. Likewise, faculty who serve on promotion and tenure committees or merit salary allocation committees may find themselves the target of a grievance.

Chairs and deans must be thoroughly familiar with the institution's grievance policy. Commonly, it is the administrator's role to advise disputants about the use of the grievance process. Indeed, even if the administrator is the target of a grievance, one should not take the matter personally. In lieu of being named in a grievance, administrators may be called as expert witnesses in grievance hearings. Whatever the grievance role performed by chairs or deans, they must realize that grievance resolution is one of their primary responsibilities.

Mini-Case

Imagine that in the department of marketing, the faculty have developed a set of procedures by which merit salary adjustments are made on an annual basis. While the procedures are democratically derived, the department has voted that an internal personnel committee consisting of the chair and two senior faculty will actually implement the procedures and make merit salary awards. This year, after the merit salary decisions are announced, Assistant Professor Hannon appeals the fact that she was given the smallest monetary award.

First, Professor Hannon can make an informal appeal to the departmental personnel committee by presenting evidence and arguments in favor of a higher salary award and asking the committee to reconsider its decision. The personnel committee can change its decision or uphold its original award. If it upholds its original award, then Professor Hannon can present her case to a formal committee of her peers. The grievance committee consists of elected faculty from a variety of departments. A three-person panel of faculty, none of whom come from the College of Business, where the marketing department resides, would be comprised as a grievance evaluation committee. By established procedures, Professor Hannon would present her case for deserving a higher merit salary award and the marketing department personnel committee chair would present the department's case for awarding the lesser amount of money to Professor Hannon. After hearing all of the facts of the case, questioning both sides, examining the marketing department's process of awarding merit salary, and deliberating about whether or not the process was applied fairly in this case, the grievance committee would either render a decision or make a recommendation to be reviewed by the college president. With such an established grievance process, conflicts can be settled objectively and quickly. Such a conflict management process would allow multiple grievances on an issue like merit pay to be handled quickly and with minimal animosity. But such a formal grievance process, with clearly articulated roles and procedures, must be established within an institution before specific conflicts can benefit from grievance hearings as a conflict management strategy.

THE CONFLICT MANAGEMENT CLIMATE IN ACADEME

Whatever methods administrators use when intervening in faculty conflicts, they must create a climate where conflict is perceived as normal, where faculty are encouraged to openly express their views and freely debate issues, and where faculty are empowered to solve their own disputes as much as possible. There must be clear incentives for dealing with conflict in professional and productive ways and strong sanctions for immature or resistant behavior. Administrators need to shape the environment to reduce conflict, develop conflict management skills in their faculty, serve a models of effective communication in conflict situations, strategically intervene in faculty conflict, and lead the institution in developing effective conflict management systems.

The sources and issues of conflict among faculty are ever-present. Faculty will continue to disagree about resources, ideologies, priorities, and policies. They will continue to find themselves in conflict over disciplinary turf, curriculum issues, tenure decisions, authorship issues, academic freedom, and the like. It is imperative that administrators understand the ways in which academic cultures fuel conflict. They need to know the forms that conflict take and the styles people use when dealing with conflict.

They need to understand and embrace their roles as managers of conflict. Finally, administrators must be familiar with a wide range of conflict management strategies so they can lead their faculty and their units toward greater harmony, satisfaction, and productivity.

REFERENCES

Anderson, J. W., Foster-Kuehn, M., & McKinney, B. C. (1996). *Communication skills for surviving conflicts at work*. Cresskill, NJ: Hampton Press.

Bergquist, W. H. (1992). *The four cultures of the academy: Insights and strategies for improving leadership in collegiate organizations.* San Francisco, CA: Jossey-Bass.

Deutsch, M. (1992). Typical responses to conflict. *Educational Leadership, 50,* 16-18.

Ehrle, E. B., & Bennett, J. B. (1988). *Managing the academic enterprise: Case studies for deans and provosts.* New York, NY: Macmillan.

Fairweather, J. S. (1996). *Faculty work and the public trust.* Boston, MA: Allyn and Bacon.

Gmelch, W. H. (1995). Department chairs under siege: Resolving the web of conflict. In S. A Holton (Ed.), *Conflict management in higher education.* San Francisco, CA: Jossey-Bass.

Holton, S. A (1995). Conflict 101. In S. A Holton (Ed.), *Conflict management in higher education.* San Francisco, CA: Jossey-Bass.

Jandt, F. E., & Kaufman, J. A. (1992). Managing grievances. In M. Hickson & D. W. Stacks (Eds.), *Effective communication for academic chairs.* Albany, NY: State University of New York Press.

Keltner, J. W. (1994). *The management of struggle: Elements of dispute resolution through negotiation, mediation, and arbitration.* Cresskill, NJ: Hampton Press.

Kennedy, D. (1995, May-June). Another century's end, another revolution in higher education. *Change,* 8-15.

Lupton, D. K. (1984). Resolving faculty disputes: The educational ombudsman proposal. *Innovative Higher Education, 8,* 94-107.

Slaikeu, K. A. (1996). *When push comes to shove: A practical guide to mediating disputes.* San Francisco, CA: Jossey-Bass.

Warters, W. C. (1995). Conflict management in higher education: A review of current approaches. In S. A Holton (Ed.), *Conflict management in higher education.* San Francisco, CA: Jossey-Bass.

Whicker, M. L., & Kronenfeld, J. J. (1994). *Dealing with ethical dilemmas on campus.* Thousand Oaks, CA: Sage.

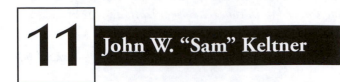

11 John W. "Sam" Keltner

VIEWS FROM DIFFERENT SIDES OF THE DESK: CONFLICT BETWEEN FACULTY AND STUDENTS

On August 15, 1996, Frederich Davidson was to meet with his major advisor and members of his graduate committee at San Diego State University to discuss problems with his master's thesis. As the session began, Davidson took a 9 mm semiautomatic gun he had hidden in a first aid kit and shot dead his major professor and the two other faculty members of his committee (Perry & O'Conner, 1996). Thus the ultimate phase of unresolved struggle was demonstrated in action. [1]

Struggles between students and faculty that are left unresolved can escalate to violent and destructive behavior. Except for the most violent situations, we rarely hear of the many struggles that occur within the student-faculty relationship throughout the educational process. The Davidson case was at the graduate level, but the various phases of struggle occur regularly at many levels of the academic curriculum. The relationships between student and faculty and the context of the teaching-learning process are at the heart of these interpersonal and intergroup struggles.

Deans and department heads, in particular, are close to the faculty-student relationship and therefore there is the potential for struggle. Within their jurisdiction falls a significant responsibility for coping with the struggles that arise from the faculty-student relationships. The costs of unresolved disputes between faculty and students can be high as demonstrated by the Davidson affair. However unique that situation was, there are many other potentially violent disputes at almost every level of student-faculty relations. Deans and department heads are administratively the closest to the territory of student-faculty disputes, and so carry a heavy responsibility for managing such disputes productively.

THE STRUGGLE SPECTRUM

Violent conflict does not occur as a singular behavior in specific recurring contexts. It has antecedents. The Davidson shooting was preceded by a number of events and conditions that led to the terminating act. As a mediator, arbitrator, and student of conflict, I have explored these antecedents and discovered that they fall into a continuum ranging from mild disagreement to violence.

Along that continuum are a number of different behaviors. For example, a mild disagreement between a student and her teacher may escalate into a more polarized dispute if it is not resolved in some fashion. That dispute may be resolved in several ways, as illustrated by Table 1, The Struggle Spectrum. The first way is through some face-to-face discussion of the matter as a joint problem. If that fails, there may follow a confrontation between the student and her teacher wherein each of them will discuss the situation and/or present arguments in support or in opposition. If this fails and either the student or the teacher feel that the dispute must be settled (sometimes this feeling may not be logical but may be based on pride and other emotionally based incentives), they may try several alternatives. An early alternative is to solicit the intervention of a third party as a mediator to facilitate the negotiations. If that fails, the parties may solicit the support of others and enter into what we can call a campaign to bring their positions to acceptance. Another alternative at this point is to go to a third party and ask that person to make a decision for them. If these alternatives fail, the parties may then move to a more stressful third party, the court. If the decisions of the third party or the court do not resolve the differences, there is a high potential for violence of some sort.

These various alternatives represent ways of dealing with the stages through which we go when we become engaged in differences. They represent

TABLE I

The Struggle Spectrum

Conditions	STAGE 1 *Mild Difference*	STAGE 2 *Disagreement*	STAGE 3 *Dispute*	STAGE 4 *Campaign*	STAGE 5 *Litigation*	STAGE 6 *Fight or War*
Processes Leading to Resolution	Discussion	Discussion Negotiation	Argument Bargaining	Persuasion Pressure	Advocacy Debate	Violent Conflict
Problem-Solving Behavior	Joint Problem Solving	Contentions over Choices	Rational Proof & Game Playing By Rules	Emotional and Logical Strategies	Selective Proofs Before Judges or Juries	Psychological or Physical Violence
Relationship Between Parties	Partners, Friends & Acquaintances	Rivals	Opponents	Competitors	Antagonists	Enemies
Goals	Includes Other	Includes Other	Excludes Other	Excludes Other	Excludes Other	Eliminates Other
Orientation to Each Other	Cooperative & Amicable	Disputative Conciliatory	Win-Lose 1 Hostile	Win-Lose 2 Estranged	Win-Lose 3 Alienated	Irreconcilable
Communication	Open-Friendly	Open but Strained	Limited Tense	Restricted & Planned	Blocked & Controlled	Closed Except for Violent Acts
Decision Making	Mutual Decisions	Joint Decisions and Agreements	Joint Decision in Mediation-Third Party Decisions in Arbitration	Vote by Constituents or Third Party Decisions	Third Party Court-room Decisions by Judge or Jury	Each Side Seeks Control by Forcing the Other
Intervention Possibilities	None Needed	Mediation by Neutral Party	Mediation or Arbitration by Neutral Party	Arbitration by Neutral Party or Election-Vote	Arbitration or Judge or Jury	Force of Police or Other Military or Power Intervention
Possible Outcomes	Integrated Agreement: Mutual Satisfaction	Accommodated Agreement with Both Satisfied	Compromise Agreement or One Wins But One or Both Dissatisfied	A Win or Draw. Winner Pleased with Loser Accepting but Dissatisfied	One Wins and Winner Celebrates. Loser Frustrated, etc.	One Prevails. Other or Both Destroyed or Harmed. High Fear in Both
Intractability Potential	Very Low	Low	Medium	High	High	Very High

	TABLE I (CONTINUED)

Notes

A. Mediation is relatively useless in Stages 1, 4, 5, and 6, but may be used in 4 under special arrangement.
B. Win-Lose escalates from Level 1 to Level 3. The longer it exists, the more intense it becomes.
C. Neutral third parties have no stake in the outcome of the struggle. They include mediators, arbitrators, judges, and juries.
D. Parties lose their joint decision-making power when mediation is no longer applicable.
E. When issues are not resolved at one stage, the tendency is to move to the right on the continuum.
F. De-escalation from right to left is possible under special circumstances (See chapter on de-escalation).
G. Disputes may become intractable (stalemated) at any stage in the process and may thus require special efforts to "unfreeze" them.

Reprinted with permission from Keltner, John W. (Sam), *The Management of Struggle: Elements of Dispute Resolution Through Negotiation, Mediation, and Arbitration.* 1994. Hampton Press, p. 5.

a spectrum of struggle. Each phase is characterized by special types of communication, by levels of polarization toward each other and the content of the argument, by attitudinal sets toward the other, by emotions, and by a number of other elements.

If the differences are not resolved, the matter may become a dispute where other types of behavior appear as the parties attempt to find resolution. At this point the intervention of a third party may be useful. The third party intervention can be of three forms: mediation, arbitration, and adjudication. Each of these types of intervention represent someone other than the parties effecting the outcome.

The intervention type that least interferes with the decision-making of the disputants is mediation. Mediators do not make decisions for the parties but serve to facilitate the parties in their own decision-making. When the parties are unable to work out a resolution themselves, they then set aside their own decision-making and rely on an outside source to make the critical decisions through arbitration, court, or administrative fiat.

The struggle spectrum chart shows the alternatives at each level of the struggle. Notice that the procedures for resolution are not universal; they are not processes that can be evoked at any stage of the struggle. Mediation, for example, is not functional when the parties are unwilling to try to settle the dispute themselves, or when they are so frozen into a win-lose structure that they are unable to negotiate and find compromise. When disputants are at a level of violence, mediation won't work until the situation is deescalated to a point where the parties are willing to negotiate with each other through non-violent means. Note the continuing stalemates in Israeli-Palestine affairs.

This spectrum of struggle is a highly useful tool for the academic administrator who must find ways to attenuate or manage the struggles between students and faculty. It facilitates the selection of approaches to the situation, clarifies the understanding of the nature of the struggle, and allows the administrator to assess the potential of a struggle.

STUDENT-FACULTY RELATIONSHIPS AND STRUGGLE

The relationships between faculty and students are often such that disputes arise easily and often. The nature of these relations emerges from many contexts in which the student and faculty member exist. Let's look at some of them.

Power Positions and Student-Teacher Struggle

The power relationship between the student and teacher plays a significant role in the struggles between them. The teacher is at least a source of information, reward, and punishment and, at various stages performs *In loco parentis*. The teacher thereby exerts considerable influence over the behavior of the student. Stress and struggle over the relationship and the consequences emerges with changing force and significance at various stages in the teacher-student relationship.

Student Attitudes toward the Learning Process

The beginning college student comes with a wide variance of perceptions of the teaching-learning process. Many of them come with high expectations of the process and of the faculty and institution in control. Others come with a "show me" attitude derived from their disappointment with secondary school education experiences. Still others come with a resentment of the process, the institution, and the faculty because they feel that they are forced to matriculate by the society in which they live. Others come with a fear and anxiety about the process because it is a new and unexplored territory for them. And still others come with a "who cares" attitude because their reason for being there has nothing to do with the academic curriculum but is centered on enjoying the social atmosphere, being athletes, and/or being political leaders.

The graduate student comes with a somewhat different set of perceptions and expectations. There is more likely to be a desire to learn more and to complete some vocationally directed areas of study with some distinction. The academic learning process has become more stabilized and usable for the graduate student. The advanced degree is seen as a more important vocational prerequisite than the undergraduate degree. The graduate student often comes with a strong concern for the amount of time to be expended in study and wants to complete the work as soon as possible.

These add up to varying styles of learning that affect the relationship between faculty and student. A faculty member I know says to his class at its first meeting: "There is nothing I can learn for you. I can learn some things for myself but not for you. You must do your own learning. I'll provide you with resources, with information, with suggestions, with coaching, with concern, and maybe affection but I cannot, even if I wanted to, do your learning for you."

This kind of approach puts a special responsibility clearly on the student. It does not, however, deal completely with those students who expect or have been accustomed to being told what to do and when to do it or those students whose learning style is to copy and replicate. Thus some stress emerges between the teacher and those students who want the teacher to do the work for them and to make all the critical decisions about what and how learning should take place. A power struggle often emerges.

Faculty Attitudes and Perceptions of Students and Learning
On the other side of the equation, the faculty in higher education represent a diverse collection of people mostly selected on the basis of their preparation in the subject matter to be taught. They have had little or no special training in the teaching-learning processes and tend to approach the classroom in manners similar to college teachers they have experienced. And those are mostly lecture-centered in their style of teaching.

A very significant part of the faculty perception is the manner in which the teacher approaches the student learning process. Some teachers see their role as the source of knowledge and the basic instrument whereby the knowledge is transferred to the student. There are many whose concept of teaching is to lecture, assign readings, and give multiple-choice tests. Among them are those who cherish being the center of attention by so many students at one time and find great ego satisfaction in putting on a show via the lecture platform. Too many college and university lecturers are not good presenters.

Still others see their role as the gatherer of knowledge (information) who shares both the gathering and the information itself only when the student conscientiously seeks it. Then there are those few who see their role as a co-seeker of knowledge who stimulates and encourages the student to share in the process of discovery as a partner.

While many colleges and universities have instituted special workshops for their faculty to assist them in developing teaching methods and styles more fitting to the learning process, the predominant teaching in the secondary schools and postsecondary schools is not primarily designed according to the process by which people discover and learn information.

Context and Contacts

The context in the postsecondary schools is also not directly facilitative of learning by the students. For many reasons, there are more and more large classes of 100 or more whereby the only way the instructor knows to teach is to lecture, either facing the mob or by videotape or multimedia productions prepared some time before. The contact between teacher and student is limited by the class size and nature of the physical arrangements of lecture halls and auditoria.

The good lecturers and presenters are those talented people who are outstanding speakers with a feel for acting, who have an organized and clear concept of their subject matter, who are skilled in the use of multimedia, and whose ego is stroked by the power they have over so many students. Unfortunately there are many who lecture who do not have these talents.

At the upper division and graduate level, the contact between the student and the teacher increases as the classes in the specialties become smaller and more contact with the faculty scholars is required in the system through advisory committees, mentoring, and other small group activities. It is here that many intense faculty-student confrontations take place.

Process and Teaching Styles

Many intense struggles arise when the student-faculty perceptions of the process and teaching styles are at odds. The egalitarian teacher encounters high resistance from students who want everything laid out with explicit directions in an authoritarian way. The authoritarian faculty member and the egalitarian student strike fire with each other at almost every turn. This latter type of struggle genesis also extends to the system itself. Many of the struggles in the 1960s and 1970s on the campuses may have begun in differences regarding the Vietnam War, but the struggles escalated when they were met with authoritarian resistance on the part of the administration and the community. The Chicago riots surrounding the Democratic convention of 1968 escalated rapidly when police resistance and countermeasures entered the streets. The Kent State debacle, where national guard troops fired on university students, demonstrated the ultimate violence that can emerge when authoritarian force is applied to highly intense differences on the university campus.

Faculty Pressures

The pressures on university faculty do not often contribute to good teaching. Although many schools now give lip service to "good teaching," it is rarely the critical element in the basic salary and promotion processes. The promotion of the teacher from instructor up the system to full professor is based primarily on research, publication, community service, and political correctness.

Teaching effectiveness is rarely actually used as the basic standard of evaluation, despite allegations to the contrary. One reason for this is the difficulty in measuring the quality and effect of teaching. Research, publication, community involvement, and political activity are easily identified and counted. The effect of the teacher on the learning of the student is much more difficult to determine.

The power relationships between faculty and students in postsecondary education are different from those that existed in the secondary and primary programs. Students are expected to be more adult. The student has more freedom of movement than before. The student also has more power of selection in relation to courses, programs, and teachers. And, because of this, students need a different kind of counseling and advising than what was available in precollege education.

What we have, therefore, is a set of conditions that are highly fertile for the emergence of struggle between many of the students and the faculties. Resolution of these struggles will depend on managing these conditions.

CONTEXTS AND STUDENT-FACULTY STRUGGLE

Student-faculty disputes arise in many contexts where students, faculty, and administration interact. Many disputes arise in relation to the making and enforcement of rules of procedure and behavior. These are the struggles we recognize as being system-based. Probably the area most frequently involved is the classroom. Here a wide array of interaction problems lead to disputes between students and their teachers. The interpersonal-social area is one where faculty and students are involved with each other in contexts removed from the classroom but affecting their relationships.

The tendency in most organizations or systems is to attempt control of disputes through procedures that seek to manage the interaction between students and faculty-administration and thereby suppress the potential for dispute surrounding it. Class syllabi, printed rules for classroom behavior, laboratory rules of procedure, rules for using equipment such as computers, attendance regulations, library rules, housing rules, scheduling requirements, grievance procedures, and others are methods of controlling the behavior of students and thereby the potential for struggles is diminished. Even so, disputes do arise over the application of such rules.

Throughout the educational process in higher education, we encounter the struggle of the students to gain control over the source and delivery of information that flows through the educational process. The underlying issues seem to have common characteristics. Power over the process appears as one of these. Student organizations on campus seek to increase their influence over many of the processes of the campus and to present the student view on many of the campus issues.

In the 1960s and 1970s, freedom of student expression and action became an issue on many campuses. Visibility of these issues seems to have subsided since, but they still exist on the campus around somewhat different themes. We have such things as the environment as a theme around which students often organize demonstrations and challenge the institution and its positions.

Students seek recognition through many avenues such as athletics, social and academic organizations, campus political activities, campus religious activity, and other outlets for their energy. The nature of the recognition seems less important than the fact of its existence.

Sexual Expression

Sexual expression is one of the powerful underlying issues on campus. This may emerge through dress codes, social affairs, fraternity-sorority relations and affairs, and personal relationships between the genders. The appearance of this issue in the faculty-student relationship is critical. Public information about them is heavily suppressed on college and university campuses. Even so, faculty-student affairs are frequent and can create serious consequences. An example of such a relationship occurred when a dynamic and attractive married faculty member fell in love with one of her graduate students. They were not discrete in their behaviors and were perceived on campus as a couple. Eventually her partner decided he wanted out of the relationship. She was greatly upset, and the two of them became involved in some almost violent encounters on campus and in the surrounding community. In the meantime her husband, getting word of the affair, sued for divorce and tried to involve the student in the legal maneuvering.

This type of student-faculty affair presents a serious challenge to the administrator because of the personal character of the behavior. The administrator struggles with the problems of intervening in private affairs even when those affairs affect the campus at large.

These student-faculty issues on the college and university campus seem to appear in several contexts: the classroom, the system, and the interpersonal-social interaction.

In each of the contexts, the struggles usually begin with mild disagreements and follow the struggle spectrum as they escalate through arguments, disputes, etc. They rarely end in violence of the type exhibited by Davidson, but they often escalate into levels that respond to different forms of intervention or become stalemated until the student leaves the scene through graduation, expulsion, or other forms of departure.

Classroom Disputes

Lori had a very difficult time in her history class. She was convinced that Dr. Tenman was a male chauvinist. She compulsively tracked his lectures for every instance where he would make references to women in what she perceived as a derogatory way and claimed she found many. Her interest in women's rights was strong, and she perceived Dr. Tenman as being an enemy of the feminist movement. In several personal conferences she had angrily faced him with her perceptions of his behavior, he became angry as well, and there was no resolution. Finally she began raising issues within the class and trying to get other students involved in attacking Tenman. The tension between Tenman and Lori was such that neither could deal with the learning experience with any satisfaction and upon advice from the dean, Lori withdrew from the class.

By far the most student-faculty confrontations occur in relation to classroom situations. Grades (evaluation of students), assignments, attendance, classroom behavior, presentational styles, misuse of property, examinations, term papers, theses and dissertations, gender issues, race and color matters, and others are matters over which faculty and students have frequent disputes.

Probably the most frequent dispute is over grades and evaluation of student performance. These occur when students perceive that they or their work have been evaluated unjustly and are willing to engage the teacher over the matter. Faculty response usually depends on the relationship with the student. When the relationship is egalitarian and cooperative, student and teacher are more likely to work out the situation. When the relationship is dictatorial, the issue may be drawn more intensely, and the teachers may then become defensive and the struggle escalates. In many cases students have attempted to go higher up on the management scale and complain to a department head or chair. Failing to get satisfaction at that level, the student may drop the issue or may take it to a dean or some appeals group in the department or school. Similar kinds of disputes arise with examinations, term papers, etc. In the case with Lori and Tenman, charges against Tenman were filed with a faculty review commission and eventually went to the president's office. By the time it reached the president's office, both parties had gathered supporters and lawyers, and were ready to do battle. Lori wanted Tenman fired. Tenman wanted Lori expelled for false allegations, and the battle was joined.

Some very intense struggles arise over behaviors in the classroom. When the student perceives the teacher behavior as being homophobic, racist, or sexist, and thus a threat to the student, there is often a confrontation of sorts. The confrontation occurs particularly in required courses where the student's freedom to choose has been limited. Many students, however, will avoid an immediate confrontation and will go directly to third parties such as ombudspersons, department heads, student affairs offices, and other faculty for intervention or help of some kind.

Most students accept the idea that academic freedom gives the faculty ultimate power within the classroom and that the student power to confront this situation is limited. Even so, many students will challenge that power when it appears that the faculty use of the power is working against the interests of the student. In such cases the student may confront the teacher, and if a settlement isn't reached, the struggle will escalate quickly (as in Lori's case) to out-of-class procedures involving third parties. Some of these third parties may be used as supporters for campaigns (both subtle and overt) against the teacher. Others may be brought in through organized procedures to assist in finding a resolution.

System Conditions

Faculty-student disputes emerge also from system conditions and classroom controls. The struggle over class schedules, the design of an academic or course program, prerequisites, religious holidays, and faculty evaluations are all system-centered in that they involve the faculty and administration with the student in a struggle over the application of campus rules and conditions. For example, a professor and his students in the beginning course in American literature were controlled by a syllabus that specifically defined everything that was to be done in the class, the lecture topics and times, the scheduling of personal conferences, the grading procedures, the times when exams were to be held, the expected behavior in the classroom, and the consequences of failure in any of the defined areas. All the beginning courses in that department were expected to follow the same syllabus. That syllabus removed a lot of variations in the teaching; it clarified for the students what was expected and what had to be done. But it also controlled a lot of learning opportunities where disputes between faculty and students could arise. It was a kind of tradeoff between controlled classrooms and student freedom.

Often these disputes erupt in demonstrations in support of some action taken or not taken by the administration. The firing of a favorite coach or faculty member, the termination of a popular academic program, the denial of access to the campus lecture system of some controversial national figure are of such nature.

Interpersonal-Social

Many struggles appearing in classroom or system contexts are also involved with interpersonal elements. Out-of-class behavior is one of the areas of interpersonal-social struggle. Contacts between faculty and student away from the class and its functions often generate struggle. This includes faculty involvement with student activities programs; with fraternities, sororities, and other social organizations; with service organizations; with religious groups; and with academic organizations (i.e., the history club, the modern language association, and other professional associations).

Interpersonal intergender contacts outside of class are a frequent source of faculty-student struggle. The faculty-student love affair, as discussed earlier, is an example. When these attractions are played out in public, the matter becomes critical, but information about them is often suppressed by the institution because of their highly personal nature.

Other areas of interpersonal-social significance include harassment, use of alcohol and drugs, sexism, racism, and homophobia. Each of these appear both in and out of the classroom. They emerge as problems and issues that bring student and teacher into confrontation. They are not relegated to one or the other of the participants. That is, students harass a teacher in many ways either singly or in groups. Teachers harass students in many ways both overtly and subtly. Sexist behaviors and attitudes may flow to and from the teacher. In one institution, a single woman teacher in a department of 25 men professors consistently graded the men in her classes at least a whole grade point below the women, called on the women to recite and ignored the men, and would not schedule conferences with the men in her classes. Male students openly but futilely confronted her in class over the matter until finally no men would enroll in her classes, and if they were assigned to the class by a computer, they would drop it.

Both students and faculty may exhibit racist behaviors both in and out of the classroom. For example, a husky African-American fellow raised in the streets of a large metropolitan city enrolled in a suburban university where there was less than a 5% black population. A white male professor who had also grown up in the streets of a large city wanted very much to help the young man get adjusted to the campus and to university education and tried to befriend him. The student borrowed a substantial amount of money from the teacher and refused to pay it back. He took classes with this teacher and did not do the work. He threatened the teacher if he did not get passing grades and made fun of the teacher to the other African-American students on campus. The professor was very patient in the face of all this, but eventually confronted the student and asked him to withdraw from school. A threatening and almost violent meeting took place involving the campus police. In another instance, a white graduate student refused to accept a black professor on her advisory committee because of the professor's race.

Homophobic behaviors are also involved in student-faculty struggles. Two male professors in the same department who, living together as partners, were often the target of off-color remarks by students, were physically threatened by a group of fraternity brothers, and had their residence attacked with graffiti, garbage, and posters.

Interpersonal-social disputes span the full range of contexts and interactions of faculty with students. The issues of power and perception in the education processes are both systemic and personal. Any procedures aimed at coping with the resulting struggles must include attention to both issues.

Other issues arising out of the interpersonal-social relationship between student and teacher are many. They exist on at least two levels: the overt and the covert. The overt are those where the struggle erupts or is played out in clear physical confrontations. The covert situations are those that are hidden, unobserved by others, but that nevertheless are significant struggles between faculty and students. Many of both types are power struggles involving students seeking to gain power by appearing to be special friends with the teacher or teachers trying to counteract overtures by the student to create a close interpersonal relationship.

A frequent issue is the presence of relations of the instructor being members of the class. Some institutions have sought to deny relatives of a teacher enrollment in that teacher's class. But frequently a teacher and member(s) of a class may belong to the same social organization, and their behavior with each other is such that others in the class become fearful that they will be discriminated against for not being a part of the "in" organization. Two students in a small animals class in a veterinary school were in the same professional fraternity as the teacher and were seen frequently with the teacher out of class. Others in the class became concerned that they would not gain the same opportunities for field work and study as the "in" group, and they complained to the dean.

The interpersonal area is a delicate one. The line separating appropriate and inappropriate interpersonal relationships is not a clear one. Most teachers seek to develop and sustain a friendly interpersonal relationship with their students. At the same time it is easy for students needing emotional support to reach out to such instructors and to attempt to establish strong interpersonal ties. Quite often, freshmen away from home for the first time will see teachers as substitutes for parents and will attach themselves and protect such attachments jealously. When the teacher rejects such advances, the student may then turn and find fault with many things the teacher does and thereby create tension that escalates to disputes between them.

MANAGING THE CONTEXTS (MENDING THE CRACKS)

A deterrent to the escalation of struggles to levels where they do damage to the people and institution is through context management. By context I mean the organizational and structural character of the institution. When students and faculty find themselves struggling with each other to the point where the struggle interrupts the teaching-learning process, steps need to be taken to deescalate the condition.

Create contexts that develop cooperative student-faculty relationships. Programs and activities aimed at bringing students and faculty together beyond the classroom are important and should include both social and professional situations. Here are some things that can be done in this respect.

Encourage Faculty Sponsorship of Student Programs

Many faculty tend to isolate themselves in their own academic cocoon and avoid seeing students outside the classroom or seminar. Students need to view and experience the faculty in as many different dimensions as possible. This allows faculty to have a clearer perception of the students as people and to understand the origins of some of the disagreements that may arise. Also, it provides a base on which the student and faculty can meet outside the attendant condition that may surround their dispute. One way of doing this is to encourage faculty to serve as sponsors or advisors to student programs and activities. Because some faculty may resist this as not being part of their contract with the institution, it may be important for such an expectation to be a part of the professional contract.

Involve Faculty in Student Advising

In these days when numbers of students put added pressure on faculty, there is a tendency to find other ways of providing advice and guidance to students in respect to their academic curriculum. Many schools have turned to student or peer advising with excellent results and substantially reduced costs. What is lost in peer advising, however, is the contact between the faculty and the student that faculty advising provides.

Faculty advising, when it is done well, can promote a sense of partnership in the learning process. Good faculty advising is a significant preventive of student-faculty struggle. It forms a relationship that is able to cope with differences and disagreements without escalation into polarized disputes. Some schools have provided special awards to those faculty members who are known and respected as student advisors. Such rewards point out the importance of good faculty advising to the institution.

Assign Students to School and Department Committees

In a large institution it is difficult for administrators to be in contact with students to the point where the administrator can solicit and/or assign the student to special committees. However, in many institutions students are chosen to serve on major university committees such as advisory committees to deans and departments, faculty senate committees, special university review and event committees, faculty and administrator selection committees, and others. It is often useful for departments to have a student advisory group composed of both majors and nonmajors. Such advisory groups can be in cooperation with the institution-wide student association or can be unique for each department or division. When these students are selected by their peers, the lines of communication and responsibility seem much more effective. Again, the presence of such groups helps to open the channels of communication and thereby provide opportunities for both students and faculty to deal with problems and differences that arise.

Set the Pattern by Keeping an Open Door

Many mild differences escalate to disputes when the parties are unable to communicate with each other early enough in the struggle spectrum to prevent escalation and polarization. This is particularly true in the academic setting. Both teachers and administrators need to be available to the students. Faculty members may complain that being available makes them more subject to student-faculty disputes. On the contrary, being available makes possible important encounters that can lead to resolution of problems that involve students and faculty.

Provide Support for Both Faculty and Students as They Seek to Perform Their Respective Functions in the Institution

One of the more provocative conditions occurs when students and/or faculty feel that there is no support for them or their function. The faculty need to feel that its administration supports its function and purpose. Students need to feel that the faculty is truly concerned with their learning experience and supports their attempts to meet requirements. The faculty member who seems aloof, uncaring, or disdainful about student concerns is quite likely to be involved in student disputes more than others.

Provide Professional Development Opportunities through Seminars, Short Courses, and Special Programs

Special seminars and short courses for faculty and students are useful in creating conditions that will prevent or diffuse disputes that could become more violent. Significant topics and themes can be developed with the help of the office of the dean of students. Joint seminars might focus on topics such as gender in the classroom, learning styles and the classroom, student expectations and the university reality, dealing with conflict on the campus, diversity on the campus, the student-faculty partnership in the learning process, and others suggested by the students and faculty.

Many universities are creating faculty development offices where programs are designed to assist faculty in their personal and professional development. Such offices can assist in the organization of seminars and special activities that facilitate faculty-student relations. A special program on conflict and dispute resolution sponsored by the faculty development office can be a highly useful project.

Special orientations on dispute resolution should be provided for all faculty and administrators. These orientations should include the nature of struggle and conflict in the academic setting, the struggle spectrum and the importance of knowing at which stage in the spectrum a specific struggle has come to the attention of the administrator, and the available processes at each stage of the spectrum (Keltner, 1994).

Special presentations and discussions at full faculty meetings are quite useful if they are targeted to faculty concerns and interests at point. Short courses or workshops offered to faculty with encouragement from the administration to attend are often quite useful in alerting the faculty to the significance of the process in this particular institution. Department heads need special assistance in understanding the etiology and nature of conflict and disputes. Specialists in conflict studies and conflict resolution need to be brought on board to educate students and faculty as to the aspects of dispute resolution. These same experts can be used in providing special seminars for students and faculty on conflict management.

Provide Systems Where Faculty-Faculty Disputes May Be Resolved Quickly and Efficiently

Faculty versus faculty disputes inevitably spill over into student affairs and involve students. A dispute between the faculty of an ROTC unit and the university senate over the role of the unit on the campus swept ROTC students and nonmilitary students into some almost violent confrontations among students, faculty, and administration.

Disputes between faculty, and between faculty and administration, do not occur in a vacuum. Faculty-faculty disputes are rarely unknown by the students, and often students are dragged into supporting the disputing teachers. Such faculty-faculty disputes must be resolved quickly and must not entangle students because that increases student-faculty tensions. The important thing here is that procedures be established by administrators (department heads, deans, directors, presidents, et al.) that discourage students from taking sides in faculty disputes and faculty from soliciting support from students. In the Lori vs. Tenman case, coalitions of faculty and students were formed on both sides. Each gathered a collection of faculty and student supporters and consequently spread the dispute as more faculty and students became involved.

Likewise with the faculty versus administration struggles. Some students are easily drawn into these problems. When this happens, disputes become more intense, and jobs and positions are frequently at stake. Similar conditions occur when intrafaculty disputes escalate and involve students in them.

A basic process for dealing with faculty-faculty and faculty-administration problems is the presence of grievance procedures and/or guidelines that define university policy and the processes for dealing with violations. These often can deescalate disputes and can be adapted to use in faculty-student relationships as well as with faculty and administration. Many universities have developed grievance procedures, policy positions on conflicts of interest in student-faculty relationships, and guidelines on consenting relationships for the campus that are useful in dealing with these kinds of disputes. [2]

Preventive Procedures for Dealing with Disputes

Faculty and students alike need to be encouraged to explore ways to prevent disputes and conflicts. By prevention I do not mean avoidance, suppression, or commands as methods. Prevention is engineering the contexts of the relationships so that the struggles do not escalate and become destructive and violent. Struggles will arise, no matter how carefully we plan the context. Even the most loving of partners will encounter differences that, if not resolved, will escalate to disputes. The essence of prevention is the containment of these conditions so that they do not destroy the relationships or the systems.

An important underlying principle of prevention is to provide opportunities for the students and faculty to share in the common problem of stopping differences from escalating into serious disputes that need intervention. Preventive services are procedures that are available or are set in motion prior to the escalation of disputes to the more violent levels of the struggle spectrum. They are the prophylactics of conflict.

Preventive methods include developing cooperative relationships, increasing skills in joint problem solving and decision-making, facilitating communication among all parties to the system, and seeking to discover and deal with differences before they escalate to the violent end of the spectrum.

Office of Student Affairs

A useful preventive by both faculty and department leaders is to understand the functions and services provided by the office of student affairs in the institution. Most such offices provide special services to deal with disputes involving students. Administrators should provide opportunities for faculty to become cognizant of the student affairs offices and their several programs, particularly those that can assist in preventing disputes between faculty and students.

Advisory Groups

Another preventive approach is for a department or division to provide for a representative group of students to serve as advisors to the administration regarding current and impending struggles arising within the department or school. Such groups are very useful in providing early warning of upcoming struggles that may escalate. Sometimes such a group within a school or division can be formed with a student from each of the departments.

Creating a context where the escalation of disputes is difficult or unlikely is important to managing struggle within the institution as a whole, but it has particular values for dealing with student-faculty problems. However, the context is not enough. Along with the atmosphere that allows for differences but encourages management of disputes, there must be special services to deal with disputes threatening to get beyond the control of the parties.

When possible, it is important to set in motion as many of these procedures as possible. Department heads can encourage faculty to discuss potential problems with their students and to build into their syllabi suggestions and methods for dealing with problems arising in class between the teacher and the students. Deans can organize student representatives and department heads in monthly overview sessions to scan the problems between students and faculty that may escalate into serious disputes. Department heads can organize special student-faculty seminars on conflict management for faculty and students within the department. Departments can work out a policies and procedures statement which involves procedures for dealing with differences and disputes and make these into a department document distributed to all faculty and majors within that department.

Preventive services should not be relegated just to single events, either large or small, or to one-time shows. It is important that the preventive services be year-round and available to the campus population as needed. Their main purpose is to find the potential disputes in the community and to create opportunities for these matters to be resolved before they become disputes. They also should provide tools and contexts where future potential disputes can be prevented from taking place or escalating to serious or destructive levels.

INTERVENTION PROCEDURES FOR DEALING WITH DISPUTES

The struggle spectrum shows that some procedures are more useful at certain stages of a dispute than at others. When the parties simply disagree and still communicate with each other with some civility, there is usually no need for an intervention. It is only when the parties become unable to deal with their dispute themselves that some form of intervention becomes important.

Mediation
Mediation is a dispute resolution form of intervention that is useful when a dispute first escalates beyond the disagreement stage to a point where it is difficult for the parties to communicate with each other, and it appears that the parties are becoming polarized.

> Mediation is an intervention by an impartial third person into an
> already existing process of negotiation in order to facilitate the joint

decision-making process between people who are becoming polarized and are colliding unproductively over differences in goals, methods, values, perceptions, and interests. The mediator makes no decisions for the parties, has no authority to direct or control the action of the parties, and can only work effectively when both parties are willing to use the process (Keltner, 1994, p. 102).

Parties to a dispute may voluntarily choose to try to resolve their dispute through this process. Properly used, the mediator facilitates the parties in continuing negotiations toward a resolution of the disagreement that has now become a dispute. A mediator or mediators should be selected by the parties themselves. It is unwise to assign a mediator to the parties when they have had no part in the selection process. I recommend that you use a mediator who has 150–200 hours of professional training and experience in the process. The selection is usually from a panel of available trained mediators provided by the university or from professional mediators in the community.

Mediators do not make decisions for the parties. They must be impartial. They assist in the negotiations but do not negotiate themselves. Their function is to facilitate the process whereby the parties work out their own solution to their problems. The intervention of the mediator into the process changes the dimensions and context of the struggle and can lead to new, more productive interactions between the parties. Before mediation can be effective, several things must occur. The parties must want to settle their dispute and be willing to meet in mediation. The mediator must be highly trained and experienced.

A campus mediation service can be organized on the campus in several ways. There may be trained faculty members who will serve as mediators. Rosters of available and adequately trained mediators can be provided by the office of student affairs, by the administration, or by an ombudsperson. It is often useful to have trained and qualified mediators from the community serve on campus rosters.

Disputants can be referred to mediation by anyone. It is still the responsibility of the parties to select the mediation process. A department head may recommend that a professor and a student go to mediation, but it is the right of the professor and the student to choose whether or not to go. This volunteerism is vital to the success of the mediation process. When parties are forced to go to mediation, it is likely to be ineffective unless there is a highly effective mediator involved.

Professor Trent and graduate student advisee Tom were at great odds over the handling of Tom's required program for the Ph.D. Rather than ask for a change of major professors, and in spite of some vitriolic exchanges between the two, Tom wanted to try to work it out before it went to his graduate committee. The department chair, upon hearing of the dispute, called the two to his office and recommended that they should go to mediation. Neither the student or the professor knew anything about mediation, so the department chair gave them some literature on the nature of the mediation process. Both student and teacher examined the material, asked questions of the chair, and talked with people who had been through mediation. They finally agreed to mediate and asked the chair to suggest a mediator. He gave them a list of several mediators who were on the faculty of other departments. It is important that both parties agree on the mediator. Trent and Tom reviewed the list and selected a woman they both knew and respected. She agreed to work with them and set a date for their first mediation session. She helped them look at the underlying interests they both had and helped them negotiate a program and set of procedures that both accepted. They wrote up their agreement and submitted it to the graduate school, where it was accepted.

When used properly and with sufficiently qualified mediators, the process can be very effective with disputants who are simply not able to work things out by themselves.

Arbitration

The arbitration process is different from mediation. It is a quasijudicial system where the dispute is heard and reviewed and a decision is made by an impartial third person or persons who are not involved in the dispute and have no stake in the outcome. In arbitration, the parties to the dispute do not make the final decision and, in most cases, agree in advance to abide by the decision of the arbitrator(s).

When a dispute goes to arbitration, it usually has progressed beyond the stage where mediation is useful. The issue(s) are usually more polarized and specific. When the parties go to arbitration, they abandon their right to resolve the dispute themselves.

A more formal procedure is followed in arbitration than in mediation. At a hearing type of meeting, the disputants present their positions to the arbitrator(s) and introduce evidence (including oral testimony, interrogation, and documents) to support these positions. The situation resembles a courtroom although it is not as formal as a court, nor does it have courtroom rules and practices. The areas of similarity with the court include the third party decision-making and some procedural processes. Likewise, some of the usual rules of evidence apply, particularly the rules regarding hearsay. The arbitrator has the right to evaluate what evidence is submitted.

Like the mediator, the arbitrator should be impartial, trained, and experienced in the process of arbitration. It helps when arbitrators of student-faculty disputes have some experience in the field or context within which the dispute has arisen. The parties must be free to select the arbitrator(s), usually from a list provided to them. [3]

On the campus, it is a useful practice to have student-faculty arbitration panels. These teams should be three-person teams. A student and a faculty member are first chosen, and these two then select the third person who will serve as chair of the panel. The panel as a whole then hears the matter and prepares the decision.

At the hearing, the parties may have representation if they so desire. The arbitrators will interrogate the parties to clarify positions and to test the evidence submitted. Usually the matter for the arbitrator to decide is framed as a question accepted by both parties as "the issue." For example, "Did Professor X violate the rights of student Y when he rejected him from class?"or "Did Professor X harass student Y during class on October 16, and if so what is the appropriate action to be taken?" or "Was student Y unfairly prevented from repeating an exam she failed, and if so what is the remedy?" or "Did Professor X denigrate the women in his class or women in general when he lectured on the Vietnam War on April 15, 1996, and if so what is the remedy?" When the parties are unable to agree on what the issue is, the arbitrators may, after hearing the beginning statements, provide a statement of the issue.

When the presentations have been concluded to the satisfaction of the parties, the arbitrators will then make a decision. Sometimes the decision is given immediately after a short break. More frequently the arbitrators will take several days or weeks to study the matter and then present a written decision concerning the dispute. This is particularly important when the decision is final and binding and when the matter involves matters of policy that affect the institution.

Ombudsperson

Many schools have an ombudsperson or an ombuds office as part of its system. Such a person can perform very valuable services to the campus student-faculty community. An ombudsperson may be a process facilitator, a spokesperson (sometimes), a problem solver, a confidential investigator, a trained listener, a protected communication pipeline to other entities, and a professional neutral. She or he may also be a mediator.

According to the University and College Ombudsman Association, an ombudsman is defined as one who has:

- The responsibility to assess grievances and conflicts and attempt to resolve them through available institutional channels or by mediation

- Access, in the performance of duties, to members of the university community and to university records

- The prerogative to recommend corrective action at any institutional level where necessary

- The authority to issue public reports concerning findings and recommendations and the obligation to maintain a standard of neutrality

The ombudsperson may either refer the parties to mediation or may, if properly trained, attempt mediation if the parties so desire. The ombudsperson maintains strict confidentiality about the matters of the disputants and the dispute. No formal or informal reports to administrators or other officers about the dispute are made without approval of the parties involved.

Ombudspersons exist in many local government offices, on college campuses, in healthcare systems, in workplace settings, and they are a valuable resource for connecting people and organizations. In recent years the function has received increased interest and application. UCLA, for example, has a campus ombuds office for all members of the university including student versus faculty disputes.

The skilled ombudsperson may mediate and/or arbitrate when selected. However, the ombudsperson responsibility is much wider than that of a mediator or arbitrator. Liaison with administration, with other agencies, with helping services, and with each of the adversaries all fall within the scope of the ombudsperson.

RESOLUTION OPTIONS IN DEALING WITH STUDENT-FACULTY DISPUTES

Generally the stage in the struggle spectrum where the resolution occurs has some effect on the form (and sometimes the nature) of the resolution. Several kinds of options occur along the spectrum: voluntary settlement-resolution agreement, mandated (third party) resolution, deescalation, punishment, and oversight.

Settlement

The voluntary settlement agreement occurs mostly as a result of mediation in the earlier stages of the struggle spectrum where mediation is used and is an agreement-resolution that the parties reach themselves. The mandated resolution emerges from arbitration and the courts where the decision is handed down by others than the contending parties.

Settlements have interesting dimensions. A settlement agreement may be conditional. It may contain conditions that are prerequisite to the final settlement as in the case of a student who had missed the final examination and agreed to retake the final exam not later than one month after the termination of the class and only after completing all other written assignments.

Settlements of disputes up through the mediation stage usually appear on the campus in the form of oral agreements or handshakes between the parties. When the dispute escalates to arbitration, the settlement is usually written.

Deescalation

Deescalation occurs when highly polarized or violent situations are defused so that the parties are able to communicate with each other and/or use third party interventions to resolve the dispute.

A basic condition of disputes that have gone to litigation, campaign, or violence is that the voluntary forms of struggle management or intervention will simply not work while the violence or litigation continues. For example, a student had charged a faculty member with discrimination, and the matter had bypassed some of the grievance process and was in the final stages of the process where the university administration was to make a decision. Both parties were strongly established in their positions, had accumulated a following among campus colleagues and students, and were anticipating the decision of the administration. The dean suggested that the faculty member attend a workshop on discrimination that was occurring on campus. The workshop impressed the faculty member so much that she made contact with the student and arranged for a private meeting to discuss the possibilities of mediation. The situation changed when it deescalated from the stage of final decision by the administration to a point where the parties worked together and solved the problem.

In situations where there is violence or high polarization in a win-lose context, there must be deescalation before any of the nonviolent processes can take place. I remember vividly one time when I thought I would intervene in a street fight and mediate the dispute. Instead I caught a wild swing in the eye and carried a lump on my head for several weeks.

It is not likely that the parties will cease hostilities to mediate, go through grievance procedures, or arbitrate when they are in the middle of a violent polarized confrontation, and each seeks to win the dispute by defeating the other. The violence must be halted before they can substantially address their differences.

Intervention. Deescalation can occur through a number of strategies. One significant process is the intervention of stronger parties into the situation. When the cops arrive, the street fight subsides. The intervention of a dean often cools down a student-faculty imbroglio. Power interventions often stop the violence or slow it down.

Level II diplomacy. Another process of deescalation is what is called "level II diplomacy" in which interested parties who are not directly involved in the violent confrontation pressure the participants to forgo the violence and seek a peaceful solution. This process is a well-known one in the field of international diplomacy (Diamond & McDonald, 1996). It is also quite useful in the interpersonal field characteristic of the campus. Many outside pressures can be brought to bear on student-faculty disputants through colleagues, administrators, fellow students, professional organizations, and the like. Deescalation occurred when a student was threatening to take her male professor to court on charges of harassment, but her roommates told her to pull back because she may have misunderstood the actions of the professor, and her testimony would not hold up in court.

Reframing. Reframing is one of the strategies that facilitate deescalation. Helping the parties reframe their dispute or alter their perceptions of what the dispute is really all about is a significant tool often used by mediators. Administrators can use it also when the dispute comes to their attention. A meeting with the department head was one of the grievance steps in a dispute over a grade. The student's position was that he had been given a grade much lower than he deserved; the teacher claimed that he got what he earned. The department head, after hearing both of their perceptions of the dispute, reframed it as "Does this affect your passing the course?"

Refined communication. Another strategy is to help the parties get into a different kind of communication with each other that is not based on a win-lose perception. Mary and her teacher refused to talk with each other about Mary's allegation that the teacher was discriminating against her in making a special assignment that Mary wanted very much. The department chair brought them together and asked them to address their particular problem to the other. Once they started talking with each other, it became clear that the nature of the assignment was misunderstood by Mary and that she could do the work she preferred to do.

Changed focus. A frequently used strategy of deescalation is to change the focus to other problems or struggles that are vital to the parties. When the parties discover that they have a common cause, they are more likely to abandon rigid or intense win-lose positions. For example, when the dean helped a professor and a graduate student discover that the program they were struggling over was going to be dropped, they joined forces to prevent that from happening. They discovered that they had joint goals in keeping the program on the campus.

Carrot and stick tactics are sometimes necessary to deescalate a difficult situation. A department chair threatened to withhold promotion recommendation for a faculty member if she continued to have difficulties with her students. On the other hand, a dean suggested that special recognition be given to faculty members who had no disputes with students over a period of two years.

All of these strategies for deescalation are usable in campus disputes by the administrators and others closely associated with the parties to the disputes. However, they depend on the existence of skilled people in the administrative offices of the student body and the institution: A student affairs office, an academic affairs office, a faculty development office, or leaders of the faculty or student senates play a very vital role. The leadership of the student body or the faculty is highly instrumental in helping to deescalate disputes. Likewise, the faculty senates themselves and other representative bodies may have considerable influence on helping faculty change their perception and conditions of disputes. It is important that the administrators take advantage of these various venues in dealing with faculty-student struggles.

Punishments

Punishment occurs as a result of court decisions and/or as a result of violence in the dispute. Oversight occurs as an avoidance. As a general rule, punishment of one or all the participants in a dispute between faculty and students may not be productive, except in extraordinary circumstances. Generally, the quiver of punishments in the hands of the institutional leadership can range from mild to extreme. For the faculty, punishments may range from warning, reprimand, unpaid leave, salary adjustment, reduction or no advancement in rank, transfer, and finally termination if all else fails. For the student, punishments may range from warning, reprimand, suspension, and when all else fails, dismissal.

Punishment for faculty-student disputes is rare and should be used only as a last resort when the unresolved dispute threatens serious damage to the institution. The institution should not use punishment as a method of controlling disputes but instead the other methods we have discussed here.

CONCLUSION

Faculty-student disputes are a constant part of the academic campus. They range in a spectrum from minor disagreements to major violent confrontations and matters that involve legal interventions. The tools for management of struggle on the campus must be widespread throughout the faculty and its leadership, the student body and its leadership, and the administration. Offices such as student affairs and academic affairs play a significant part in setting up the dispute resolution processes, providing instruction in the use of the processes, and offering a constant resource for service.

The most important way to deal with student-faculty struggle on the campus is to create an atmosphere (context) of partnership among administration, students, and faculty in the teaching/learning process. This partnership runs the length and breadth of the institution. It needs to be accented in all the campus affairs of the institution and by all the officers of the system.

The purpose of such systems is not to eliminate conflict but to manage it so that healthy struggle and productive disagreement can exist without escalating to violence and destruction of the essential inner body of the learning institution. Had there been better dispute management tools and concepts known by and available to Fred Davidson, his graduate advisor and committee might still be alive.

ENDNOTES

1. See discussion of The Struggle Spectrum in Keltner, John W., *The Management of Struggle*. Also see The Struggle Spectrum, Program #1 of a series of videotapes depicting the role of mediation and mediators in facilitating the resolution of divorce-family, labor-management, and community disputes. Produced by the Communication Media Center, Oregon State University, Corvallis, Oregon.

2. Most large universities have grievance procedures. A characteristic one is the Grievance Procedure for Faculty, Fellows, and the Student Body of Johns Hopkins University Medical School. Many schools have student grievance committees. The University of Maine has a set of Guidelines on Counseling Relationships. The University of Victoria (Canada) has a set of Guidelines on Conflict of Interest in Student-Faculty Relationships.

3. The usual procedure for the selection is to flip a coin as to who has the first choice of rejection, and then the parties alternatively reject arbitrators

until one remains, and that arbitrator becomes the one chosen. The usual list includes five or seven arbitrators so that after each disputant has equal rejections, one arbitrator remains.

REFERENCES

Diamond, L. & McDonald, J. (1996). *Multi-track diplomacy: A system approach to peace* (3rd ed.). West Hartford, CT: Kumarian Press.

Keltner, J. W. (1994). *The management of struggle: Elements of dispute resolution through negotiation, mediation, and arbitration.* Cresskill, NJ: Hampton Press.

Perry, T., & O'Conner, A. (1996, August 17). Suspect in campus killings angry over criticism. *The Oregonian,* p. 3.

STUDENT-STUDENT CONFLICT: WHOSE PROBLEM IS IT ANYWAY?

DEANS AND CHAIRS AS PROBLEM SOLVERS: CHALLENGING THE MANAGERIAL PARADIGM

The American university is in the process of being reconceptualized. While multiple rhetorics are being generated to explain and justify this transformation, economic necessity is the primary force driving much of this discourse. There is no longer any serious debate about the fact that institutions of higher education need to be managed, that they are similar to corporations and companies, and that the tools of modern management should be applied to universities which are no longer being understood as remote, ivory towers. In this context, deans, chairs of departments, and other administrators are no longer thought of as intellectual leaders, but as managers and supervisors. Institutions are divided into separate departments, and the organizational chart reflects a structure and chain of command which allocates responsibility and power in ways that purport to be rational and manageable. As a managed institution, the power relations between the various constituents also needs management. In this context, grievance procedures are developed, rights and responsibilities are delineated and protected in various policies and procedures, and appeals processes are built into most institutional dispute resolution systems.

Managerial administration has its limitations. As managers, deans and chairs are required to oversee the daily operation of their part of the larger bureaucracy and they are rewarded for their efficiency. But bureaucracies create problems for people, particularly for students who, because they are the least experienced with bureaucratic processes, are the most vulnerable constituency on campus. The managerial model of administration contributes this vulnerability, as this approach tends to obscure the need for problem solving skills. Deans and chairs are called upon to mediate conflicts, yet are not trained or educated to see themselves as troubleshooters or problem solvers. As a consequence, students and others are frequently forced to cope with concerns on their own. If deans and department chairs are involved in situations, it is too often the case that their role becomes adversarial. To succeed as a managerial administrator, deans and chairs need to understand their work and define themselves as multidimensional: As agents of the institution, their task is to administer efficiently; as agents of the faculty, their task is to lead effectively; and, as agents of the students, their task is to facilitate their academic and social success, goals which can be met only if the administrator is available to them. This last task is the easiest to ignore, yet it is perhaps the most important.

While the organizational structure of colleges and universities differ among institutions, institutions of higher education are grappling with increasingly complex economic, demographic, and social factors that challenge many of the traditional assumptions about academic life. As part of this tradition, institutions are built around prototypical organizational models, in which hierarchically structured and specialized units have jurisdiction over very defined subject matters and subjects. Most universities, for example, are divided into separate units, such as academic affairs, student affairs, administration and finance, and continuing education. In this context, administrators focus on the concerns and issues relevant to their bailiwick, the primary goal of which is the protection and guardianship of their turf. While there is collaboration, cooperation, and some joint planning across these units, there is also an undercurrent of tension and competition for resources and recognition among these respective administrative units. While strategic planning attempts to address some organizational problems, it often reinforces this segmentation. Rather than developing holistic approaches to institutional change and development, strategic plans tend to ignore the ways that the organizational structure itself impedes the achievement of the goals formulated in the plan. There is a logic which drives this organizational approach, as the division of colleges and universities into specialized units can clarify divisions of labor, delineate varying tasks, and give coherence to administrative roles and job responsibilities. But this approach is also potentially damaging, as administrators at different levels of the institution are forced to think and act myopically, thinking primarily of what is in the best interest of their unit. As a consequence, colleges and universities are bureaucratized, and administrators begin to think and function as bureaucrats.

The bureaucratized university is particularly problematic for students and for those who work with them. Educating students is at the heart of a university's mission, and that responsibility, in theory, drives the activities of the institution as a whole. The primary responsibility, however, for student life resides in the student affairs sector, within which are housed the administrative units that deal with residential life, student activities, student health, discipline, and other areas involving student related functions. The staff in these units are generally considered to be the professional experts regarding student affairs, and the institutional expectation is that this staff will attend to and resolve most student related issues. Indeed, student affairs administrators do, in fact, attend to most of these concerns, providing students and the institution with oversight and responsibility for managing complex activities and resolving complex problems. At the same time, however, the institution may rely too heavily on student affairs professionals not only to do the work related to students' concerns, but to be the people who are primarily responsible to think about these concerns as well. As a consequence, administrators and staff in academic affairs tend to relinquish their responsibility to be educated about the social realities of students. One result is that they are either unprepared for some of the issues they might face or uninterested in problems that are brought to them, leaving many matters to fester and deepen.

Academic deans and department chairs, in particular, are involved in both day-to-day and long-range activities which involve and affect students and their interests. Their concerns, however, are primarily attached to academic matters. Although they are required to negotiate a range of complex issues relating to curricular, faculty/student, and other academically oriented tasks, they do so with little reference to policies and practices administered within the arena of student affairs. In many cases, decisions are made without the full knowledge of relevant policy. Without a comprehensive, multi-institutional perspective, academic administrators may make incomplete and inappropriate decisions. This can be particularly problematic in the area of student-student conflict, an arena of trouble which is generally understood to be within the jurisdiction of student affairs. But student-student conflicts cross into the academic sector as well, and administrators in this sector are likely to be unprepared for the problem because they do not fundamentally believe that problems between students are problems for which they are responsible. In addition, those few academic administrators who accept responsibility for conflicts of this type are often untrained and unprepared to actually deal with student-student related concerns.

STUDENT-STUDENT CONFLICT: WHY DEANS AND DEPARTMENT CHAIRS SHOULD GET INVOLVED TO HELP RESOLVE THESE PROBLEMS AND WHAT THEY SHOULD DO

While many students flourish in college environments, they inevitably face myriad situations which challenge their ability to coexist with others, to develop constructive relationships with their peers and mentors, and to thrive both academically and socially. Perhaps those who are most disconnected from the daily realities of student life are academic deans and department chairs, despite the fact that they are central to students' academic programs, the most essential part of students' life. And one of the most neglected and least understood arenas involves student-student conflicts which are pervasive, diverse, potentially violent, often inflammatory, and always painful. Academic administrators need to be educated about the nature and effect of these kinds of conflicts and to develop some managerial and problem solving approaches for their selective facilitation. Some may argue that this is a job for student affairs administration. While the management and resolution of student-student conflict should primarily reside within student affairs, academic administrators need to intervene in certain types of these disputes and would be well-served to know more about the rules and norms of student life.

Some working in academic administration will ask why they should bother to pay attention to these kinds of problems. This is indeed a legitimate question given the complexities and burdens of their jobs. There are, however, a number of examples which may illuminate why deans and department chairs should interest themselves in some aspects of student-student conflict. Consider the scenarios to follow, each of which is fictional, but drawn from a composite of situations that have occurred on campuses throughout the country. They are meant to represent types of situations involving student-student conflict that academic deans and department chairs confront. They also raise questions about the obligation and role of the academic administrator. For example, is this the type of conflict that belongs within their jurisdictional arena? If not, in what jurisdiction does it belong? If it remains with the dean or the chair, what should that person actually do about the situation? What are the consequences of referring the problem elsewhere? What if there are no clear-cut avenues for the problem's management? What questions should the dean or the chair be asking? Whom should they be questioning? What and whose counsel should they seek? While administrators need to consider problems and their response on a case-by-case basis, it can be helpful to have a more general conceptual reference point to guide individual decision-making. The following steps are offered as a frame of reference and as a potential analytic and strategic tool that a dean or a department chair might use in fashioning a response to a specific situation.

1. Problem Clarification and Information Gathering: What Kind of Problem Is This?

While this seems simple, what many overlook is that these concerns can be answered only if the right questions are asked. It is important to not only think about what is asked but how questions are asked, setting a tone and creating a context so that people feel comfortable talking. This is an information gathering stage, and as such, it is important that the parameters of confidentiality are delineated. (If confidentiality does not apply, it would be helpful to be clear about that.)

2. Option Generation: What Are Some Ways of Dealing with the Concerns Presented?

During this phase of the discussion, the dean or department chair should be thinking about what avenues exist for resolving the problem. What other administrators or campus services might be useful here? It is important to consider a broad range of options. Rather than narrow the problem to a limited solution, generate a list of possibilities. In order to do this, it is important to think about communication style, ensuring that parties involved feel able to participate in this phase of problem solving.

3. Closure: What Options Will Be Pursued to Achieve Resolution, and Who Is Going to Do What?

After choosing the course of action that makes the most sense, make sure to clarify specifically what the respective parties agree to do. It is important to be clear about what next steps, if any, the administrator has agreed to pursue in order to avoid any potential future confusion. While not always necessary, it can be helpful to write up an action plan. It is also helpful for the administrator to keep personal notes, rather than to rely on memory.

4. Follow-Up: Has the Administrator Followed Through and Kept the Student Informed?

Lack of follow through is a frequent source of conflict. It is important that the student is made aware of the steps that the dean or chair has taken, even if this involves nothing more than a referral to another office. Again, communication is a critical part of this process.

SCENARIO #1

In a large, introductory general education course, which includes a writing requirement, the professor requires that students occasionally work on group projects. In one such project, the students were required to do a series of peer evaluations of each other's first draft of a writing assignment. The professor was brusque, and many students felt he was unapproachable, albeit a good teacher. Toward the latter half of the semester, a female student made an appointment with the department chair and told him that she wanted to drop the course, a requirement for her major as well as a university requirement, because a male student had been writing sexually offensive comments on her peer evaluation papers. She felt that she was being sexually harassed, and rather than pursue anything formal, she wanted to drop the course. She showed the chair one of the papers. The comments stated "you look better than you write. I love it when you sit next to me. I'm going to ask to critique all of you, not just your papers." She didn't want to talk to the professor who seemed uninterested. The teaching assistant had told her to "grow up and do your work." She was trying to move off campus, because the student who had written these comments apparently knew where she lived and had been seen hanging around her dormitory. Although it was technically too late in the semester to drop the course, department chairs can often bend the rules.

Problem Clarification and Information Gathering

The primary issue here involves the allegation of sexual harassment, and although it is not necessarily the academic administrator's job to handle it, the institution is required by law to take immediate and effective action once having been made aware of a sexual harassment claim. In this case, it is the department chair's legal obligation to address this allegation. Because few administrators understand the parameters of this type of problem, an important first step is to contact the agency on campus responsible for sexual harassment complaints. This is usually the affirmative action office, but may vary from campus to campus. If the student does not wish to disclose her identity, it is not required to reveal her name during this information gathering phase. It is, however, important to discuss with the student what her needs are concerning confidentiality.

Option Generation

During this phase, chairs should make sure that they are aware of the relevant university policies and procedures, so that the student can be informed of her rights. At this point, it might be appropriate to alert the dean or other appropriate persons in the chain of command, making sure that the student is informed of these disclosures. Both the dean and the department chair need to expand their knowledge and understanding of sexual harassment and its management on their campus in order to generate as many appropriate options as possible. Another important option to consider is whether the chair has an obligation to intervene with the professor and teaching assistant about the tone of the classroom exchanges and about the classroom dynamics. Many chairs and deans feel reluctant to get involved in this kind of problem on the grounds of interfering with academic freedom. But not taking action may result in more problems and interference with the education of students.

Closure

At this point, the chair should consider which interventions make the most sense. While taking direct and personal action on some of the more academically related aspects of this matter, the chair might call upon other campus agencies—the ombuds office, for example—for assistance with other parts of this problem, such as pursuing formal action or mediation on the harassment issue.

Follow-Up

The chair should let the student know what has been done or is in the process of being done. It would be helpful to find ways to discuss this matter with the faculty member as well. It might be helpful to raise the general problem of student harassment with the department as a whole, to explore how to use certain pedagogies, such as peer critiques, without surfacing these kinds of problems.

SCENARIO #2

In an upper level seminar in the English department, students were required to make several oral presentations during the course of the semester. The class was composed of 20 students, 18 of them white, one African-American, and one exchange student from India. The professor was a white woman who had been teaching Narratives from the Third World for the past few years. The professor had found it effective to have students give each other feedback at the end of their presentations, the goal of which was to present a coherent, articulate, well-argued analysis of one of the assigned readings. During the second presentation by the African-American student, a couple of the other students began to snicker and write notes to each other. These students interrupted the presentation several times asking the presenter to clarify points, to speak up, and to repeat things. During the critique, these students monopolized the discussion. They said that they felt that this student's presentation was weak, incomprehensible, and that this student should take some basic courses in proper English. The student was visibly upset and ran from the room. At this point, the student from India shouted that this was a racist attack, that these students had been antagonist and hostile since the beginning of the semester, that the professor was complicit in this racism by having allowed the students to attack the black student, and that she was going to the dean right after the class to demand that something be done.

Problem Clarification and Information Gathering

One of the primary issues to be clarified is whether the behaviors of the students constituted a violation of any university policy. The dean needs to investigate what policies are applicable, and the first step in this process is to ask the right people at the institution, including the dean of students or whoever is in charge of administering the disciplinary system for the campus. During this phase, the dean should also meet with both the complaining and accused parties. These meetings would allow the dean to do some fact finding and to make the symbolic statement that what goes on in the classroom is part of what an academic dean cares about and is the kind of matter about which the dean will take action.

Option Generation

The academic dean might decide to turn part of the conflict over to the dean of students for investigation and processing. In this event, however, the academic dean needs to stay apprised of the situation and not relinquish her interest in the problem. During this phase, the dean should explore whether there is any formal or informal recourse for the claim of racial harassment, as this is generally a murky area at most institutions. This would require discussions with other agencies on campus as well as discussions with the parties, as the dean may have to decide the answer to this question. Although there may be no clear institutional policies on this issue, nor clear actions that the dean should take, it is important to create some options, such as sponsoring ongoing discussion groups on the issue, guest speakers, symposia, or brown bag lunch sessions. By taking an active role in the creation of more options, the dean or the chair is in the position to help deescalate racial conflict.

Closure
As in the first case, the dean may want to use the services of the ombuds office or other advocacy agencies on campus that focus on questions of civility and social justice. Since there may be no other recourse, the dean may want to act as a facilitator of some ongoing discussions of these issues.

Follow-Up
The dean needs to ensure that the measures that have been promised actually occur. This is a watchdog role for the dean, a time-consuming job, but one that will likely have benefits for future racial encounters.

SCENARIO #3

In Business 241, the professor assigned two group projects which counted for 50% of the students' grades, as well as a midterm and a final exam which accounted for the other 50%. At the end of the semester, several students complained to the department chair that their grades were unfair, that they had done all the work for the two group projects, and that one member of the group had done no more than copy a few graphs and tables. They were outraged that this student had received the same grade as they had. In addition, they complained that this student had plagiarized some of the material he had used in the introduction of the first project. They were concerned that they not be held accountable for his acts, even though all of their names were on the project.

Problem Clarification and Information Gathering
This is a case in which the pedagogical method of the faculty member, while meant to enhance student learning, creates conflict among students. The mandates of academic freedom limit what the chair can actually do here. For example, the chair should not change the students' grades, alter the syllabus, or interfere with the faculty's teaching. The chair cannot unilaterally punish any of the parties, nor can the chair take action on the academic dishonesty charge. But the chair should nonetheless investigate the complaint by talking with all the parties to clarify what it is that they are

actually seeking. Are they seeking a change of grade? A charge of academic dishonesty? A grievance against the professor? What type of outcome would satisfy them?

Option Generation

Depending on the type of relief being requested, there are a number of options the chair can explore. One option would be to contact the academic honesty board or its equivalent. On some campuses, it would make sense to contact the dean of students, or whichever office oversees discipline. The chair may want to explore with the faculty member possible ways to restructure the course to avoid these dilemmas. On some campuses, there are faculty workshops which focus on how to design these projects, and the chair may want to make such a resource available to the faculty member.

Closure

If it turns out there is little formal recourse for these students, the chair needs to be clear to them about this fact. The chair might let the students know what steps are being taken not only in regards to their complaint, but more generally as well.

Follow-Up

The chair needs to be available to the students for future discussions if necessary. While this might seem obvious, many students complain not so much about the unavailability of department heads, but about their invisibility. Chairs are in a unique position to facilitate the kind of conflict presented in this case because they have no formal power to adjudicate or mandate a resolution for this type of dispute. Because, in this type of case, they are not charged with the obligation to make or impose the rules, their role is advisory and can be potentially mediative. To ignore this problem is to undermine the academic goals of the institution and the quality of education being provided.

SCENARIO #4

In an experimental freshman writing class, students were expected to keep on-line journals which they would email to their professor once a week, with the expectation that the professor would email his comments in return. Although the university issues passwords to students on the condition that they are to be kept confidential, one student in this class got another student's password and started using that student's account. Using this stolen account, the student began to send threatening messages to other students in the class. The department chair became aware of this situation and went to the dean for advice.

Problem Clarification and Information Gathering

The first step for both the chair and the dean is to investigate whether the institution has any formal policies that address the misuse of electronic media. The dean of students' office would be a good source of information, as would the office of information technology or its equivalent. In addition, the office which manages computer accounts should be notified as it probably has relevant information.

Option Generation

Based on the information gathered, this problem may be referred to the office which has authority for investigating these types of complaints. In addition, the appropriate office may be notified to determine whether the student's computer privileges should be revoked. The specific member, as well as the entire faculty, should be informed about the rules related to computer use. This information can help avoid problems in the future, as faculty can include appropriate notice in their syllabi, giving students advanced notice of the consequences of a violation. If it turns out that there are few relevant policies, the dean may want to develop and implement a separate policy for her particular school or college. Some department chairs may want to create departmental level policies. But in either case, the policies need to conform to university policy and practice. Finally, the dean may want to contact university counsel.

Closure

The dean should try and meet with the students involved to get input from them on what types of institutional policy would make sense. These meetings could take place as a face-to-face discussion, but an on-line discussion might also be an appropriate and useful option.

Follow-Up

The dean might want to monitor whether these kinds of problems are becoming more frequent, as the university becomes more reliant on electronic technologies. The dean might consider forming a standing faculty committee with student representation that could track issues related to emerging technology.

CONCLUSION

All of these examples point to the value of involving academic administrators in some student-student conflicts. Their involvement is not usually formally mandated, nor is it necessarily geared to a formal resolution of the problem. It is important, nonetheless, as it signifies the interest of the academic sector in student issues. It signifies that these issues are not to be relegated to one part of the university, and that the administration is a whole which interacts and collaborates dynamically on a range of concerns and problems. But these examples also point to the need for deans and department chairs to gain competence in handling student-student disputes. To do this well requires that deans and department chairs define themselves, at least in part, as managers of communication, a role that requires some systematic approach to both conversational interaction and to action. The principles explored in this discussion will help to create a social context for students to enhance their academic and overall experience.

Joel M. Douglas

CONFLICT RESOLUTION IN THE ACADEMY: A MODEST PROPOSAL

THE NATURE OF CONFLICT

Tension in faculty and staff employment relationships is growing within American colleges and universities, and the pivotal issues are similar to those confronting other segments of the economy: downsizing, job security, financial independence, and compensation and benefits. Fueled by the economic conditions of the 1980s and 1990s, colleges and universities have reduced personnel costs as a means of ensuring their financial security. They have cut the number of tenure track positions and use more nontenure-stream faculty lines and adjuncts, and other forms of outsourcing. At the same time, workloads have been increased while traditional forms of academic job security and due process rights have been reduced. This new environment, while not universal, is sufficiently widespread to cause concern.

The academy is engaged in acts of workplace warfare that are being played out on the national scene:

- Yale University—graduate student unionization

- Harvard University—strikes by clerical employees

- University of Minnesota—threats to remove tenure

- City University of New York—litigation regarding the imposition of retrenchment and financial exigency violating university guidelines

- Adelphi University—dismissal of the board of trustees and subsequent removal of the president

- University of California, Berkeley, and University of California, Los Angeles—strikes and job actions by unions of graduate student employees

- State University of New York—prolonged negotiations over threats to privatize various functions including academic medical programs

The litigation potential is enormous. Many observers external to higher education express incredulity when learning of these difficulties. The romanticized vision of the academy as a bucolic workplace where faculty conduct research and teach without interruption persists, for the most part. Though this paradigm may exist at a handful of prestigious institutions, it is increasingly the exception rather than the rule. On most campuses the traditional industrial prototype of labor relations, with some modifications in the areas of governance and peer review, has been superimposed onto the academic model and has generated significant problems and increased the likelihood of litigation.

This chapter does not attempt to pass judgment on whether the fictionalized account of academic life is worth preserving. Instead, it concentrates on what happens when controversies over these issues erupt into clashes among the professoriate, staff, students, administrators, and agents of the employer, and how those conflicts are ultimately resolved. The chapter focuses on conflict resolution in the unionized setting of higher education and refers to the nucleus of alternative dispute resolution (ADR) techniques available in the academic workplace. It sets forth an organizational framework to assess conflict in higher education employment relationships and addresses concerns of supervisors and middle- to upper-level management, predominantly chairs, deans, and provosts. Acknowledging the role of external legal elements, including the collective bargaining agreement, decisions of labor boards, administrative agencies, courts, and arbitrators have on the process, the major concerns raised are addressed from a legal/structural perspective.

FACULTY RIGHTS VERSUS ADMINISTRATIVE POWER: THE EQUILIBRIUM TEST

Understanding power relationships within the academy is critical to assessing conflict resolution mechanisms. Faculty rights transcend the institution or employer and are rooted in the profession or academic discipline. In theory this premise is rarely disputed; in practice, it is frequently breached. In matters such as academic freedom or the ability to pursue independent research, faculty rights are recognized and pursued according to an established set of normative values. If administrators or boards of trustees attempt to interfere with these rights, then recourse within the profession, labor boards, arbitrators, or even the courts is not dependent upon the sanctity of the employing institution.

Additionally, the interests and investments of the faculty are not synonymous with those of administration or the institution. Faculty chose the professoriate for a variety of reasons, economic security being one of them. Few selected the academy as a means to accumulate wealth or to compete in a business setting with a focus on profits and the bottom line.

But faculty are now routinely required to perform certain business functions that formerly were not considered part of the job. For example, where the admission staff has been decimated, or the counseling staff drastically reduced, faculty may be required to assist in student recruitment. These assignments can, at times, be successfully performed by faculty who are interested in these areas and activities. The problem arises when these functions are made an integral part of the job description and must be performed at a time when teaching loads and research expectations have also increased. Faculty and administration rights clash, and while faculty may claim a shield of immunity from administrative and ministerial duties, management—often under pressure from a board of trustees—argues the opposite.

Many of these academic/business decisions are made by administrators who were schooled in a scholarly discipline and find themselves in supervisory positions where they are required to make judgments for which they have no training or experience. They in turn seek assistance from an unwilling faculty, thereby compounding the problem. Imagine a pharmaceutical research firm relying on laboratory scientists for support in selling and marketing their product; the company might soon collapse. Yet in the academy, historians, biologists, and economists may be required to counsel students and market programs that are unrelated to their professional training. It is this type of expectation that is often responsible for the conflicts in higher education.

These dilemmas are further compounded by the near total lack of leadership training programs within the academy. College administrators have traditionally risen through the ranks of the faculty, and while there is value in home-grown leadership, there is also danger in the paucity of training for the job. When the institution seeks direction from a business executive, government official, or military leader, the predicament is often exacerbated as the cultural clash and environmental differences may be too great to surmount. For example, when General Dwight D. Eisenhower became president of Columbia University, he welcomed the faculty by referring to them as *employees* of the university. He was quickly corrected—in no uncertain terms—that the faculty *were* the university. Equilibrium between faculty rights and administrative power is still a difficult subject for many on both sides of the issue to address, a fact about which those who seek to manage conflict in higher education conflict must be cognizant.

THE QUANDARY OF ACADEMIC MIDDLE MANAGEMENT: CHAIRS, DEANS, AND PROVOSTS

Collective bargaining and unionization have not been kind to department chairs, deans, and provosts. Anecdotal evidence suggests that on unionized campuses, the authority and power of chairs, deans, and provosts has diminished. What had been a strict hierarchical pyramid employment relationship with a well-defined chain of command and span of control has now been replaced, at least in theory, with faculty representatives enjoying a position that is level with agents of the college. This egalitarian relationship is legally enforceable before administrative agencies and courts and has placed academic managers in the ponderous position of not knowing where their own individual interests may lie. Although the economic condition of administrators at unionized campuses may have improved as a result of faculty bargaining, there is a scant evidence to suggest that chairs, deans, provosts, supervisors, and managers have otherwise benefitted.

In order to secure their own employment relationships, on some campuses chairs, deans, and provosts have attempted to unionize, either as a separate administrators' bargaining unit or as part of the faculty unit. Public sector academic managers have predominantly been found to be employees with the same commonality of interest for collective bargaining purposes as other faculty and, at times, have been placed within the faculty bargaining unit. For example, at the Connecticut State University system there is a unit dedicated to administrators. At the City University of New York, State University of New York, and Nassau Community College, administrators are included within rank-and-file faculty units; however, the administrators represented include chairs and some assistant or associate deans, but not academic deans or provosts.

At private colleges the supervisory and managerial exclusions reach far deeper, and it is rare to encounter bargaining units, either comprehensive or autonomous, which include department chairs. Private sector employers, including colleges and universities, are not required to collectively bargain with units containing supervisory or managerial employees. Supervisory employees have been statutorily excluded from coverage of the National Labor Relations Act (NLRA) since the enactment of Taft-Hartley Amendments in 1947. Affording statutory collective bargaining rights to managerial employees such as academic deans in either sector is far less likely and is virtually unheard of for provosts. The restriction against managers and supervisors collectively bargaining pursuant to the NLRA is not new and does not reflect a legal change. The qualifications are rooted in private sector labor law, and while academics may claim that the interpretation is fresh, managerial employees have never enjoyed the protection of the NLRA.

In *National Labor Relations Board v. Yeshiva University*, the United States Supreme Court found the faculty at Yeshiva University, a private institution under the jurisdiction of the NLRA, to be managerial employees and therefore not entitled to bargain collectively under statutory protection. Justice Powell, writing for the majority, noted that in any other setting the authority of the faculty would be managerial and that "... to the extent the industrial analogy applies, the faculty determines within each school the product to be produced, the terms of how it is to be offered, and the customers who will be served" (*National Labor Relations Board*, 1980). Until then, private sector faculties were able to retain union representation and fully participate in institutional governance. *Yeshiva* did not alter the rights of managers and supervisors but found that faculties were within those groups and reaffirmed the implied exclusion from the act for representatives of management. In subsequent cases the exclusion was applied to academics who possess supervisory authority (*Boston University*, 1984). Where then do chairs, deans, and provosts go to secure job security rights? Academic managers lack a union shield or any other organization framework to protect their employment interests. They are at-will employees who serve at the pleasure of the institution, and except for certain constitutional and statutory protections, they can be terminated for good reason, bad reason, or no reason. In most scenarios they are blocked either legally or administratively from enjoying the statutory right to bargain with their only job security limited to statutory rights, personal employment contracts, or on some campuses the right to depart their administrative post and retreat to their tenured faculty line.

CONFLICT RESOLUTION IN HIGHER EDUCATION

The labor relations model of the United States is adversarial and provides for a series of laws and regulations designed to ensure the uninterrupted flow of commerce, goods, and services while permitting employees the right to organize and take action—including the right to strike—to achieve their goals. Promulgated in the 1930s and 1940s, the National Labor Relations Act and its amendments presume adversarialism and establish a series of referees, including the National Labor Relations Board, to administer and interpret the law. Nearly all of the 40 states that have enacted legislation that permits public sector faculty and staff bargaining have based their laws on the NLRA, and while state statutes may be narrowly tailored and are jurisdiction-specific, the essential legal elements between the private and public sector statutes are parallel. This paradigm has been applied to private sector colleges and universities and regulates labor relations in 504 institutions covering 1,115 unionized campuses. Represented are approximately 250,000 faculty, most of them at public institutions and none at Ivy League colleges (Hurd et al., 1996). The labor relations model remains firmly ingrained in academe and is viewed as a major element of academic human resources management.

The most distinctive characteristic of higher education employment relations and conflict resolution is that decisions pertaining to academic judgment are historically not reviewable. While appeals may be taken on claimed procedural violations, determinations dealing with substantive matters are not appealable. The term *academic judgment* has traditionally come to mean findings concerning faculty appointment, reappointment, promotion, and tenure. In those areas the decision of the academic body is controlling and final. Thus any conflict resolution model must recognize that unless there is a definable procedural violation, appeals are restricted.

Conflict resolution within higher education has become ever more prescribed and legalistic and habitually involves participants external to the campus. Whether it is a matter of seeking to invoke discipline against a faculty member for alleged misconduct, or an attempt to introduce a new curriculum that may be challenged by civil rights groups or other interested parties, the actions of the administrators rarely, if ever, go unchallenged. Most of the disputes in academia involve adverse personnel actions including the following:

- Denial of appointment or reappointment

- Denial of promotion

- Denial of tenure

- Selection of administrators

- Hiring in compliance with affirmative action plans

- Sexual harassment claims

- Discipline for alleged misconduct or incompetence

- Removal for moral turpitude

- Access to personnel files

- Equal pay for equal work

- Age discrimination

Although some of these actions may be substantively nonreviewable, there may be multiple forums for litigation. These venues may include the following:

- Negotiations

- The faculty senate

- College ombudsman

- Standing or ad hoc internal committees

- Boards of inquiry

- Mediation

- Mediation/arbitration

- Contractual grievance arbitration

- Employer promulgated arbitration

- Courts and administrative agencies

Regardless of venue, chairs, deans, and provosts often find themselves at the heart of the problem. Either as witness, charging party, or responsible agent of the employer, they may be pressured to articulate and defend the institutional position. In the forums discussed below, an analysis of the roles of chairs, deans, and provosts are set forth.

Negotiations

Considered the least confrontational of all procedures, the use of negotiations as a persuasive tool is effective in reducing conflict and reaching agreement. Direct negotiations, without the intervention of a third party, should be attempted first as they encourage communication and education. The opportunity to listen to each other's opinion may assist in arriving at a solution, even at another level.

Strategies may vary, but it is critical that the process be noncompetitive, conciliatory, and cooperative. Should the parties fail to reach a consensus through the use of direct negotiations, then they are free to select any outlet available to them; however, it is suggested that negotiations be a prerequisite for entry into any other forum.

The Faculty Senate

One cannot assess conflict resolution within higher education without exploring the role of the faculty senate. Institutionalized at virtually every college, senates have traditionally been the mechanism by which collegial decisions, peer review, and shared governance are implemented. A widely recognized boundary exists between senates and unions, and although there is some overlap, both bodies have acknowledged their exclusive areas and respective spheres of interest: Senates have traditionally addressed the pursuit of education and related academic matters, while on unionized campuses, the bargaining agent negotiates the terms and conditions of employment.

Chairs, deans, and provosts are often concurrently faculty members, college senators, and supervisory or managerial agents of the employer. Dependent upon which hat one wears, administrators may run afoul of existing labor law if they attempt to exercise control over the senate in such a manner as may be construed as dealing with the terms and conditions of employment of bargaining unit members.

Faculty senates do not consider contractual relationships and were not created as sham unions or as a means to deny faculty representation rights under the NLRA (*DuPont*, 1993). Yet on some campuses, college administrators have attempted to control the faculty senate or other faculty committees, thereby raising questions of unlawful domination by administration over college committees. Concerns have also arisen among some labor relations practitioners over the collaborative role demonstrated between the faculty senate and the college administration. This chapter theorizes that under current labor law, faculty senates may be prohibited labor organizations within the meaning of the NLRA in that they deal with the employer over some conditions of employment (Douglas, 1995). The record further supports the belief that many faculty senates receive free office space, material support, released time for the faculty presiding officer, some degree of clerical assistance, and other benefits from the college administration (*Electromation,* 1992). In an industrial setting, these acts may qualify as indicia of management's unlawful domination or support of a labor organization.

Senates can be a valuable forum for resolving conflict or exerting pressure, including the imposition of censure, on various college constituencies. However, chairs, deans, and provosts must exercise extreme caution while performing their senatorial duties so as not to dominate, control, or influence the terms and conditions of faculty employment.

College Ombudsman

Many colleges have fashioned a system whereby a distinguished member of the faculty is asked to serve as the campus ombudsman in order to unravel a particular problem. This procedure is widely used, and if acknowledged and sanctioned by the faculty, chairs, deans, and provosts and other administrators, it can be successful in minimizing campus conflict. The advantages of this model are many and include:

- Resolving the problem promptly

- Maintaining the issue within the organization

- Alleviating the necessity of outside agency, arbitrator, or judicial intervention

- Opening communication channels among various campus constituent communities

- Reducing organizational bureaucracy, jurisdictional lines, and traditional administrative hierarchy

- Relieving pressure on existing complaint and grievance resolution administrative channels

- Serving as a check for the college president on ineffectual subordinate administrative practices

There are national and international societies of ombudsmen including the University and College Ombudsmen Association. The process is becoming firmly established within the conflict resolution and alternative dispute resolution communities.

The key to a successful ombudsman program is the willingness of all members of the college community to accept virtually unchallenged the results of the independent ombudsman's inquiries and findings. If these are second-guessed or not widely accepted, then the authority of the ombudsman is diminished and the process viewed as nothing more than a management arm. Although many university and college administrators are willing to welcome ombudsmen systems to resolve student disputes, they are apparently less welcoming if the dispute involves faculty and staff employment relationships.

Structural and legal problems associated with the ombudsman system, although few, may be significant. Campus ombudsmen are appointed by and supported by the college president, and although the model provides for an independent office, the source of authority and funding is vested in the administration. This link to management may be viewed as a threat to ombudsman autonomy. Additionally, in some instances the ombudsman may be precluded by the collective bargaining agreement from discussing any terms or conditions of employment that may be addressed by that agreement. A faculty senate or union may also feel threatened by an ombudsman inquiry and be uncooperative. Furthermore, problems can also arise over the right-to-privacy, with the ombudsman exercising a shield of confidentiality which may not be recognized by courts or administrative agencies. College management is encouraged to use the ombudsman model as an effective means to resolve or lessen the impact of campus conflict.

Standing or Ad Hoc Internal Committees

On virtually every campus, both union and nonunion, there exists standing and ad hoc committees designed to address an expressed predicament. These bodies may be creatures of the collective bargaining agreement or the faculty senate or established by the central administration. They are charged with a specific mandate and, at times, given an inflated title in order to bestow distinction. Under this category one can find a variety of commissions, councils, conclaves, congresses, and assemblies.

Perhaps there is a technical distinction among the various groups. However, their function is traditionally limited to investigating a specific problem, such as retrenchment or financial exigency, issuing their findings and, in some cases, making recommendations. Their guidance and advice, although technically not binding, do carry the weight of the appointing authority. That existing power relationship may be upset by the introduction of a new campus participant is a related problem.

External Boards of Inquiry

The use of external boards of inquiry has traditionally been limited to school visits or investigations by various groups including accrediting agencies, discipline based professional associations, and the American Association of University Professors (AAUP). These groups call on the campus for a specific objective, and with the exception of requisite accreditation procedures, they usually are investigatory. In the case of the accrediting agencies they may also inquire into a wide range of employment personnel actions which may ultimately impact the accreditation decision. Thus, a Middle States' accreditation team examination might result in a question regarding campus life diversity. This finding may in turn be queried by a campus group challenging the accreditation body's finding which can then advance the dispute to a forum other than the one in which the problem was originally heard. Such a situation arose at Baruch College of the City University of New York when the Middle States' team, concerned over the alleged lack of cultural diversity among the professoriate, found themselves and their procedures challenged by a faculty committee who in turn took the problem to the accrediting agency's parent body and ultimately to the United States Department of Education.

AAUP investigations are traditionally performed in response to a faculty protest that the college has violated academic freedom, the right to free association or speech or another academic civil right. Such an inquiry can lead to a finding by the AAUP that a transgression has occurred and, as a result, the institution may be sanctioned for infringement of governance standards. The purpose and objectives of sanctions are stated in *Academe,* the journal of the AAUP, as follows:

> The publication of these sanctions is for the purposes of informing Association members, the profession at large, and the public that unsatisfactory conditions of academic government exist at the institutions in question (Staff, 1996).

AAUP sanctions should not be considered frivolously by college administrators as the process is public, and if the institution is sanctioned, it can have injurious effects not only to the college but to the careers of individual chairs, deans, provosts, and presidents. The standards for censure vary but include a finding that the institution is "... not observing the generally recognized principles of academic freedom and tenure endorsed by this association, the Association of American Colleges and Universities, and more than 150 other professional and educational organizations."

The AAUP often works in concert with other faculty organizations including the American Federation of Teachers, the National Education Association, and other independent faculty associations. When seeking to resolve conflict on both the unionized and nonunionized campus, AAUP involvement can be a positive and constructive force.

Mediation

Mediation as a conflict resolution technique is widely established and is incorporated in virtually every dispute settlement model. For the process to be fully effective, one must accede to the lack of mediators' authority beyond that of the power of persuasion. While the mediator can require that meetings be held and that information be produced, the forthcoming recommendations, if any, are not binding and are used primarily to narrow existing differences and force the parties to focus on settlement.

Mediation generally does not involve individual rights, and as such, the rules of evidence play a minimal role. It is a more unstructured and freer process and relies on the interpersonal and intergroup skills of the mediator to separate the participants from the problem. In higher education employment relationships, the mediator traditionally enters a dispute in one of four ways. If controversy relates to a term or condition of employment, then the mediator may be assigned by the administrative agency charged with the responsibility of regulating labor relations and negotiations of bargaining agreements. In this scenario, supervisors and managers may find themselves as members of a bargaining team working with the mediator in an attempt to settle a particular contract impasse.

Mediators may also be used as conveners to initiate an exchange between campus factions and the external community. Mediation may be used for a considerable range of potential problems, and after a dialogue is initiated, the mediator/convener will remain as a process monitor until a resolution is made.

A third role that the mediator may play on the campus is akin to that of the ombudsman in that he or she has a wide range of discretion in deciding what groups should be brought together to attempt to reach a settlement. Mediators may also be assigned to a particular problem by an administrative agency or judicial body and charged with oversight functions by the appointing authority.

Although mediators function primarily in an informal manner, their use is not widespread in the college community. Considering its value as an effective conflict resolution mechanism, and its minimal cost, more attention should be devoted by academic managers to institutionalizing the use of mediation.

Med/Arb

This ADR (alternative dispute resolution) technique is fairly recent and synthesizes the best of mediation and arbitration into a single process. The same individual functions as the mediator and arbitrator and initially attempts to obtain resolution through a mediated settlement. Until this juncture, med/arb and mediation are similar; however, under med/arb the mediator states that if a finding were required, then it would likely resemble the one she is now suggesting in mediation. This announcement gives the mediation proposal added weight. Knowing that the mediator has the ultimate power to issue an arbitration award on this issue, the parties are more likely to work with her in arriving at a mediated solution. Should the process fail, then the information obtained during the mediation process will be used to fashion an arbitration award.

Grievance Arbitration

On the unionized campus, the collective bargaining agreement and its grievance arbitration provision are the most frequently used forums for dispute resolution. Grievance arbitration, a quasiprivate judicial system used to resolve industrial conflict, is both less formal and more cost effective than using the court system. As such, it is now widely established, a matter of public policy, and is encouraged and protected by statute and case law.

Most grievance procedures set forth a three- to five-step system culminating in binding arbitration. Although there are some minimal divergences in the process, traditionally, the parties have incorporated a select panel of arbitrators (five to seven names) into their contract, or have otherwise agreed to use the arbitration services of a recognized agency such as the Federal Mediation and Conciliation Service or the American Arbitration Association. Arbitrators selected may or may not have demonstrated expertise in higher education. Time restrictions and procedural requirements to move the grievance through its various steps are similar to those used in other employment settings. Limits on arbitrability are specified, and academic judgments issues are normally exempt from the process. Different processes more analogous to industrial settings may be available for units of classified staff and other non-faculty employees. Critical to the process is the recognition that awards issued by arbitrators are binding and enforceable in courts of law.

Employer Promulgated Arbitration

Although not widely used in academe, this model is gaining acceptance in both university and industrial ADR. Those arguing in support assert that the procedure brings final and binding arbitration, an acknowledged dispute resolution system, to the campus without faculty unionization. Opponents maintain it is nothing more than a management attempt to maintain a union-free environment by denying faculty unions a primary organizing instrument. The balanced approach maintains that the system imposes symmetry between the interests of a faculty and the administration in that it brings about a sought-after faculty goal while at the same time permits the college to remain nonunion and not impose the limits of a collectively negotiated collective bargaining agreement.

The procedure is in place at several institutions and appears to be working well. For example, the faculty at Columbia University and Northeastern University have enjoyed arbitration under these systems since the 1970s and are reportedly satisfied with the process. Where available, faculty members who are labor relations neutrals may be asked to serve as either arbitrators or hearing officers on their own campuses. At times, a widely recognized labor arbitrator from another institution, or one from outside academe, is brought onto the campus and, although not arbitrating faculty grievances that have been raised pursuant to a collective bargaining agreement, they are nevertheless asked to bring their dispute resolution expertise to the table. Predominately used in resolving individual rather than campus-wide disputes, the system can be effective only if the decision, although technically not binding, is accepted by all parties as dispositive.

Courts and Administrative Agencies

Unless there is specific contractual language forbidding access to other forums, chairs, deans, and provosts must prepare to defend their actions in a variety of alternative arenas including the most expensive and time-consuming option of all—courts of competent jurisdiction and administrative agencies exercising jurisdiction over the claim. This forum is the least preferred, the most litigious and costly, and can result in the maximum financial liability and exposure to the institution and individual litigant. Contested in external arenas, the college is often forced to disclose records and other data that heretofore were maintained under their direct control. For example, when the University of Pennsylvania denied tenure to a Professor Tung, the United States Supreme Court ordered the university to produce records of faculty tenure committee deliberations to the Equal Employment Opportunity Commission (EEOC). Although the university asserted a shield of confidentiality, the EEOC's position that ordered the university to conduct a full investigation into claims of academic discrimination filed by Professor Tung was upheld.

The propensity of academics to litigate claims of academic discrimination are well-documented and should be of concern to all administrators (LaNoue & Lee, 1990). Not only can chairs, deans, and provosts be compelled to produce their own notes and those of committees that they serve on, but also they may be individually liable and accountable. In cases that involved the violation of individual statutory rights, the traditional belief that when one acts as an agent of the employer, he or she is shielded from personal culpability is not always controlling.

A New Conflict Resolution System

Existing conflict resolution systems must be modified and used to alleviate further confrontation in academe. None of the existing procedures and forums identified herein can by themselves be productive unless structural and environmental changes are made within the academic workplace ADR model. Critical to the process is the development of a new strategy designed to reduce the current level of internal organizational conflict. Additionally, the level of adversarialism that exists between faculty, staff, middle management, other administrators, and boards of trustees is excessive, far worse than exists in many other employment settings.

What then should the new conflict resolution system for higher education contain? The following concepts are suggested as guidelines to be incorporated and used in conjunction with any or all of the above referenced forums. The initial conflict resolution process should be unceremonious and unpretentious with formality and codification becoming part of the system only as it moves toward finality. Limited funding should be provided to pay the costs of administering the procedure, but finances should play only a very minor role in the settlement process. The procedure must be codified, with all citizens of the campus community made aware of its contents. Conveners and facilitators should be identified and made accessible. In matters of perceived employment or academic discrimination, written charges with the opportunity to respond must be accorded all parties. The right to participation and representation by all parties to the dispute must be guaranteed. Confidentiality must be encouraged, with limitations developed to restrict nonparticipant access to the process. Grievances, complaints, and inquiries must be addressed and promptly resolved. Claims of employment or academic discrimination that may affect one or more individuals should be expedited and immediately analyzed to see if there is potential for class action suits. With the exception of forums such as arbitration or the EEOC that may prescribe options and limits on appeal, the parties to campus disputes should be made aware of the existence of appellate procedures and rights. Experimentation with any of the weapons in the arsenal of conflict resolution should be encouraged.

Academic managers must assess the nature of campus conflict and determine its impact on individuals and the institution. Building cooperative systems and teamwork to manage conflict within the college community is an indispensable goal. Questions pertaining to the failure to resolve friction, and the associated long-term consequences of such failure, should be fully addressed. Appreciation that the primary purposes of the college are teaching and research, and that students can learn ADR by observation from the way campus conflict is managed, should be an implied educational goal. All members of the college community should strive for systems designed to manage conflict in a beneficial manner and to establish a constructive conflict resolution model. Furthermore, in many situations, the costs of conflict litigation, the risks of increased public exposure, and the potential for the development of causes célebres are so prohibitive that alternative dispute resolution is no longer optional: It is necessary.

In developing a campus conflict resolution system, partnerships should be encouraged and strategies developed to seek assistance from existing campus groups and bargaining agents, as well as external professional bodies such as:

1) American Arbitration Association

2) American Association of University Professors

3) American Association of University Women

4) American Federation of Teachers

5) Association of Governing Boards

6) Baruch College National Center for the Study of Collective Bargaining in Higher Education and the Professions

7) National Association of College and University Attorneys

8) National Education Association

9) National Institute for Dispute Resolution

10) Society of Professionals in Dispute Resolution

Chairs, deans, and provosts must reexamine the definition and costs of winning from an economic and sociological perspective and acknowledge that administrators viewed by their peers as firm but fair are more likely to gain respect and enhance their professional standing. The decision to defend a contested adverse middle management decision should be weighed against the costs of settlement. The negative impacts of testifying, both for the individuals and institutions, as well as the associated economic costs, must be measured against a negotiated or brokered agreement.

Faculties will invariably form alliances and coalitions to articulate their interests. Whether this takes the form of unionization, senates, committees, or professional organizations, the inescapable fact is that chairs, deans, and provosts must acknowledge faculty solidarity and representation and acquit themselves in such a manner so as not to exploit their authority, or act in an arbitrary or capricious manner that invites judicial or regulatory agency intervention. If solutions replace winning as the key to successful academic management, then chairs, deans, and provosts have an immense opportunity to minimalize campus adversarialism and devote their efforts toward their primary purpose of teaching, research, and service.

REFERENCES

Douglas, J. M., (1995, February). Faculty senates as labor organizations: An investigation of governance structures in higher education. *Labor Law Journal, 46* (2), 116-124.

E. I. DuPont De Nemours & Company and Chemical Workers Association, Inc., International Brotherhood of DuPont Workers, 311 NLRB 88 (1993).

Electromation, Inc. and Teamsters Local 1049, AFL-CIO, 309 NLRB 163, 142 LRRM 1005 (1992).

Hurd, R., Forest, A., & Johnson, B. H., (1996, January). *Directory of faculty contracts and bargaining agents in institutions of higher education (22),* New York, NY: City College of New York, Baruch College, National Center for the Study of College Bargaining in Higher Education.

LaNoue, G. R., & Lee, B. (1990). *Academics in court.* Ann Arbor, MI: University of Michigan Press.

National Labor Relations Act, P. L. 198, 74th Congress (1935) as amended by Labor Management Relations Act, Taft-Hartley Act, 61 Stat. 156 (1947).

National Labor Relations Board v. Boston University. (1984). 1-CA-11061.

National Labor Relations Board v. Yeshiva University. (1980). 444 U.S. 672.

Staff. (1996, September/October). *Academe: Bulletin of American Association of University Professors, 5,* 62.

University of Pennsylvania v. EEOC, 493 U.S. 182 (1990).

ACADEMIC MORTAR TO MEND THE CRACKS: THE HOLTON MODEL FOR CONFLICT MANAGEMENT

Conflict in higher education is inescapable. As you have learned throughout this book, conflict exists at every level of our academic world.

And while conflict can be negative and can cause deep rifts in the framework of the institution, it can also be used as a tool to take the institution and the people in it from stagnation to a new level of effectiveness. What makes the difference is conflict management.

The purpose of this chapter is to introduce a process for managing any conflict which you may encounter. While it is aimed at your role as a department chair or dean, the model given is equally effective in your role as partner or parent, a board member or a volunteer. I will first give a brief overview of the model and then show how it can be used to manage a conflict in higher education.

The Holton Model for Conflict Management is one which can be used with any conflict in any setting.[1] It is important that all parts of the model are used. Attempts at conflict management often fall apart when the conflict is not clearly identified or understood. The saying "a problem well defined is half solved" is certainly true for conflict. Because only after identifying the conflict can anyone begin to manage it. Often the presenting conflict, the one that is the most visible, is either a mask for other conflict or only one of a number of conflicts facing the institution.

After the conflict is identified and understood, it is necessary to identify possible solutions. My years of training in creative problem solving reinforce the notion that no problem has only one solution. It is the responsibility of the parties in conflict to find the range of alternative solutions, and then to work with a process to determine which solution is best.

But the parties in conflict are not yet finished. Unless there is a clear, specific plan of action, the conflict management process can again fall apart. The third step in the process is to create that plan of action and to follow it. Who is responsible for what, when? Exactly what is going to happen to implement the solution? A map for this step is necessary.

With the following three steps of the Holton Conflict Management process, any conflict which you face can be managed.

1) Identify the conflict

2) Identify solutions

3) Implement solutions

At the core of this model is communication. All people involved in the conflict must work on effective communication, including both speaking and listening. In order to understand the conflict, one must first speak clearly and honestly about their issues and then must listen intensely to the others involved in the conflict.

1. IDENTIFY THE CONFLICT

The identification phase of conflict management is a six-step phase, and all of the steps are necessary to understand the conflict.

Who Is Involved?

Identify all of the parties who are involved in the conflict, as well as all who are not directly involved but may be affected by it. What is the relationship of those who are involved? In what ways are they interdependent? Has their relationship changed? What are their roles and responsibilities in relationship to each other and to this conflict situation? What are their prior interactions? Have they been adversaries before? Is this a new conflict? Do they trust each other? Are they polarized? What are the motivations of those involved in the conflict? What do they say are their goals and objectives? How does their behavior support or negate those? What sources of power do those in conflict have? Who are the people not directly involved in the conflict, but likely to be affected by it? Who are those who are likely to be brought into the conflict if it escalates? Are there "ghosts" involved in this conflict? Are there people who were a part of the origins of the conflict (or another related conflict) who are now gone?

What Is the Conflict?
What happened? What are the specific, observable data about the conflict? What are the feelings and emotions surrounding the conflict? What are the presenting issues? What are the secondary (and tertiary...) issues?

When Did It Happen?
When did the conflict begin? Is there a specific incident which can be identified? Is it ongoing? Is it cyclical? Is it intermittent? Does it escalate or die down?

Where Did It Happen?
Where physically did the conflict occur? Where, within the organizational structure, did it occur?

What Management Attempts Have Been Made?
What attempts have been made to manage the conflict? If it is a recurring conflict, what attempts have been made in the past? In what ways were they successful? In what ways were they not?

What Are the Consequences of the Conflict?
What will happen if the conflict is not managed? What will happen if it is? What gains and losses are perceived to exist as a result of solutions?

When you have identified and analyzed the conflict, it is necessary for those directly involved in the conflict to work together (often with a neutral third party) to identify solutions.

2. IDENTIFY SOLUTIONS

The development of solutions is rarely a simple process. Setting the stage and getting parties to communicate and work together is a necessary part of this phase of the conflict management process.

Develop a Positive Attitude

Unless those involved in a conflict are willing to work together toward a mutually agreeable solution, no management is possible. And so the first step is to work with the parties to develop a positive attitude. This may require a discussion about ways in which they might benefit from working together in the future and about the positive outcomes which are possible as a result of the management of this conflict.

Establish Ground Rules

Conflict produces a feeling of chaos. It is therefore important to work with the parties to establish ground rules for the conflict management. Ground rules typically include agreements on communication and structure.

Identify Interests of the Parties

Parties must understand their priorities and the outcome(s) they want. Fisher and Ury (1981) have written extensively about the importance of interests versus positions. A position is an entrenched stand (e.g., I will never work with that professor again!). Interests, on the other hand, are the underlying concerns of the parties (e.g., I want Professor Snyders to acknowledge my expertise in dance and show respect for my work and my abilities). Parties need to understand what they truly want as a result of the management of the conflict. This includes an understanding of what Fisher and Ury refer to as the Best Alternative to the Negotiated Agreement (BATNA). Sometimes it helps to explain to parties what will happen if they don't come together to manage the conflict. Often the threat of externally imposed solutions are enough to get parties to agree to work together.

Develop Alternatives

Now that the issues of the conflict are understood, it is important to identify alternative solutions for managing it. Brainstorming is the best process to develop alternatives. In an environment of trust (usually facilitated by the neutral third party), disputants can work together to develop multiple alternatives. It is also helpful to identify ways that similar issues have been managed in other situations. This gives the disputants an acknowledgement that solutions are possible and may expand their concepts of possible alternatives. This phase must be separate from the decision-making based on criteria.

Identify Criteria

Not all of the ideas generated during the previous stage will be appropriate to manage this conflict, so it is necessary to identify appropriate criteria and use those criteria to determine the best solutions. First, there are often objective criteria, given the nature of the conflict. Some criteria are also subjective. These are often overlooked to the peril of the conflict management. After the criteria have been developed, they should be prioritized; not all criteria will carry equal weight in the decision-making.

Weigh Solutions Against Criteria

The solutions should be weighed against the prioritized criteria, and a best solution will result. It is important to determine whether that solution is, in fact, felt to be the best by all parties. Too often, after a solution has been agreed upon, parties realize that they left out some important criteria. They may, for example, have identified only rational, logical criteria and ignored any emotional aspects of the decision. Or they may agree on a solution, but realize that they don't have the time to implement it.

3. IMPLEMENT SOLUTIONS

Too often this is the phase of conflict management that is neglected. Even when significant time is spent on identification of the conflict and identification of potential solutions, the implementation phase is too often rushed. To have a successful conflict management, the parties must be diligent about the implementation phase.

Develop a Plan of Action

It is not enough to agree to a nebulous solution; all parties in the conflict must agree to the specifics. The plan of action should include:

- Who is going to be involved in the implementation of the solutions? If some people outside the immediate system of the parties are involved, how are they going to be brought in to the solution phase?

- What exactly is to be done? Be as specific as possible about the actions that are to be taken.

- When the parties are going to act? Develop a very clear and concise timeline. What is going to be done tomorrow? By what date will the complete solution be in place? What checkpoints do the parties have along the way? Include in the timeline some check-in dates, when the parties will get together to talk about the solution, about the progress that is being made, and work with any issues that arise during the implementation phase.

- Who is responsible for mediating any differences between the parties during the implementation phase?

The plan of action should be written up and signed by all parties, including any neutral third party. This document will be more valuable if every aspect of the agreement is clearly spelled out, in terms that will not be debatable down the line.

Determine How to Handle Future Conflict

As a part of the conflict management process, the parties should agree on a way to deal with conflict in the future. They may, for example, agree to go to the university ombuds officer, to appoint a conflict management committee, or to meet monthly to discuss issues and avert problems.

THE CASE OF COMPETING INTERESTS

How does this model actually work? The Case of Competing Interests is a fictional compilation of challenges and opportunities found in institutions throughout the continent. Any resemblance to a specific institution or conflict merely underscores the fact that conflict occurs everywhere in academia today.

Appropriation of and use of space is a problem at many institutions and was the presenting problem with a midsized university where many programs were competing for space.

Multiple groups, both on- and off-campus, were competing for performance space. On-campus groups included the music department, the theater department, the dance department, the Troubadours, the Crue (a student performance group), the student activities office, and the office of institutional planning. Off-campus groups also wanted to rent the space for community theater groups, dance recitals, commerce department speakers, and others.

For many years, all parties involved in the conflict were feuding about space—all feeling that there was not enough space and what space that existed belonged to "me." Everyone had excellent rationales for the precedence that their program should take. For academic departments, performance was required for course work. The cocurricular activities of clubs and programs were considered vital for student development. Making space available to community civic groups established necessary good will to the community.

Annually, internecine warfare erupted at calendar-setting time. Typically, everyone came to the table with positions firmly established: They had their list of events and dates and the space they must have. Everyone emerged from the meetings unhappy—no one got everything they wanted. And so during the academic year, people in each of those areas worked behind the scenes to get special favors, to swap whatever they had, and to figure out any way to get the space when and how they wanted it. It was a conflict that only escalated yearly and one that had to be managed. They decided that they needed help.

Whenever I am involved in conflict management, I begin with an extensive information gathering phase in which I interview everyone connected to the conflict.

1. IDENTIFY THE CONFLICT

Who Is Involved?

You must first identify who is involved by department or division. The conflict under discussion here crosses most major divisions in the institution. The space is maintained by the department of facilities, the student affairs division handles student performance groups and all programming of events for students on campus, the academic affairs division is in charge of any academic program and their subsequent performance related to course work, and the office of institutional planning works with external groups who want to come to the university.

People who are directly involved. Within each of those areas, who are the people involved in the conflict? In facilities, it was the building scheduler. In student affairs, both the director of student programming and the advisor for student clubs were involved. In academic affairs, the chairs of the departments of dance, music, and theater, as well as the individuals in charge of the performances came to the group, as well as a representative from the office of institutional planning who worked with both on-campus and off-campus programming.

Who else was involved in this issue? There were some people in each department or division who had no formal role, but who were pivotal to the conflict. The technical director was involved as was the director of the alumni association who interacted with the alumni who wanted to host events at the university.

Students. In what ways are the students involved? In this conflict, the students felt that they were in the middle and often heard anger among their professors and advisors as space issues were discussed. Many students, as double majors or participants in more than one performance activity, felt torn in their loyalties between professors and programs.

The history. In looking at relationships with this issue, a tangled history of cooperative and competing efforts was discovered. Although each competed for the limited spaces on campus, there was also cooperation.

Many of the professors involved in performance classes were also advisors of student clubs. They also frequently collaborated on programming and helped each other out with performances. There was a range of academic and performance experience among the faculty and advisors. Some professional jealousy was present; some felt that their experience and background were far superior to that of anyone else. There was also a strong element of entitlement. Some professors and advisors felt that they were entitled to the space they requested because their program or activity was, in their eyes, the most important on campus and far superior in quality to other performances.

This was the sentiment expressed by the student activities people as well. They felt that their programs served all students at the university, not just the few who were in performance programs.

And so the adversarial—and the cooperative—relationships have existed between all involved for a long time. In fact, the adversarial relationships existed long before most of the current players came to the university. In listening to everyone tell their story, it was discovered that there were a few ghosts in this conflict.

More than 30 years ago, the chairs of the departments of music and dance were in conflict. There were no other programs, no student activities office, and no outsiders competing for their space. Their conflict, therefore, was more limited than the current one, and perhaps more fierce. There were legendary battles about performance space and stories of pianos being moved and equipment being sabotaged. Annually, battles were waged about whose performances would get prime-time scheduling.

It was bad enough when it was just the two departments. As the university grew, student affairs began student programming, more departments with performance components were established, and more people wanted the same spaces. As the departmental historian says, "All hell broke loose."

Almost no one involved in the original conflict was still in the university. But the tales, possibly embellished, of the fights in the early days are legion.

This is an example of the ghosts—the parties of conflict which are truly present in spirit, but no longer so in body. When this happens, you can only ask, "And how does that affect our work today?" Bring those ghosts out of the closet and into open discussion. It is interesting for the history of the department, and for the history of the conflict, to thoroughly understand how those ghosts impact today, and then to let go of them, their history, and their power to impact the present.

In this conflict, there was ambiguity in roles. There needed to be a clarification of ultimate responsibility. Who was responsible for the decisions about the performance spaces at the institution? That person needed to be involved in the conflict management. What role do others have in the space allocation? Conflict often occurs because two people (or two divisions or departments) believe that they are in charge of the same area. The conflict is sometimes easily managed at this point by clarifying the roles and responsibilities of the people involved.

The role of power. Power, or lack of power, is often the cause of conflict between people in academia (as well as outside of it). What sources of power do those in conflict have? Is the conflict really a power play, with one person desirous of the power or perceived power of another? The music department chair believed that the external programmer was listened to, got more prime-time performance space, and was therefore more powerful than she. In a power conflict, often the true issue is a lack of affirmation for the self or the program. The music department chair needed to hear that she and her program were valued by the university.

It is sometimes difficult to get people to recognize that power is infinite and that the more people with power in a department, division, or school, the better! The translation from power *over* to power *to* changes the perception not only of power, but of ways to use power as a positive force in conflict management. Power *to* enables everyone to determine ways in which they have the power to work effectively. After many hours of working together, the people in this conflict decided that they were going to have to work together in order to manage the conflict. Working together, they had power to make decisions that were best for all performance programs. If they did not, some external power broker was going to come in and do it for them—which meant that they would have no power to decide their fate and that of their programs.

Motivations. Next, determine the motivations of those in conflict. What are their goals and objectives in this conflict? What do they hope to gain? It is important to determine whether their actions support or negate those goals and objectives. Perhaps the person is too close to the battle to see how she/he is acting. And some clarification of that reality will help the person to understand her/his behavior, and subsequently change that behavior. In this conflict, it was important to show how the behavior of the faculty and administrators was affecting the students. Virtually everyone said that their stance was for the good of the students. But their behavior created negative modeling for the students. They needed to see how their positional conflict behavior was in fact hurting the students.

It is important to identify who is not directly involved in the conflict, but likely to be effected by it. In this case, and in academia in general, it is often the students who are one heartbeat away from the conflict. It is almost always desirable to keep the conflict out of the classroom and away from the students. The job of learning is complex enough; students do not need to add taking sides in a conflict to their busy schedules.

You now have information about who is and isn't involved. It is time to determine the "what."

What Is the Conflict?

In this phase it is important to identify exactly what happened. What are the specific, observable facts about the conflict (who, what, when, where, why, how)? In interviewing each person, ask for that individual's version of what happened. If a specific incident ignited the conflict, then you will find out. If the conflict is a more diffuse one, it will become obvious either that there is no clear "what," or that the "what" happened long ago. At lower levels of conflict, it is relatively easy for people to define the conflict (e.g., I am always scheduled for an 8:00 class and am the only one in the department who has to teach at that time). As the conflict level increases, it will be more difficult to isolate an exact instance.

In this case, the facts are diffuse. Faculty complaints included: "They always get the dates they want," "We never have enough opportunities for performance," "There is no place for our students to experience what it is to sing before a live audience," "The university is for all students, and we can't program enough for them all." After intense questioning, it became clear that while there were a few specific incidents, the larger problem was one of a feeling of inequality rather than specific instances of it.

It was also clear that emotions were running high. Virtually everyone in the process felt slighted, overlooked, unimportant, and undervalued. Almost everyone argued that her/his students were hurt (no one, of course, argued that he or she was hurt personally).

While gathering information it is important to hear not only what we scientifically refer to as facts or those things which are specific, measurable, and observable, but also to gather the feelings and emotions that surround the conflict. Conflict is never emotion-free, and emotions are an important part of the identification process. The emotional reactions are also likely to be different from the various parties involved, so it is important to identify emotional response from everyone involved.

As a part of this phase, ask people what they perceive to be the issues. It is helpful to ask an objective question while you are gathering these facts,

"What is happening?" and "What are the issues facing the department/ division/ school?" are objective questions that will get wider responses than just asking "What's wrong?"

In this case, the parties identified issues of lack of performance time, lack of adequate space for concerts, plays, recitals, and programs, lack of opportunities for students to present their work, lack of cooperation among the departments and divisions of the university.

When Did It Happen?

It is sometimes difficult for parties to pin down the beginning of the conflict. You need to try to determine when the conflict began. Was there a specific incident which started the conflict (e.g., During the meeting on Friday, when we were discussing the strategic plan, Glenn said that the computer science department was the only one that needed new computers)?

Also determine whether the conflict is ongoing. Sometimes parties cannot identify the specific time when the conflict began, but say it feels as if they have always been in conflict. Such was the case in the conflict under consideration.

As noted earlier, this conflict was longstanding. It predated the university's student activities division and almost everyone now involved in the departments and divisions on campus. The ghosts of previous players were called up to support the conflict, to fuel the fire.

This is a clear case of a cyclical conflict. It became stronger every spring semester when calendar-setting time began. Weeks before the scheduled meeting, people began to be stressed and tense, and to complain about "them."

Where Did It Happen?

If the parties involved can identify what happened and when, they might also be able to determine where the conflict occurred. Does it always occur when we meet on the stage in the Black Box theater? Might there be a reason for that? If you probe a bit, you might find that the space for the Black Box theater originally was dance department performance space, and someone (no one remembered who or why) gave it to the theater department. Being in the space reminded the dance people of the inequities they feel they have suffered. We decided to meet in a different place.

It is also important to determine where in the organizational structure the conflict occurs. Does it always occur between department chairs? If so, it may mean that there is not a clear role and responsibility identification for those chairs. Or if it always occurs between the student clubs, it may be that there is a lack of clarity of the goals of the student clubs. If the conflict frequently occurs in the same place on the organizational structure, then there is a problem of clarity in the responsibilities and roles of the people involved and a lack of communication between the people in these roles.

In this case, the conflict occurred on a more diffuse level. It had been going on long enough to permeate relationships at every level.

Have There Been Management Attempts?

People often try to manage a conflict before it becomes public knowledge. In this instance, the chairs of dance and music talked and tried to come up with a time that each wanted to do their performance. Unfortunately, each wanted to do the annual Easter concert on the same weekend.

While it is good for people in conflict to work together to manage the conflict, such unsuccessful attempts might also make people more entrenched in their position. When both chairs tried to work together and came up with no answer, they both felt "see, I tried, and he was totally unreasonable." Or perhaps the theater department and the student affairs department both feel that in the past they have given in to the demands of the other and rescheduled so that the other could do some programming. And they feel that even though they gave up their first choice, the other was never satisfied. They go into another conflict feeling that this is going to fail also.

So it is helpful to know what previous attempts have been made and the level of success and failure that the parties have felt. They have also probably had some successful negotiations over the use of space, and it is important to really try to articulate those experiences.

In this case, one such instance stands out. The regional commerce department wanted to schedule its annual meeting showcasing the people and companies in the area who had made outstanding contributions to the region during the year. But the dance department had a lavish performance, complete with elaborate sets, ready for the same weekend. After much conversation and the help of a third party, the two came up with an amicable solution. The sets would remain and the dancers would come to perform for the commerce department event. The department's work was showcased, the commerce department could use the space, have free, quality entertainment, and all went away happy.

Recalling such successful management of conflict helped the parties to realize that they could work together, and that they in fact had done so in previous instances.

What Are the Consequences of the Conflict?

Finally, all parties have to think about the consequences of the conflict. What will happen if the conflict is not managed successfully? In this case, the conflict is only going to escalate and the frustration level of everyone involved will increase. But in some conflicts, the consequences of not resolving the conflict is negligible. Sometimes it is just easier and more politic to let the conflict go.

In this case, the gains of managing the conflict far outweigh the losses. A process needed to be identified and put into place which would be used in the future for the management of all of the possible performance spaces at the institution.

After this information about the nature of the conflict has been acquired, the conflict can be understood. Then it is necessary to work with the parties directly involved in the conflict to identify solutions. Those directly involved in the conflict must work together (often with a neutral third party) to identify solutions.

2. IDENTIFY SOLUTIONS

The development of solutions is not a simple process. Setting the stage and getting parties to communicate and work together is a necessary part of this phase of the conflict management process.

Develop a Positive Attitude

Is everyone willing to work together toward a mutually agreeable solution? If not, this process won't work. In the identification phase, I mentioned finding some instances where the parties did work together effectively. The group came up with a number of such instances so that they began to realize that the conflicts can be managed, and that they had a history of working together. Working together, the parties created a long list of performances and events where everyone worked together, where they negotiated space and time, and where people did come away satisfied.

It sometimes helps to list the benefits of working together. The people competing for performance space acknowledged a long list of the reasons that working together was in the best interest of everyone involved. So they went into the solution identification phase with a positive attitude.

Establish Ground Rules

The chaos of conflict had been experienced frequently by everyone involved in this case, so they were willing to establish ground rules for their work together.

Communication. Everyone thinks that they know how to listen effectively, so it is important to approach a lesson in active listening and feedback as a reminder to everyone to use information they already have. We had a brief session on these and had everyone practice it. In the practice sessions, I asked everyone to engage in active listening as their partners spoke of the most exciting performance experience they had been involved with at this institution. Then I had them give and receive feedback as their partners discussed a way in which they had worked together or seen the other person work positively. There is plenty of time for negatives; at the early part of conflict management it is important to get people to affirm each other.

Structure. People in chaos want structure. In this case, we agreed to meet every Tuesday afternoon from 3:00 to 5:30 for two months. We agreed that at the end of the two months, we would meet to assess the progress and determine whether it was necessary to keep meeting. The entire group stated that they would stay with the process and come to every meeting. The meetings would take place in the library's conference room, a neutral space which was not owned by anyone in the discussion.

Identify Interests of the Parties

It is vital that the conflict manager find out the true interest of people in the conflict. In their seminal volume, *Getting to Yes*, Fisher and Ury (1981) talk further about interest bargaining.

One way for me to capture interest versus positional bargaining involves one piece of cake and two people. I offer moist chocolate cake with thick chocolate icing to two people. But I only have one piece of cake. So what do I do? Of course, I cut it in half! I give it to the two people and watch them eat it. But I see that one eats only the icing and the other eats only the cake. What would have happened if I asked each person why they wanted the cake? Then I would have discovered the interest of each—that one wanted icing and one wanted cake—and would have managed the "conflict" differently.

You must find out the interest of each person involved in the conflict. In this case, I had to determine what all involved truly wanted. Did they want their students to have at least three performances a semester? Then it may not matter which space it is in. Did they want the students to feel the experience of performing on the largest stage at the university? Did they want to break the record for the largest musical performance every held at the university? Did they want to provide a variety of entertainment experiences for the students?

It is necessary to get away from positions (e.g., We must have the Easter concert on the main stage on the first Saturday of April) to interests (e.g., I want the students to have an opportunity to perform their music, and I want to do it soon after spring break).

Develop Alternatives

We now understand the interests of everyone involved; we understand the conflicts and have identified the issues. It is now time to identify alternative solutions.

We did this in a number of ways. I suggested that people find out the ways that performance space is handled at other institutions. They returned with information that identified ways in which performance space was used in other institutions of the same size with comparable needs. Some other people looked into the history of performances and programs at the university and discovered what had been done in the past.

Everyone went to their departments and their classes and asked for input from their colleagues and their students. Often those who are involved in the programs—but not directly involved in the conflict—can shed some wonderful light on solutions.

After everyone spoke about the information they gathered, we held a brainstorming session and covered the walls with newsprint containing possible solutions.

It is important that an atmosphere of trust had been established so that people could do true brainstorming: coming up with ideas which were outrageous, improbable, and creative without judging themselves or each other.

Identify Criteria

We now had these wonderful ideas, but had to do some gleaning. The first thing we did at our next session together was to establish criteria that would be used to determine the best ideas. With the newsprint taped to the wall, we first eliminated all ideas which were clearly illegal or immoral. Then we decided on objective criteria: Implementation of the solution had to possible by April of the following year when planning was to begin; it had to cost less than $3,000 to implement (so we couldn't build a new building, for example); it had to fall within the mission of the university and the mission of all of the departments and divisions involved; and it had to have a positive effect on the students.

Then subjective criteria must be included. The most important of the subjective criteria was that everyone involved had to like the idea. While no one could specifically define what that meant, it was clear that a solution that didn't feel right to the people around the table would never be successfully implemented.

Weigh Solutions Against Criteria

It does take a long time to weigh each solution against the criteria. But it is important to discuss each of the ideas and see how they fit the established criteria above. After we did that, the best solutions emerged. They included both long-term and short-term solutions. The long term (which did not fit the immediate criteria of time, but came about as a result of the discussion) was to thoroughly investigate the entire campus and the city in which the university was located to see if alternative performance space could be found.

There were multiple short-term solutions agreed upon: to establish a rotation system for major performances; to expand the "seasons" so that more programming could be done within the framework of a "special" time; to establish a ranking system for all other use of space with priority given to academic programs, then to student affairs, and then to external programming; and to establish a performance space committee, charged with making the decisions about the space.

The solutions decided upon above were much too amorphous, as is often the case. The implementation phase must make them more concrete and determine exactly what will be done, by whom, and by when.

3. IMPLEMENT SOLUTIONS

Develop a Plan of Action

Each of the solutions agreed upon the need for a specific plan of action. In order to explain the process, let me take just one of their agreed-upon solutions, that of establishing a ranking system for use of space.

Who. A committee was formed, including representatives of the conflict management team and two additional representatives from each department and division involved. We decided that everyone who was a stakeholder in the process was included in the original conflict management group, but that it was important for the vice presidents to be alerted to the agreed solutions so that they could buy into the implementation phase. They were informed and invited to be a part of this process.

What. The group was to establish a ranking system so that every event considered for the currently existing performance spaces would be ranked. The top-ranking events would have scheduling priority.

When. The group began working immediately, using the same time as the conflict management group, Tuesdays from 3:00 to 5:30. They agreed to have a ranking system in place in one month which would be brought back to the original conflict management group for its consideration. After the plan was approved by the group, it would be sent to the vice presidents and president for final approval.

Mediation. The conflict consultant would be called upon to mediate if further conflict ensued. However, the group felt strongly that it could now manage the conflicts that might erupt as it worked on this solution.

The plan of action was written up and signed by all parties. The document served as a check for the process and the procedure.

Determine How to Handle Future Conflict

This group of people, representatives from many departments and divisions across the institution, successfully worked together to manage a conflict that had haunted them for years. They agreed that, for the first year, they would meet monthly to check on the progress of the subcommittees and to discuss any conflicts which occurred.

I agreed that they could call me to talk through the process and the problems if and when they occurred. A contact person was chosen so that everyone would not call me, thus possibly fueling other conflict.

They also agreed that if significant conflict surfaced, they would call in the consultant at the beginning of the process, rather than wait until they were ready to declare war on the other divisions and departments.

AND THEY ALL LIVED HAPPILY EVER AFTER

Well, yes and no. As the institution grows, conflicts continue to surface. But this group now has a process to work through conflicts. And the people who were involved in the original conflict management team are committed to working together. They have also modeled for the entire institution a positive implementation of a conflict management process and have been called upon by others to talk about their experience.

The cultural shift from an antagonistic to a cooperative environment was a significant one for all involved. And that is one of the benefits of effective conflict management.

The appropriate mortar of an effective conflict management process can work to mend the cracks in the ivory tower.

ENDNOTE

1. It is also important, however, to know when the conflict is beyond your abilities. Some conflicts are easily managed by the parties involved or by inviting an interested third party from the institution. In your role, you are

often that "interested third party." But sometimes the conflict has reached a level of distress where someone from outside the institution must come in. When that happens, I cannot stress enough the importance of getting a conflict management expert to come in to help you. Find someone who works with conflict in academia—because as you well know, academia and "big business" are not the same.

REFERENCES

Fisher, R., & Ury, W. (1981). *Getting to yes.* New York, NY: Penguin Books.

Appendix

Conflict Management Programs for Administrators

By Gillian Krajewski

This list of training programs was assembled from responses to a broadly distributed survey. All programs listed are affiliated with an academic institution. If your institution has a conflict management training program open to administrators, contact me to be added to the database, which will be updated regularly.

Institution and Program	Contact Information	Training Description	Location & Schedule	Duration	Cost
Bryn Mawr College HERS, Mid-America Summer Institute for Women in Higher Education Administration	Dr. Cynthia Secor Director HERS, Mid-America University of Denver Park Hill Campus 7150 Montview Blvd. Denver, CO 80220 Phone: 303-871-6866 Fax: 303-871-6897 E-mail: csecor@du.edu	A residential program on the Bryn Mawr College Campus offering women faculty and administrators intensive training in education administration. The curriculum prepares participants to work with issues facing higher education, including issues of conflict, with emphasis on the growing diversity of the student body and the workforce.	Bryn Mawr College Bryn Mawr, PA Summer sessions only	Four weeks	$5,500 Includes tuition, room & board, instructional materials
Bryn Mawr College NACWAA/HERS Institute for Administrative Advancement	Jane Betts Director 17410 Shiloh Pines Drive Monument, CO 80132 Phone: 719-488-3420 Fax: 719-488-3495 E-mail: ejbetts@aol.com	NACWAA/HERS Institute for Administrative Advancements. A week-long residential program offering women coaches and athletics administrators intensive training in athletic administration. The curriculum prepares participants to work with issues currently facing intercollegiate athletic administration with emphasis on leadership skills, including conflict resolution and professional development.	Bryn Mawr College Bryn Mawr, PA Offered in June	One week	$2,100 Includes tuition, room & board, instructional materials, application fee
California State University, Dominguez Hills	David Churchman BSGP California State University Dominguez Hills, CA 90747 Phone: 310-243-3779 Fax: 310-516-3449 E-mail: dchurchman@dhvx20.csudh.edu	30 semester-unit M. A. addressing policy research and applied conflict management skills and theories and specialized electives in family, neighborhood, labor, organizational (including higher ed), public policy, and international conflict. Delivered by traditional on-campus instruction or throughout California by interactive television.	On-campus or throughout California by interactive television. Fall and spring semesters	Three to four academic semesters for M. A. classes held in the evening	Please call for details (costs are generally lower for California residents)

Program	Contact	Description	Location/Schedule	Duration	Cost
Catonsville Community College National Institute for Conflict Resolution Conflicts in Education: Identification, Management and Resolution	Patricia A. Miller, Esq. Director 1160 Spa Road, Suite 1-B Annapolis, MD 21403 Phone: 410-268-1461 Fax: 410-267-9454 E-mail: pamiller7@aol.com	Conflict resolution training for senior administrators in higher education as well as senior education officials in federal and state government. Program uses a model in which conflict management skills or techniques are discussed, demonstrated, and then practiced. Nationally recognized presentation team provides both legal and psychological perspectives and has more than 20 years experience training management in business, courts systems, and government.	At Catonsville Community College. Several 40-hour training sessions each year.	40 hours	$750 to $1,250 per person
Columbia University International Center for Cooperation and Conflict Resolution (ICCCR) Graduate Studies in Conflict Resolution	Ellen Raider Training Director ICCCR Box 53 Teachers College Columbia University New York, NY 10027 Phone: 212-678-3289 Fax: 212-678-4048 E-mail: er127@columbia.edu	Teachers College, Columbia University Offers conflict resolution education at two learning levels. Level one (4 courses) is for those who want to learn these skills for themselves. Level two (2 additional courses) is for those who wish to train others.	Teachers College, Columbia University Weekends in fall and spring, July 7–25 in summer	40 hours, each course	$800 per course for non-credit. $1,740 for credit (three)
Duquesne University Graduate Center for Social and Public Policy, concentration in Conflict Resolution and Peace Studies	William R. Headley, CSS, Ph.D. Associate Professor, Department of Sociology, Duquesne University 313 Administration Building Pittsburgh, PA 15282 Phone: 412-396-5286 Fax: 412-396-6577 E-mail: headley@duq2.cc.duq.edu	Conflict Resolution and Peace Studies program introduces students to the theory and skilled practice of the emerging discipline of conflict resolution. Students are equipped with a theoretical framework, supervised experience in mediating conflicts, and a sharpened sense of their own motivation for conflict resolution work.	Held at Duquesne University Mostly evenings	Semester-long	Cost includes tuition and fees and is based on student status. Please call for details

Institution and Program	Contact Information	Training Description	Location & Schedule	Duration	Cost
Franklin Pierce Law Center Dispute Resolution Institute and Education Law Institute	Sarah E. Redfield, Professor Director Education Law Institute 2 White St. Concord, NH 03301 Phone: 603-228-1541 Fax: 603-228-1074 E-mail: sredfield@nh.ultranet.com	The Education Law Institute at Franklin Pierce Law Center offers training specifically for educators in mediation and other forms of dispute resolution. The basic course is training for mediation. Advanced courses are training to train others and to implement system-wide ADR initiatives.	Concord, NH or elsewhere, by arrangement: This year's training includes "Mediation for Educators," July 8–18, 1997	Two week, 1/2 day, two credit course. Other programs available.	$375 per credit; other options available.
Fresno Pacific University Center for Peacemaking and Conflict Studies	Duane Ruth-Heffelbower Associate Director 1717 South Chestnut Avenue Fresno, CA 93702 Phone: 209-455-5840 Fax: 209-252-4800 E-mail: duanerh@fresno.edu	CPACS specializes in training educators in restorative discipline techniques. Offers graduate certificates and an M.A.	Fresno, CA, various locations across the U.S. and also via the Internet. See *www.fresno.edu/pacs* for schedule	Varies	$230 per unit of graduate credit or as arranged.
Georgia State University, College of Law $E=mc^2$, a program of the Consortium on Negotiation and Conflict Resolution	Carolyn Benne Assistant to the Director Consortium on Negotiation and Conflict Resolution Georgia State University College of Law P.O. Box 4037 Atlanta, GA 30302-4037 Phone: 404-651-1588 Fax: 404-651-2092 E-mail: cbenne@gsu.edu	$E=mc^2$ offers consultation and training in the following areas: • Negotiation • Mediation • Consensus building • Facilitation • Managing campus conflict • Conflict management system design • Collaborative problem solving • Conflict management skills for deans and department heads • Effective communication for resolving conflict • Respecting differences on campus: Resolving conflict across cultures	At GSU, DeKalb College, Kennessaw State, U of Georgia, Macon College, and elsewhere, by arrangement. Mediation training winter and spring semesters. Other training available.	Mediation training, 20 hours. Other courses vary in length.	Please call for details.

Program	Contact	Description	Dates	Duration	Cost
Hamline University Hamline University School of Law Dispute Resolution Institute	Kitty Atkins Associate Director, Dispute Resolution Institute Hamline University School of Law 1536 Hewitt Avenue St. Paul, Minnesota 55104-1284 Phone: 612-641-2897 Fax: 612-641-2435 E-mail: katkins@gw.hamline.edu	The Hamline University School of Law Dispute Resolution Institute was established in 1991 to provide high quality dispute resolution training for law students, lawyers and other professionals. This is accomplished through regular law school course offerings, collaborative training with the Mediation Center of Minneapolis, encouragement of faculty research in dispute resolution, and the sponsorship of intensive two-week summer, and one-week winter courses taught by nationally recognized practitioners and scholars in the ADR field.	Hamline University School of Law. Summer institute begins in June. Winter institute occurs in January.	Summer: depending on course, up to two weeks; Winter: depending on course, up to one week.	Varies. Includes tuition and course materials. Please call for details.
Harvard Law School Program on Instruction for Lawyers	Linda Casey Associate Director 1563 Massachusetts Ave Pound Hall 207 Cambridge MA 02138 Phone: 617-495-3187 Fax: 617-495-2869 web: http://www.harvard.edu/academics/cle	Offered by Professor Frank Sander with the collaboration of Linda Singer and Michael Lewis, two experienced lawyer-mediators, the mediation workshop consists of a blend of theory and practice and introduces participants to mediation as a concept and as a skill. Training program is intended for professionals of all backgrounds.	Harvard Law School 1998: March 23–27	Five days: 9 a.m. to 5 p.m. each day.	$1,850
Massachusetts Institute of Technology Negotiation: Theory and Practice	Elizabeth Martin Program Manager, Short and Custom Courses MIT Sloan School of Mgt. E52 110 50 Memorial Drive Cambridge MA 02139 Phone: 617-253-7345 Fax: 617-252-1200 E-mail: sloanexceed@mit.edu	Topics addressed: Types of negotiations, theoretical concepts, power, personal style, constructive relationships, integrative bargaining, mixed motive situations, performance feedback, and appraisal, collaborative decision-making, difficult people, ethical dilemmas, dispute resolution systems.	MIT (Cambridge, MA), June 9–13,1997	Five days	$3,500 incl. all program materials, continental breakfasts, luncheons, and some dinners at the MIT Faculty Club.

Institution and Program	Contact Information	Training Description	Location & Schedule	Duration	Cost
Massachusetts Institute of Technology The MIT Executive Short Course in Negotiation: Theory and Practice	Elizabeth Martin Programs Manager Short and Custom Courses MIT Sloan School of Mgt. E52-17 50 Memorial Drive Cambridge MA 02139 Phone: 617-253-7166 Fax: 617-252-1200 E-mail: sloanexeced@mit.edu	Course topics include: negotiations species, theoretical concepts, power, personal style, constructive relation-ships, integrative bargaining, mixed motive situations, performance feedback and appraisal, collaborative decision-making, difficult people, ethical dilem-mas, dispute resolution systems, and other topics	MIT (Cambridge, MA) June 9–13, 1997 and each year at about the same time	Five days	$3,500 includes tuition, all program materials, breakfasts, luncheons, and some dinners.
Massachusetts Institute of Technology mediation@MIT	Carol Orme-Johnson Director MIT W20-549 77 Massachusetts Avenue Cambridge, MA 02139 Phone: 617-253-6777 Fax: 617-258-8391 E-mail: mediation@MIT	The mixed class of undergraduates, graduate students, junior and senior staff, and faculty learn conflict resolu-tion skills. Principal themes of the train-ing include self-awareness, a disputant-centered focus, and multi-cultural issues. Of the 11 training sessions, four are devoted to classroom exercises, and seven are role play.	Cambridge, MA Twice a year in June and January	35 hours	Please call for details.
Michigan State University Building Mutuality and Resolving Conflicts between Graduate Students and Faculty: A Proactive Approach	Karen Klomparens Assistant Dean The Graduate School 118 Linton Hall Michigan State University East Lansing MI 48824-1044 Phone: 517-355-0301 Fax: 517-353-3355 E-mail: kklompar@msu.edu	Graduate students and faculty learn interest-based conflict resolution skills and use these skills to collaboratively develop explicit expectations about graduate education and personal inter-actions. The program uses video vignettes to focus on conflicts that arise from unclarified expectations.	At MSU several times each semester. Also at other locations, by arrangement. Please call for schedule.	Varies: from three hours to one and 1/2 days	Please call for details.

Program	Contact	Description	Location/When	Duration	Cost
Montclair State University Master of Arts in Legal Studies with a concentration in Dispute Resolution	Barbara A. Nagle Graduate Advisor Montclair State University D1348 Upper Montclair, NJ 07043 Phone: 201-655-4152 Fax: 201-655-7951 E-mail: nagle@saturn.montclair.edu	Negotiation Theory and Practice: in-depth study of negotiation theories and practical applications. Includes an examination and comparison of various negotiation theories and critical skills needed to be an effective negotiator. Extensive role plays. Study of ethical and policy issues. Mediation Theory and Practice: in-depth examination of the theory and practical applications of mediation. Integration of ethical and policy issues and applications through role plays.	Upper Montclair, New Jersey (approx. 1/2 hour from New York City). Negotiation is offered in the fall, one evening per week. Mediation is offered in the spring, also one evening per week.	15 weeks, four hours per week	Cost per credit is $158 if NJ resident and $200 if not a resident. Each course is three credits. (Tuition only)
Northwestern University Negotiation Strategies for Managers	Executive Programs J. Kellogg Grad. School of Mgt. Northwestern University James Allen Center Evanston, IL 60208-2800 Phone: 847-467-7000 Fax: 847-491-4323 E-mail: execed@nwu.edu web: http://www.kellogg.nwu.edu	Training in negotiation and dispute resolution; emphasis on planning and implementing strategy; creating mutual gain and claiming a fair share of that gain.	Northwestern campus 4 times per year	Three days	1997: $2,750
Pitzer College Conflict Resolution Studies Program	Susanne Faulstich Director, Conflict Resolution Studies Program Pitzer College 1050 N. Mills Ave. Claremont, CA 91711 Phone: 909-621-8807 Fax: 909-607-7058 E-mail: Susanne_Faulstich@pitzer.edu	Conflict resolution training of various kinds is offered to students, staff, and faculty at various times during the year. Complete training which can lead to certification is offered every two years, depending on need and interest. Offers short workshops on a variety of topics relating to conflict management with an emphasis on education both in post-secondary and K-12 institutions. These are free and open to the public.	Pitzer College fall and spring at various times	Variable depending on need/interests	Please call for details.

Institution and Program	Contact Information	Training Description	Location & Schedule	Duration	Cost
Pitzer College (continued)		Maintains a resource center which provides consultation, referrals, and published materials for circulation. Please call for information on upcoming programs and to request brochures.			
Pepperdine University School of Law Straus Institute for Dispute Resolution	Professor L. Randolph Lowry Founder and Director 24255 Pacific Coast Highway Malibu, CA 90263 Phone: 310-456-4655 Fax: 310-456-4437	The Straus Institute offers professional training, a professional certificate program, and an M. A. degree in dispute resolution. Educators regularly participate in all programs. A special one-week intensive program, "Dispute Resolution in Education," is presented each summer. More than 500 students from 20 states study at the institute each year. Faculty for all courses are practitioners as well as academics.	On campus in Malibu, CA Professional certificate program, M. A. degree program, and special training courses offered year round.	Three days to full semester courses	$295–$1,500 per course includes tuition, some materials, and food.
Rochester Institute of Technology Student Ombudsman	Dr. Barry R. Culhane Assistant to the President Ombudsman 254 San Gabriel Drive Rochester, NY 14610 Phone: 716-475-7202 Fax: 716-475-7316 E-mail: brcnge@ritvax.isu.rit.edu	Practical set-up and operation of ombudsman functions	Trainings conducted at RIT Schedule varies	Varies	Please call for details.

Program	Contact	Description	Location / Timing	Duration	Cost / Details
Southern Oregon University Mediation and Conflict Resolution Training	Dr. Michael Belsky, Program Coordinator and Instructor, Southern Oregon University Psychology Dept. Ashland, OR 97520. Phone: 541-488-5676. Fax: 541-955-8651. E-mail: jwilson@wpo.sosc.oshe.edu	Mediation and conflict management skills. Teaches skills used by professional mediators, negotiators, and conflict managers. Provides a comprehensive introduction to negotiation and mediation and meets the requirements of the basic mediation curriculum set out by the Oregon Dispute Resolution Commission.	Southern Oregon University, summer and winter terms	40 hours: Mediation & conflict management; 30 hours: Divorce & family mediation	$550: Mediation & conflict management; $395: Divorce and family mediation
Syracuse University Program on the Analysis and Resolution of Conflicts	Robert A. Rubinstein, Director, 410 Maxwell Hall, Syracuse University, Syracuse, NY 13244. Phone: 315-443-2367. Fax: 315-443-3818. E-mail: parc@mailbox.syr.edu	Training in conflict management and negotiation. Special emphasis on interpersonal conflicts, organizational development, and cross-cultural issues in conflict. Simulations and expository lectures are modes of training.	Syracuse, NY; New York, NY; Washington, DC. Offered year round.	Various durations, from one or two days to semester-long	Various levels. Please call for details.
Temple University Communication & Conflict Processes Department of Communication Sciences	Joe Folger, Professor; Tricia Jones, Professor; Temple University Department of Communication Sciences; 265-62 Weiss Hall; Philadelphia, PA 19122; Phone: Joe Folger 215-204-1890; Tricia Jones 215-204-7261; Fax: 215-204-5954; E-mail: folger@vm.temple.edu; v5431e@vm.temple.edu	Offers a 24-hour basic mediation training using role plays and videotaping. Case studies are contextualized for university settings and are appropriate for students, faculty, and administrators.	Temple University main campus & Center City campus. Each spring and fall semester	Two to three days (typically three days)	Sliding scale includes training & materials, sometimes refreshments.

Institution and Program	Contact Information	Training Description	Location & Schedule	Duration	Cost
University of Hawaii Program on Conflict Resolution	Karen Cross Associate Director Bruce Barnes Professor of Conflict Resolution 2424 Maile Way, # 523 Honolulu, HI 96822 Phone: 808-956-2437 Fax: 808-956-9121 E-mail: program@hawaii.edu bbarnes@hawaii.edu	PCR's special expertise is in training university personnel in basic to advanced mediation and facilitation techniques. From organizing facilitation for 170 top administrators and faculty creating curriculum consensus, to 15 years of university-based mediation, facilitation and consultation system-wide, PCR shares its extensive experience base with other campuses via training and workshops.	University of Hawaii Schedule varies	From 1/2 to five day trainings	Please call for details.
University of Iowa Office of Faculty & Staff Services	Jim Goldman Director The Office of Faculty & Staff Services The University of Iowa 5101 Daum Iowa City, IA 52242 Phone: 319-335-2085 Fax: 319-335-2056 E-mail:jim-goldman@uiowa.edu	Provides interactive opportunity for looking at the antecedents of conflict, personality styles, environmental influences, integrative strategies to deescalate and/or resolve differences through compromise, cooperation, constructive confrontation, disciplinary action.	University of Iowa campus. Schedule varies.	Three to six hours	Please call for details.
University of Manitoba Conflict Resolution Skills for University Administrators	Dan Bradshaw Org. and Staff Development Officer and Coordinator, University Mediation Service. Room 309 Admin Bldg. University of Manitoba, Winnipeg, Manitoba, Canada R3T 2N2 Phone: 204-474-6634 Fax: 204-275-0789 E-mail: Dan_Bradshaw@ UManitoba.CA	Provides skills and practice in the resolution of interpersonal and departmental conflict. Participants • Develop communication skills for effective conflict resolution • Learn and practice an interpersonal negotiation model • Practice various models of intervention including "coaching" parties in conflict and facilitating "face-to-face" discussions	University of Manitoba Twice a year	Two days	Please call for details.

Program	Contact	Description	Location / Schedule	Duration	Cost
University of Massachusetts, Boston — Graduate Programs in Dispute Resolution	Gillian Krajewski, Assistant Director, Dispute Resolution Programs, UMASS Boston, 100 Morrissey Boulevard, Boston, MA 02125-3393, Phone: 617-287-7421, Fax: 617-287-7099, E-mail: disres@umbsky.cc.umb.edu, http://www.umb.edu/disres/	Senior level administrators in higher education join with other senior and career professionals to learn and implement dispute resolution concepts and skills. Classes include mediation, negotiation, dispute resolution systems design in organizations, as well as internship opportunities managing real mediation cases.	UMB campus in Boston. Year round (mostly evenings) Programs begin in fall, spring, and summer	Varies (minimum 36-hour class)	From $650
University of Minnesota Humphrey Institute of Public Affairs Conflict and Change Center	Dr. Thomas Fiutak, Director, 252 Humphrey Center, 301 19th Avenue S., University of Minnesota, Minneapolis, MN 55455, Phone: 612-625-0362, Fax: 612-625-3513, E-mail: ccc@tc.umn.edu	Provides administrators, faculty, and staff with cooperative options for managing internal disputes. Starts from the assumption that universities are unique conflict cultures balancing the often competing needs of its bureaucratic and collegiate mandates. Therefore, wherever possible all training is open to all members of the community.	Humphrey Institute, Twin Cities and regional campuses. New chairs orientation in fall. Monthly day-long seminars on conflict management and negotiating in higher education	Varies from one hour to more than a year	Varies: day-long seminar costs range from $50 – $100
University of New Mexico UNM Mediation Clinic	Jean Civikly-Powell, Professor, Dept. of Communication and Journalism Director, UNM Mediation Clinic, Dept. of Communication and Journalism, University of New Mexico, Albuquerque, NM 87131-1171, Phone: 505-277-3437, Fax: 505-277-4206, E-mail: jcivikly@unm.edu	Training in mediation skills for academic leaders and senior administrators; focus on conflict experiences; planning a mediation; the mediation process, phases, principles and language; saving face; the role of the mediator; practice sessions and feedback.	At UNM two or three times per semester.	1/2 day to two days	Please call for details.

Institution and Program	Contact Information	Training Description	Location & Schedule	Duration	Cost
University of Texas at San Antonio Problem solving/Conflict Resolution Program	Dr. Norma Guerra Associate Vice President for Admin and Planning University of Texas, San Antonio 6900 North Loop 1604 West San Antonio, TX 78249-0604 Phone: 210-458-4664 Fax: 210-458-4655 E-mail: nguerra@lonestar.utsa.edu	The 40-hour mediation training includes an introduction to the varying levels of conflict and addresses appropriate resolution options. Active listening, problem solving, and ombudsing are addressed, along with collaborative problem solving and group facilitation. Scenarios have been designed to address higher education campus community issues. Facilitators work with each group to practice skill development. Participant practice and trainer feedback are important commitments made with this training.	University of Texas, San Antonio Annually each summer	40 hours	Please call for details.
University of Utah Dept. of Communication Conflict Resolution Certificate Program	Michelle Hawes Program Director Dept. of Communication Conflict Resolution Certificate Program 2810 UNCO Building University of Utah Salt Lake City, UT 84112 Phone: 801-585-9662 Fax: 801-585-6255	The Conflict Resolution Certificate Program is a series of three courses that teach basic methods of conflict resolution and the communication skills required to use each method effectively. The emphasis is on mediation, the most common form using a third party neutral. It also covers facilitation, conflict management, arbitration, ombudsing, advocacy, and other less formal resolution methods.	Salt Lake City, University of Utah. Begins September, through May.	Program duration varies from nine weeks to nine months (held in the evenings).	Up to $2,800

University of Washington Law School Professional Mediation Skills Training Program	Julia Gold, Director Mediation Clinic Continuing Legal Education Washington Law School Foundation University of Washington School of Law 1100 NE Campus Parkway Seattle, WA 98105-6617 Phone: 206-543-0059 800-CLE-UNIV Fax: 206-685-3929 E-mail: discover@ u.washington.edu	Course focuses on collaborative, face-to-face, interest-based style of mediation. Participants learn the challenging practice of mediating with parties in joint session, using caucuses when appropriate. Class consists of mix of short lecture, demonstrations, and extended opportunities to role play in simulated mediation sessions, with individualized coaching and feedback. Participants are typically attorneys, human resource managers, counselors, business managers, senior administrators, and law enforcement.	In Seattle, WA, trainings offered three times per year, usually in the fall, winter, spring, or summer	36 hours (four and 1/2 days)	$749 per person
Wayne State University, Detroit Program on Mediating Theory and Democratic Systems (MTDS)	Bill Warters Associate Director Program on Mediating Theory and Democratic Systems 3140 Faculty-Admin. Building, Wayne State University, Detroit, MI 48202 Phone: 313-577-5313 Fax: 313-577-8269 E-mail: warters@cms.cc.wayne.edu	Campus mediation and conflict resolution skills training workshops of various lengths are provided by university-based trainers with over a decade of experience designing and implementing campus dispute resolution systems in a wide range of university settings, public or private, urban or rural, large or small.	Wayne State University in Detroit. The MTDS program offers yearly institutes on various dispute resolution topics, in June or July.	Most are 20 to 25 hours over the course of several days.	$500–$1000. Please call for details.

Institution and Program	Contact Information	Training Description	Location & Schedule	Duration	Cost
Wayne State University, Detroit Master of Arts and Graduate Certificate in Dispute Resolution	Dr. Frederic S. Pearson Michaelene Pepera Academic and Program Directors, Center for Peace and Conflict Studies College of Urban, Labor, and Metropolitan Affairs 2320 FAB Wayne State University Detroit, MI 48202 Phone: 313-577-3453 Fax: 313-577-8269 E-mail: fpearso@cms.cc.wayne.edu www.mtds.wayne.edu	The program requires a minimum of 32 credits for MA, 24 in the core curriculum plus a minimum of three electives. The curriculum is informed by a multicultural perspective, interdisciplinary course offerings, and an emphasis on democratic theory and dispute management. All students participate in a practicum experience bringing theory to practice. Fields include labor, education, legal, commercial, family, and diplomatic specialties.	On campus and at extension centers Year round	15-week semesters	Please call for details.
Wellesley College HERS New England Management Institute for Women In Higher Education	Dr. Cynthia Secor Director Wellesley College Cheever House Wellesley, MA 02181-8259 Phone: 617-283-2529	An integrated series of five seminars offering women administrators and faculty professional management training, including conflict resolution.	Wellesley College Wellesley, MA Weekend seminars in October, November, January, March, April.	12 days (Five seminar weekends)	$2,150 Tuition, materials, meals & breaks
Western Connecticut State University Conflict Resolution Project	R. Averell Manes Associate Professor, Dept. of Social Sciences and Director of Conflict Resolution Project 23B White Hall 181 White Street Danbury, CT 06810 Phone: 860-350-1410 Fax:203-837-8526 manes@wcsub.ctstateu.edu	Level 1: Listening, information sharing, rapport building, nonverbal communication, assertion, creative problem solving, conflict management, ethics and conflict resolution, and an introduction to conflict intervention techniques. Level 2: Negotiation, mediation, facilitation, arbitration, ethical considerations, and dealing with difficult people.	Danbury, CT spring and fall semesters\ as well as winter and summer intersessions	One week (intersession) to semester long	Varies: $440 for matriculated students per three credits $350 for matriculated students per 37.5 hours

CONTRIBUTORS' ADDRESSES

1. *What's It All About? Conflict in Academia*
   Dr. Susan A Holton
   Department of Communication Studies & Theatre Arts
   Bridgewater State College
   Bridgewater, MA 02325
   508-697-1750   fax: 508-697-1729
   sholton@bridgew.edu

2. *Administration in an Age of Conflict*
   Dr. Gerald Graff
   University of Chicago
   5801 South Ellis Avenue
   Chicago, IL 60637
   312-702-8671   fax: 312-702-9861
   ggraff@midway.uchicago.edu

3. *The Janus Syndrome: Managing Conflict from the Middle*
   Dr. Walter H. Gmelch
   College of Education
   University of Washington
   Pullman, WA 99164-2136
   509-335-1738   fax: 509-335-9172
   gmelch@mail.wsu.edu

4. *Chairs as Department Managers: Working with Support Staff*
   Dr. Mary Lou Higgerson
   Department of Speech Communication
   Southern Illinois University
   Carbondale, IL 62901-6605
   618-453-2291   fax: 618-453-2812
   mlhigg@siu.edu

5. *Spanning the Abyss: Managing Conflict Between Deans and Chairs*
   Dr. Ann F. Lucas
   Department of Organizational Development
   Fairleigh Dickinson University
   Teaneck, NJ 07666
   201-569-4747   fax: 201-569-3521
   AnnLucas@aol.com

6. *The Cutting Edge: The Dean and Conflict*
   Dr. Nancy L. Sorensen, Dean
   School of Education
   College of Charleston
   66 George St.
   Charleston, SC 29412
   803-953-8047   fax: 803-953-5407
   Sorensonn@ashley.cofc.edu

7. *And Never the Twain Shall Meet: Administrator-Faculty Conflict*
   Dr. Judith A. Sturnick
   The Sturnick Group
   15 Portofino Circle at The Shores
   Redwood City, CA 94065
   415-631-6071   fax: 415-631-7072
   judith@sturnickgroup.com

8. *Managing Conflict on the Front Lines: Lessons from the Journals
   of a Former Dean and Provost*
   Dr. Clara M. Lovett, President
   Northern Arizona University
   PO Box 4092
   Flagstaff, AZ 86011-4092
   520-523-3232   fax: 520-523-1848
   Clara.Lovett@nau.edu

9. *Student Affairs and Academic Affairs: Partners in Conflict Resolution*
   Dr. Lynn Willett, Vice President for Student Affairs
   Bridgewater State College
   Bridgewater, MA 02325
   508-697-1281   fax: 508- 279-6107
   lwillett@bridgew.edu

10. *Can We Agree to Disagree? Faculty-Faculty Conflict*
    Dr. Cynthia Berryman-Fink
    Department of Communication / ML 0184
    University of Cincinnati
    Cincinnati, OH 45221-0184
    513-556-4455   fax: 513-556-0899
    Cynthia.Berryman-Fink@UC.Edu

11. *Views from Different Sides of the Desk: Conflict Between Faculty and Students*
    Dr. John W. "Sam" Keltner
    Consulting Associates
    Box 842
    Corvallis, OR 97339-0842
    541-757-8623   fax: 541-757-8623
    keltnerj@ucs.orst.edu

12. *Student-Student Conflict: Whose Problem Is It Anyway?*
    Dr. Janet Rifkin
    Associate Dean of Social and Behavioral Science
    Legal Studies Department
    University of Massachusetts
    Amherst, MA 01003
    413-545-5881   fax: 413-545-4171
    jrifkin@legal.umass.edu

13. *Conflict Resolution in the Academy: A Modest Proposal*
    Dr. Joel M. Douglas
    School of Public Affairs
    Baruch College (CUNY)
    17 Lexington Ave, Box 322
    New York, NY 10010
    212-802-5985   fax: 212-802-5903
    Profjmd@aol.com

14. *Academic Mortar to Mend the Cracks: The Holton Model for Conflict Management*
    Dr. Susan A Holton (see above)

Appendix: Conflict Management Programs for Administrators
    Gillian Krajewski
    Graduate Programs in Dispute Resolution
    University of Massachusetts
    100 Morrisey Blvd.
    Boston, MA 02125-3393
    617-287-7421   fax: 617-287-7099
    krajewski@umbsky.cc.umb.edu